AT HOME IN THE COSMOS

AT HOME IN THE COSMOS

DAVID TOOLAN

ORBIS BOOKS
Maryknoll, New York 10545

The Catholic Foreign Mission Society of America (Maryknoll) recruits and trains people for overseas missionary service. Through Orbis Books, Maryknoll aims to foster the international dialogue that is essential to mission. The books published, however, reflect the opinions of their authors and are not meant to represent the official position of the society. To obtain more information about Maryknoll and Orbis Books, please visit our website at www.maryknoll.org.

Published in 2001 by
Orbis Books
P.O. Box 308
Maryknoll, New York 10545-0308

Manufactured in the United States of America

Library of Congress Cataloging-in-Publication Data
Toolan David,
    At home in the cosmos / David Toolan.
       p.   cm.
    Includes bibliographical references and index.
    ISBN 1-57075-341-5
    1. Human ecology – Religious aspects – Christianity. 2. Nature – Religious aspects – Christianity. 3. Environmental ethics. 4. Religion and science. I. Title.

BT695.5 .T66 2001
231.7 – dc21
                                                                        00-044084

In memory of
Pierre Teilhard de Chardin, S.J.
(1881–1955)

How can we contrive to be at once
astonished at the world and yet at home in it?
How can this queer cosmic town...
give us at once the fascination of a strange town
and the comfort and honour of being our own town?

— G. K. CHESTERTON, *Orthodoxy*

Contents

Acknowledgments   xiii

Introduction   1

Part I
THE BIBLICAL VISION
OF CREATION   7

1. Does Yahweh Care about Whales?   9

Is Christianity to Blame for the Problem? / 10
New Developments / 15
The Priestly "Steward" vs. the Yahwist's "Service" of Nature / 17

2. Nature Symbolic of Promise   22

Not Anthropocentrism but Theocentrism / 26
Promise and the Land / 27
Transcendence and Negation / 29
Nature as Sacrament / 32
Sacrament as Human Deed / 38

Part II
THE DEVELOPMENT
OF SCIENTIFIC MATERIALISM   41

3. Imperial Ecology and the Death of Nature   45

Literacy and Detachment from the Earth / 46
Imperial Ecology / 48
Enter Isaac Newton: The Death of Nature / 50
Classical Physics and Economic Materialism / 55
The Clockmaker God / 57

4. The Competitive Ethos Triumphant   59

How the Industrial World Works / 62
Arcadian Ecology / 64
The Harsh Lesson of the Galapagos / 67
Are Ecologists the Good Guys? / 70

Part III
STATE OF THE EARTH   75

5. Is There an Environmental Crisis?   79

The Case against Environmental Hype / 80
Reading Earth's Vital Signs: Soil and Food Production, Water,
  Forests, Biodiversity / 84

6. Pushing the Limits   92

Built-in Blindness to Limits / 92
Energy Consumption / 94
Pollution and Other Garbage / 97
Global Warming / 98
Preventive Action? / 101

7. The Dynamics of Unsustainability   104

Scientific Uncertainty / 105
Fitting into the Great Economy / 107
Driving Forces behind Environmental Damage / 109
Malthusian, Structuralist, and Economistic Arguments / 111
The Debate Continues / 113
The New Colonialism / 116
Sustainable Development vs. Sustainable Communities / 119
Civilizing the Global Marketplace / 121

Part IV
THE NEW COSMOLOGY   127

8. Evolution and Theological Repair   132

Theology in a Static Cosmos / 133
Time and the Chancy Universe of the Prophets / 135
Hubble's Expanding Universe / 137
The Cosmic Clock / 139
No God of the Gaps or Big Explainer / 144
Christian Spirituality in an Evolving Universe / 146
Causality vs. Vision / 150

9. **A Physics of Promise** 156

   Cosmic Pessimism / 159
   Arrows of Time: Darwinian vs. Thermodynamic / 164
   Open, Nonequilibrium Systems / 166
   Dissipative Structures and Emergent Complexity / 168
   The Big Bang and the Anthropic Principle / 173

10. **The Voice of the Hurricane** 178

    The Unpredictability and Interconnectedness of Matter-Energy / 180
    A Semiotic Universe / 182
    Order Out of Chaos / 184
    The Anthropological Fallout / 186

Part V
EARTH ETHICS:
DOING JUSTICE TO CREATION 193

11. **The Fallout for Spirituality** 195

    A Big Enough God and the Spirituality of Ascent / 199
    Pneumatology and a Spirituality of Descent / 202
    Christology and the Dream of Earth / 205
    Eucharist: Oneness with Earth / 210
    Converting Matter-Energy into Sacrament / 213

12. **Citizens of Earth** 220

    Love of the Wild / 223
    Extending the Social Contract to Earth / 226
    What a Sustainable Society Would Look Like / 231
    The Great Work / 236

Appendix A: The Relationship between Science and Religion 241

Appendix B: The Churches in the Environmental Movement 244

Index 249

Acknowledgments

I wish to thank a number of people for their support in writing this book. First, many thanks to my former editor-in-chief at *America* magazine, George W. Hunt, S.J., who in 1997 generously gave me a year's sabbatical (with pay) so that I could work full-time on the project; and to his successor, Thomas Reese, S.J., who in early 1999 was equally accommodating in giving me a month off to finish things up. Next, thanks to my provincial superior, Kenneth Gavin, S.J., who kindly subsidized sundry upgrades of my computer and periodic raids on bookstores for materials vital to my research.

Much gratitude to former colleague and friend Professor Frank Dinan of the chemistry department at Canisius College in Buffalo, New York, who read through an early version of my manuscript and saved me from a number of scientific howlers. (I take full credit for those remaining.)

My heartfelt thanks also goes to Eileen Simpson and Robert Giroux of New York City and Professor John F. Haught of Georgetown University, who graciously (and successfully) recommended me to the Rockefeller Foundation for a grant to spend a month at the Villa Serbelloni in Bellagio, Italy, where I was able to work on the manuscript in undisturbed splendor and among entirely stimulating good company. And thanks as well to Susan E. Garfield, manager of the Bellagio Study and Conference Center in New York City, and the able and ever-gracious Italian manager-in-residence, Gianna Celli.

For their constant support, encouragement, and tact (in knowing when not to ask too many questions about finishing the project), my thanks to the members of the West Side Jesuit Community on West 98th Street in New York City, whose good company and conversation I have happily enjoyed for the last seventeen years. And finally, for inspiring my love of nature in the beginning, loving thanks to my grandmother, Gertrude Cunningham Maher — for summer days amid tidal pools in Cape Elizabeth, Maine; and to my parents, John and Gertrude Toolan — for the gift of a boyhood spent in orchards, gardens, and woods by the Navesink River in New Jersey, and for extraordinary vacations in the Big Horn Mountains of Wyoming and in sugarcane fields in Cuba.

Introduction

"History," says the cultural historian Thomas Berry, "is governed by those overarching movements that give shape and meaning to life by relating the human venture to the larger destinies of the universe. Creating such a movement might be called the Great Work of a people."[1] In listing some examples, Berry cites the work of classical Greece in the creation of the Western humanist tradition; the work of Israel in expressing a new experience of the divine in human affairs; the work of Rome in gathering the diverse peoples of the Mediterranean and Western Europe under the rule of law; and the work of the medieval period in giving the Western world its first Christian shape as symbolized by the great Gothic cathedrals. In India, he says, the great work was "to lead human thought into spiritual experience of time and eternity and their mutual presence to each other," while Chinese Confucianism "created one of the most elegant and most human civilizations we have ever known as its great work." "The Great Work now," says Berry, "as we move into a new millennium, is to carry out the transition from a period of human devastation of the Earth to a period when humans would be present to the planet in a mutually beneficial manner."[2]

The historical change that we face, argues Berry, will be more dramatic than the transition from classical Rome to the medieval period, or from the medieval period to modern times. For a parallel we must go back to the geobiological transition that took place 67 million years ago when the era of the dinosaurs ended and a new biological age began. With the opening of this third millennium humankind must respond to a new calling — a new vocation.

> The Great Work before us, the task of moving modern industrial civilization from its present devastating influence on the Earth to a more benign mode of presence, is not a role that we have chosen. It is a role given to us, beyond any consultation with ourselves. We did not choose. We were chosen by some power beyond ourselves for this historical task. We do not choose the moment of our birth,

1. Thomas Berry, *The Great Work: Our Way into the Future* (New York: Bell Tower, 1999), 1.
2. Ibid., 3.

1

who our parents will be, our particular culture or the historical moment when we will be born. We do not choose the status of spiritual insight or political or economic conditions that will be the context of our lives. We are, as it were, thrown into existence with a challenge and a role that is beyond any personal choice. The nobility of our lives, however, depends upon the manner in which we come to understand and fulfill our assigned role.

Yet we must believe that those powers that assign our role must in that same act bestow upon us the ability to fulfill this role.... Our own special role, which we will hand on to our children, is that of managing the arduous transition from the terminal Cenozoic to the emerging Ecozoic Era, the period when humans will be present to the planet as a participating member of the comprehensive Earth community. This is our Great Work and the work of our children.[3]

What, I want to ask in this book, is humanity's place in the great scheme of things, in the new cosmic story that is now being narrated by the natural sciences? And what might provide a basis for the ecological ethic that our earth cries out for? The Enlightenment view of nature that we have been living with for the last two centuries — nature as mechanistic and deterministic — is dissolving before our eyes. In its place contemporary science is discovering a world that is irreversibly temporal, dynamic, interconnected, self-organizing, indeterminate, and boundlessly open to evolutionary transformation. The material world is once again sacramental, a field of promise, and hence it can be contextualized far more effectively by a creation-centered biblical religion — with its future orientation and sense of God's fidelity to promise — than by the alienating cosmic pessimism advocated by scientists like Steven Weinberg, Richard Dawkins, and Jacques Monod.

The new cosmic story requires some theological repair work, notably a shift to a God of the future who, as the great Exodus story proclaimed, leads us by going "up ahead" of his people. We are invited to pass a new threshold, to rediscover both our profound kinship with the rest of nature and a heightened responsibility toward it. Environmentalists have confronted us with a false choice in this respect: between anthropocentrism and biocentrism. In the twenty-first century, the construction of the very conditions of life and survival — what the weather will be, the state of the soil, of the air, the forests and the water — will depend upon us, whether we like it or not. In an age of possible ecological crisis, how do we prepare ourselves for this gigantic extension of

---

3. Ibid., 7–8.

moral responsibility — from the personal to the ecosystem? This book looks at the historical origins of our ecological predicament and argues that both science and religion, the culture-forming factors behind our environmental problems, are even now converging on a positive reconception of Western culture's relationship to the natural world; in effect, we are in the process of forging a new social contract with nature.

In Part I, "The Biblical Vision of Creation," I consider the principal objection to a joint effort between scientists and believers on behalf of the ecosystem, namely, the suspicion that the Bible's conception of human "dominion" over nature is responsible for our current ecological problems. Christianity's ambivalent attitude toward the material world is certainly part of the problem, but in the big picture the Bible provides a much better basis for an environmental ethic than is generally realized. The Bible leads us to ground our ethics in the elemental promise that is ingredient "in the heavens and the earth."

Part II, "The Development of Scientific Materialism," argues that the biggest obstacle to an ecological ethic lies less with Moses and Jesus than with the ideas of the great forefathers of modernity: Francis Bacon, Isaac Newton, and Adam Smith. The central cultural source of our current environmental problems, I will claim, can be attributed to the scientific materialism that developed in what Alfred North Whitehead called the "century of genius," the seventeenth century of the scientific revolution. And what has been the impact of this scientific and economic materialism? Classical science and liberal economics provide the major rationalization for environmental exploitation and destruction.

In Part III, "State of the Earth," I try to assess the current consequences of scientific and economic materialism. I confront the present argument by economists and industry (and Gregg Easterbrook) that environmental doomsayers have exaggerated our ecological predicament. What are the facts? Do we face ecological meltdown? What is the state of the question, and what are the structural factors that make for unsustainable economies in the developed and developing worlds?

Part IV, "The New Cosmology" begins the constructive part of the book, a study in cross-fertilization or mutual influence between science and theology. First, Christians must begin to stress certain neglected aspects of their tradition, and even revise their conception of God. Second, if classical physics and the materialism it gave rise to are part of today's ecological crisis, the "new physics" of our century is also part of the solution. In this section, I try to show that science itself, as an engine of cultural change, is breaking down the old Cartesian dualism that has so distorted the relationship between Western society and the natural environment. This section reviews developments in big bang theory, quantum physics, thermodynamics and information theory, nonequilibrium thermodynamics and chaos theory to conclude that the new physics gives us a worldview of possibility and big chances in which the Hebrew prophets and the Christian tradition can be fully at home. Why? Because nature itself, from beginning to end, exhibits a promissory character. What is emerging, I argue, is a new post-Einsteinian cosmology that is fully congruent with the historical and eschatological thinking of the Bible. From this perspective, human identity can be understood as kin to all sentient beings, and human destiny as intimately related to the fate of the cosmos as a whole. At the same time, human beings have a unique role in the unfolding of nature's story as creators of justice and beauty.

Part V, "Earth Ethics: Doing Justice to Creation," connects elements of the Christian theological tradition to the new cosmology and develops the implications of the new theo-cosmological vision for a new social contract with nature. Like it or not, we are the authors of ongoing creation. From here on in morality must mean accepting responsibility for constructing the basic givens — the objective facts — of life, things like the climate, the state of ocean fisheries, a breathable atmosphere, and the diversity of species.

Behind our ecological problems, I will assume, lie four factors (not necessarily in order of importance): (1) the need to feed, clothe, house, and provide a livelihood for a world population that will probably reach 10 to 14 billion by the year 2050; (2) institutional arrangements, particularly the political economy that is based on the assumption of unlimited economic expansion; (3) cultural values, beliefs, and ideologies that legitimize social arrangements, such as the materialist notion that consuming (and throwing away) more is always to be preferred, since it makes the market economy work; (4) the technology that enables us to transform the environment more than any other species.

The strain of population is just one aspect of the problem, and not the worst. The toughest part of the problem, I will argue, consists of ingrained cultural beliefs and attitudes toward the natural world. But population is a factor that aggravates every other aspect of our difficulties. At the start of the agricultural revolution some twelve thousand years ago, the population of the planet is estimated to have been about 5 million. By 1650 c.e., at the inception of the scientific revolution in Europe, earth's population had multiplied a hundredfold to 500 million. Two hundred years later, by 1850, we had doubled that number, reaching the first billion. By 1930, a mere eighty years later, human numbers doubled again, to 2 billion. By 1975 that 2 billion had become 4 billion, thus adding in forty-five years as many humans as had lived since the beginning of human evolution. Just lately we passed 6 billion.

That a population twice the size of our present one will put enormous, perhaps unacceptable, strains on the biophysical capacities of the planet seems to me obvious and in need of no extended argument. And that our present productive technology threatens to deplete nonrenewable resources and pollute the atmosphere at unsustainable rates seems equally plain. My analysis, therefore, will pay special attention to the cultural factors, our ways of understanding nature and our relationship to nature, the ideas and attitudes, in other words, that stand behind our ecological problems. What attitude toward the ecosystem in general does science itself promote? And what attitude does my Christian religious tradition foster? Is religion friend or foe of the environmental movement? Is science the friend that Carl Sagan seemed to suppose? In what sense is nature to be taken as sacred?

The key question, however, is this: How large is the circle of our moral concern? Does it restrict itself to human society? Will it stretch no further? Can the biophysical world be included within our moral compass? Does the ecosystem of which we are a part have moral standing? What is our obligation, if any, toward the air, soil, water, plants, and animals that sustain us? Without which we could not exist? Can nature be said to have "rights"? And therefore make moral claims? These will be the central questions of the following chapters. We dwell within a promising universe, I will argue, and our function, our great work, is to make something beautiful of it, to pour soul and spirit into it.

Part I

The Biblical Vision
of Creation

These first two chapters are expository and reconstructive. I will take up the charge that Christianity is mainly responsible for the planet's deteriorating ecological situation. The Bible, I will argue, has been given a bad rap by mainstream environmentalism. It is not the final word we require for an ecological ethic, but it offers a starting point that can and should be built upon. I shall argue that the biblical vision, which has so shaped Western culture, includes the natural world within its moral compass. God's salvific will, I will claim, reaches out to embrace all of creation, not simply humankind. And all of creation reflects the God of promise.

ONE

Does Yahweh Care about Whales?

Be fruitful and multiply and fill the earth and subdue it; rule over the fish of the sea and the birds of the sky and all of the animals created on the earth. — Genesis 1:28

The Cosmos is all that is or ever was or ever will be. Our feeblest contemplations of the Cosmos stir us — there is a tingling in the spine, a catch in the voice, a faint sensation, as if a distant memory, of falling from a height. We know we are approaching the greatest of mysteries. — CARL SAGAN, *Cosmos*

We are close to committing — many would argue we are already committing — what in religious language is sometimes called Crimes against Creation.

— *An Appeal for Joint Commitment in Science and Religion*

In January of 1990, as I was sorting through, and throwing out, the daily office mail, I came across something worth keeping. It was a message from twenty-four distinguished scientists, including the late Carl Sagan, Nobel laureate Hans Bethe, physicist Freeman J. Dyson, and biologist Stephen Jay Gould, appealing to the world's spiritual leaders to join the scientific community in protecting and conserving an endangered global ecosystem.[1] "We are now threatened," the signatories wrote,

> by self-inflicted, swiftly moving environmental alterations about whose long-term biological and ecological consequences we are still painfully ignorant — depletion of the protective ozone layer; a global warming unprecedented in the last 150 millennia; the

---

1. See "Preserving and Cherishing the Earth: An Appeal for Joint Commitment in Science and Religion," reprinted in Carl Sagan, *Billions and Billions* (New York: Random House, 1997), 143–45.

9

obliteration of an acre of forest every second; the rapid-fire extinction of species; and the prospect of a global nuclear war that would put at risk most of the population of the Earth. . . . We are close to committing — many would argue we are already committing — what in religious language is sometimes called Crimes against Creation.

"Problems of such magnitude," said the scientists,

> . . . must be recognized from the outset as having a religious as well as a scientific dimension. Mindful of our common responsibility, we scientists — many of us long engaged in combating the environmental crisis — urgently appeal to the world religious community to commit in word and deed, and as boldly as required, to preserve the environment of the Earth.[2]

What did the scientists want church, temple, and synagogue to do? "We understand," they said,

> that what is regarded as sacred is more likely to be treated with care and respect. Efforts to safeguard and cherish the environment need to be infused with a vision of the sacred. At the same time, a much wider and deeper understanding of science and technology is needed.

The scientists' appeal was warmly welcomed around the world, in some eighty-three countries, by hundreds of cardinals, bishops, rabbis, lamas, patriarchs, mullahs, and chief muftis.

Is Christianity to Blame for the Problem?

The Sagan appeal to Jewish and Christian leaders must have struck many environmentalists as odd. For ever since the late 1960s it has been a staple of the environmental movement that the Judeo-Christian tradition is not part of the solution but part of the problem. Historian Lynn White Jr.'s famous 1967 article, "The Historical Roots of the Ecological Crisis," is supposed to have shown exactly that.[3] White had argued that the West's ecological fall from grace began with the Book of Genesis. In the first of two versions of the creation story in the Book

---

2. The Sagan appeal seems to presuppose that science and religion do not conflict but can be seen as complementary. For three different ways of construing the relationship between science and religion, see Appendix A.

3. Lynn White Jr., "The Historical Roots of the Ecological Crisis," *Science* 155 (1967): 1203–7.

of Genesis, the so-called Priestly account, God sets humans off from other creatures and then gives us dominion over them.

> God created humanity in his image; in the image of God he created it; male and female he created them. And God blessed them and God said to them, "Be fruitful and multiply and fill the earth and subdue it; rule over the fish of the sea and the birds of the sky and all of the animals created on the earth." (Gen. 1:27–28)

No biblical text has been quoted more often or discussed more avidly in recent debates about biblical religion and ecology than this one. Regrettably, interest in the Priestly viewpoint has dominated the debate despite the fact that Genesis 1 (the so-called Priestly account) is only one of many creation accounts in the Bible (also in the Psalms, Isaiah 40–66, Job, and Proverbs), all of which differ from each other and from Genesis 1. Psalms 77, 89, and 93, for instance, describe creation as a cosmic battle with the forces of chaos (a common theme in the Bible and in the literature of Israel's neighbors). In this tradition God's victory in the battle is the act of creation. In turn, Isaiah 40–55 uses creation-by-combat to interpret the revival of Israel after the sixth-century exile. In general, all of these texts show that God's great redemptive deeds are always acts of creation.

Most notably, however, the brief Priestly account (Gen. 1:1–2:4a) is immediately followed by Genesis 2, the story of Eden, the initial episode of the so-called Yahwistic epic (referred to as the J editor-author), which represents an independent version of creation and reflects a view of the human role in nature that differs markedly from the Priestly editor's (referred to as P). White paid no attention to this second account of creation.

Using the Priestly version of creation as paradigmatic of the whole Bible, White argued that no religion had been more anthropocentric than Christianity, and none more rigid in excluding all but humans from the realm of divine grace and in denying any moral obligation to the lower species. "By destroying pagan animism," said White, "Christianity made it possible to exploit nature in a mood of indifference to the feelings of natural objects." If we are looking for the source of our environmental problems — the enemy of ecological sensitivity, the friend of extractive capitalism — Christianity is it. "We shall continue to have a worsening ecologic crisis," concluded White, "until we reject the Christian axiom that nature has no reason for existence save to serve man."

Environmental historians have tended to agree with White that Western culture is fundamentally hostile to the earth. They differ among themselves only on when the West's fall from grace occurred. Some historians (with whom I agree) hold that neither Abraham nor Moses was to blame; it was the Renaissance and the seventeenth-century scientific revolution, they argue, that doomed the earth to be treated as a machine that would never stop running, however it was used and abused.[4] A few other historians contend that the problem of human domination is not limited to the West, but includes every settled, agricultural society, from the irrigation-mad ancient Chinese to the irrigation-mad ancient Sumerians.[5] Only the Paleolithic cave-dwellers, for whom the whole earth was held to be sacred, are typically exempted from this original sin of plowing up Mother Earth. But otherwise, current environmental history tends to tell the same dismal story of the West's animus against nature. It is a tale of land seized, exploited, and exhausted, of traditional cultures said to have lived in harmony with the soil being displaced by the reckless individualist, the capitalist exploiter. But is this an accurate picture?

What Lynn White has right is just this: Early Christianity was deeply influenced by apocalyptic consciousness, and the split of the world into two ontological realms became foundational for the Christian West. As Theodore Hiebert puts it in his study of Yahwistic thought:

> Combined in various ways, first with Neoplatonic thought that separated soul from body and later with other forms of idealism, Christianity developed at its heart a profound metaphysical dualism. Here, too, the spiritual world assumed primary importance and the natural world took on secondary or temporary significance. In its more extreme forms, Christian dualism even perceived the material world as alien to authentic human experience and therefore dispensable, if not downright evil.[6]

White was therefore right to criticize Christianity; we have some long overdue reparation to make.

The second thing that White's thesis has very right is that it highlights the fact that the environmental problem is primarily cultural, situated in our basic beliefs about human nature and destiny. The

---

4. See Carolyn Merchant, *The Death of Nature* (San Francisco: Harper & Row, 1980). Also Victor Ferkiss, *Nature, Technology, and Society: Cultural Roots of the Current Environmental Crisis* (New York: Oxford University Press, 1993); and Donald Worster, *Nature's Economy: A History of Ecological Ideas*, 2d ed. (Cambridge: Cambridge University Press, [1977] 1994), 26–55.

5. See Max Oelschlaeger, *The Idea of Wilderness: From Prehistory to the Age of Ecology* (New Haven: Yale University Press, 1991), 1–67.

6. Theodore Hiebert, *The Yahwist's Landscape: Nature and Religion in Early Israel* (New York: Oxford University Press, 1996), 153.

modern crisis, in other words, cannot be explained as simply due to deficiencies in managerial skill among scientists and technicians. It has to do with the basic ideas and values that have determined how science and technology have developed and been put to use. As White correctly pointed out,

> Both our present science and our present technology are so tinc-
> tured with orthodox arrogance toward nature that no solution
> for our ecological crisis can be expected from them alone. Since
> the roots of our trouble are so largely religious, the remedy must
> also be essentially religious, whether we call it that or not. We
> must rethink and refeel our nature and our destiny.[7]

The aim of this book is to "rethink and refeel" our place within nature and our common destiny with nature as a whole — from a Christian perspective. In her presidential address to the fifty-first annual convention of the Catholic Theological Society of America in 1996, Elizabeth A. Johnson of Fordham University directed her remarks to what she called a "vital theme largely absent from the thinking of most North American theologians, namely, the whole world as God's good creation." She pointed out that the sixteenth-century Reformation signaled an anthropocentric turn, and since then the vision of theology, both Protestant and Catholic, has not kept pace with new scientific developments. Increasingly, the focus of theology was confined to God and the self, and theologians exhibited more and more estrangement from ongoing thought about the universe. The doctrine of creation was for all practical purposes separated from the doctrine of redemption.

Throughout most of the twentieth century, one could go through a whole course of study in college, seminary, or university, Johnson claimed, and never encounter the subject of nature, which came to be treated as no more than the stage on which salvation history is played out. This neglect of the cosmos in recent mainstream theology blocked "what should be theology's powerful contribution to the religious praxis of justice and mercy for the threatened earth, so necessary at this moment of our planet's unprecedented ecological crisis." "What is needed now," Johnson insisted, "is...a fully inclusive turn to the heavens and the earth, a return to cosmology, in order to restore fullness of vision and get theology back on the track from which it fell off a few hundred years ago."[8] This book will take up Johnson's

---

7. White, "The Historical Roots of the Ecological Crisis," 1207.

8. Elizabeth A. Johnson, "Turn to the Heavens and the Earth: Retrieval of the Cosmos in Theology," in *The Catholic Theological Society of America: Proceedings of the Fifty-First Annual Convention,* 1996, 1, 5.

challenge to return to that vital missing theme, to cosmology — or to
what the Bible refers to as "heaven and earth."

In retrospect, it is clear that Lynn White's indictment of the biblical
worldview was too sweeping by far. By and large, with the exception of
the apocalyptic Book of Daniel, the Hebrew Bible exhibits no dualism
that would oppose two distinct ontological orders: human vs. world,
history vs. nature, spirit vs. body, mind vs. matter. The Bible does
not limit redemption to human beings; as the primordial "rainbow"
covenant with Noah makes clear, it conceives of redemption reaching
out to embrace "every living creature to be found with you, birds,
cattle and every wild beast with you; everything that came out of the
ark, everything that lives on the earth" (Gen. 9:10). In short, nature is
included within salvation history.

The separation of history from nature or redemption from creation
is largely a modern phenomenon, something that nineteenth century
exegetes took over from influential idealists like Hegel. Within the Hebrew Bible itself, such dichotomies are not to be found. The liturgical
calendars preserved in the Yahwistic account in Exodus 34, the Priestly
account of Leviticus 23, and the Deuteronomist account in Deuteron-
omy 16 are all agricultural calendars, their structure established by
the seasonal harvests of barley, wheat, and fruit. In turn, the idea of
redemption is firmly grounded in the agricultural landscape to which
humans are intrinsically related from the very beginning. That is, redemption depended entirely on a fertile and secure land and a lasting
and stable relationship with this arable land and the bountiful harvests
it produced. The Yahwist's deity, for instance, cannot be understood
apart from his theophanies at particular places — Shechem, Bethel,
Hebron, and Beersheba — and through a remarkable array of natural
forms: the tree, the mountain summit, the wind, fire and smoke, and,
above all, the thunderstorm.

It was only with the rise of apocalyptic thought late in Israelite history that the Hebrew tradition's unitary viewpoint and deep valuation of
earthly reality was broken. The apocalyptic worldview, whose clearest
expression in the Hebrew Scriptures is the Book of Daniel, comes within
inches of despairing of life in this world and conceives of salvation in
terms of a complete transformation of earthly reality and/or as a new
existence in another, supernatural sphere of reality. For the first time
in biblical history you get a clear notion of life after death and a sense
that earth is no longer the true human home. Ultimate salvation for the
faithful was to be found in another metaphysical plane. This becomes
the dominant viewpoint of mainline Christianity, but it is important to
see that it is only marginally the viewpoint of most of the Hebrew Bible.

New Developments

Now a lot has happened since White made this charge in 1967. For one thing, the churches and the synagogue have become active in the environmental movement.[9]

Second, the assumption that Western culture has been congenitally hostile to nature can no longer be sustained. It is simply not true, as was often asserted until very recently, that Western culture evolved by sloughing off its nature myths. In his magisterial book *Landscape and Memory,* Harvard University's Simon Schama has shown that all those myths and cults which environmentalists seek out in indigenous, traditional cultures — of the forest primeval, of the river of life, of the sacred mountain — are in fact "alive and well and all about us if only we know where to look for them."[10] Schama indicates where we are to look for these myths: in the architecture of Gothic cathedrals, the royal hunting forests of Europe, in the mystique of England's "greenwood," the landscapes of *la douce France,* and in our national parks (places like Yellowstone Park and Mt. Rushmore) and the broad sweep of Western art and architecture. The West's cultural habits have included the idea of dominating nature, yes, but they have also made ample room for the sacredness of nature. Schama writes:

> All our landscapes, from the city park to the mountain hike, are imprinted with our tenacious, inescapable obsessions. So that to take the many and several ills of the environment seriously does not, I think, require that we trade in our cultural legacy or its posterity. It asks instead that we simply see it for what it has truly been: not the repudiation, but the veneration, of nature.[11]

More important in the long run, biblical scholars have reexamined the whole issue of how the Bible understands the relationship between human beings and what we call "nature." They have come to very different conclusions from those that were standard among scholars in the 1960s. In 1973 Lynn White recognized this himself. In his article "Continuing the Conversation," he clarified a remark found in his first essay, that "since the roots of our trouble are so largely religious, the remedy must also be essentially religious." In amplifying that remark, White, a church-going Presbyterian, refers to the potential for change inherent in Judeo-Christianity. "In its doctrine of the Holy

---

9. For a brief sketch of religious involvement in the environmental movement, see Appendix B.
10. Simon Schama, *Landscape and Memory* (New York: Vintage Books, 1995), 13.
11. Ibid., 18.

Spirit, Christianity fortunately makes provision for continuing revelation. Or, to phrase the matter in a more orthodox way, it recognizes the progressive unfolding of truths inherent in an original deposit of revelation." Further on, White observes:

> In every complex religious tradition there are recessive genes which in new circumstances may become dominant genes. In my 1967 discussion I referred to St. Francis's abortive challenge to the anthropocentric concept of God's world. Scattered through the Bible, but especially the Old Testament, there are passages that can be read as sustaining the notion of a spiritual democracy of all creatures. The point is that historically they seem seldom or never to have been so interpreted. This should not inhibit anyone from taking a fresh look at them.[12]

Scholars have been taking that fresh look.[13] The current consensus about the Hebrew Bible's attitude toward nature is well summed up in Evan Eisenberg's *The Ecology of Eden:*

> Far from rejecting nature, the Hebrews embraced her as a whole, thorns and all. No place is godforsaken, unless it be the cities of men. However bleak, the sands and stones have sermons to preach. Nor do they preach self-mortification or the vanity of the world. What they say is: Go back to your fields. Go back to your vineyards and orchards. Only this time do it right. This time, let there be justice and peace.[14]

Eisenberg is worth citing, in fact, at some length:

> One of the things that have kept the Bible fresh, while most of ancient Near Eastern literature withered or was embalmed, is the gust of country air that hits the reader the moment he opens the book — the smell of cedar, sheep dung, sun-baked wheat, and olives bruised beneath one's sandals....In all the ancient Near East, only the Hebrew writers have dirt under their fingernails. Amos drove goats ("a herdsman and a piercer of figs," he called himself, referring to the gashing of sycamore figs to hasten their ripening). David was tending sheep when Samuel discovered

---

12. Lynn White Jr., "Continuing the Conversation," in *Western Man and Environmental Ethics: Attitudes toward Nature and Technology,* ed. Ian G. Barbour (Reading, Mass.: Addison-Wesley, 1973), 61.

13. For a useful overview of current thinking, see the essays collected in Dieter T. Hessel and Rosemary Radford Ruether, eds., *Christianity and Ecology: Seeking the Well-Being of Earth and Humans* (Cambridge, Mass.: Harvard University Center for the Study of World Religions, 2000).

14. Evan Eisenberg, *The Ecology of Eden* (New York: Vintage Books, 1999), 129.

him.... Indeed, prophets such as Amos may present some of the few cases in the ancient world of an honest-to-God rural point of view finding its way into writing.

In looking at the Hebrew view of nature, it is a common mistake to pay more attention to the form — the bare idea of a single transcendent god — than to the content, both legal and poetic. The content of the Bible shows, as the great nineteenth-century naturalist Alexander von Humboldt noted, a greater and more sweeping sense of the grandeur of nature than is found among the Greeks, even at their most "pagan."[15]

The Priestly "Steward" vs. the Yahwist's "Service" of Nature

Most biblical scholars in the 1960s, unconsciously influenced by nineteenth-century idealist categories, set up a sharp dichotomy between nature and history. The Bible, they thought, exhibits no interest in nature in its own right; nature is merely the stage upon which the historical drama of human redemption is carried out. Or worse, nature is a mere launching pad that human beings abandon as we soar off toward an incorporeal supernatural realm. The thesis was that unlike their Canaanite neighbors with their "nature religion," the biblical writers were exclusively concerned with historical events and so-called "existential" questions. Current biblical scholarship, however, has radically revised this assessment. As just noted, the early Israelites were thoroughgoing citizens of earth who conceived of salvation as a "stable, healthy relationship with the earthly environment, not as the transcendence of it."[16]

Well up through the mid–twentieth century, though, biblical scholars had followed Gerhard von Rad, G. Ernest Wright, Albrecht Alt, and Roland de Vaux in imagining that Israelite religion was unique in the ancient Middle East in distancing itself from the natural world of space and place. Much was made of the idea that the locus of Israelite religion was desert nomadism. Assuming a desert setting of stark solitude and barrenness, these scholars alleged that it was impossible for either Israel or its patron deity to develop close and lasting bonds to specific sites in the phenomenal world. Israel, it was thought, had to anchor itself

---

15. Ibid., 131.
16. Hiebert, *The Yahwist's Landscape*, 155. See also Richard J. Clifford, *Creation Accounts in the Ancient Near East and in the Bible* (Washington, D.C.: Catholic Biblical Association of America, 1994); Ronald A. Simkins, *Creator and Creation: Nature in the Worldview of Ancient Israel* (Peabody, Mass.: Hendrickson, 1994).

exclusively in its transcendent God and God's mighty acts in history. This whole interpretation, however, has not passed scrutiny.

On the contrary, argue contemporary scholars like Theodore Hiebert and others, the Yahwist creation account (Gen. 2–3) shows no such detachment between the society and its environment. The desert has little to do with it. The picture, in fact, is just the opposite. The original Israelite was a "small farmer whose society and its well-being, and whose religious life itself, are solidly rooted in the arable land of the biblical hill country and in the rhythms of the agricultural economy that it sustained."[17]

> In the narrative of ancestral society that unfolds in the first, primeval age, the relationship between these early farmers and their land — in particular, the link between human morality and the soil's fertility — is every bit as important as the relationship between these farmers and their deity. Of course, these relationships are inseparably bound up with one another; one can hardly be characterized as the backdrop of the other. Furthermore, the great etiological narratives of the postflood era, which explain and authorize the realities (or alleged realities) of the Yahwist's age, are designed not just to validate political orders and events, but also to establish bonds between people and their environs. In Israel's case, the connection between its ancestors and the arable highlands of biblical Israel is continually reiterated by these narratives. In fact, this land assumes a central role in the Yahwist's theology of promise and blessing that dominates the postflood age. Outside of this setting, the survival of Israel's ancestors is always in jeopardy, a fact illustrated most vividly in the southern narratives of exile in Egypt and the desert that conclude the epic. From the offerings presented to God by Cain and Abel in the epic's first generation to the great liturgical prescriptions promulgated to the epic's last generation, the agricultural economy of those highlands provides the basis of Israelite worship.[18]

The Yahwist author, it is important to note, understands the human place within nature quite differently from the Priestly author. For P, the crucial fact about human nature is that it is imprinted with the image of God (Gen. 1:26–27). Given the absence of dualism between spirit and matter, soul and body, in Hebrew thought, this does not import to humans a special ontological status within creation; rather, it assigns to

---

17. Hiebert, *The Yahwist's Landscape,* 155.
18. Ibid., 150.

humanity a special function, that of serving as God's representative or steward in the created order. But it does distinguish human life from all other forms of life, drawing humanity into a unique relationship to God.

By contrast, the essential thing about human life for the Yahwist author is that it emerges out of arable soil. The Yahwist traces Israel's ancestors, and the human race as a whole, to "the farmer," *ha adam,* who was made from arable soil, *adama,* and designated by God to be its cultivator. Adam's descendants and the narrative's central characters — Cain, Noah, Abraham, Isaac, and Jacob — are all landholders engaged in the mixed agriculture of herding and cropping. In their basic nature, therefore, humans are associated with the earth and all living things. The breath blown into the first human being by God is the same breath by which all animals live; it bestows no unique divine status upon humanity. What is stressed is humanity's kinship with the rest of creation.

These contrasting notions of human nature are connected with differing conceptions of the relationship between human and animal life. P's view of the relationship is decidedly hierarchical. In the beginning humans are commanded by God to rule (*rada*), to exercise dominion over animate creatures. By contrast, the Yahwist conjures up a more communal relationship. Seeing that both humans and animals are made from the earth's topsoil, they possess no distinct ontological status but are referred to jointly as "living beings" (*nepes hayya;* Gen. 2:7, 19). Animals are regarded as helpers or companions in the task of agriculture. The act of naming them (2:19) does not indicate power and control but identification and relationship.

The relationship between humans and the earth is also opposed. For the Priestly author, agricultural work is understood as subduing (*kabas*) the earth (1:28). The verb *kabas* is a powerful word implying the coercive subjection of another. It is used in the Bible to describe defeating an adversary in battle, making slaves, and raping women. For P, then, the land is viewed as an adversary to be pressed into service (a view that Francis Bacon will later accent, as we shall see). The Yahwist adopts an entirely more modest and humble attitude toward the land. Agriculture is understood as serving (*abad*) the land (2:5, 15; 3:23; 4:2). The land must not be overused; it, too, must have its rest period, its sabbatical.

> For six years you may sow your land and gather its produce; but in the seventh year you shall let it lie fallow and leave it alone. It shall provide food for the poor of your people, and what they leave the wild animals may eat. You shall do likewise with your vineyard and your olive-grove. (Exod. 23:10–11)

For J, the land is viewed on the analogy with a king; the land is a sovereign to be served. As Hiebert puts it, "For P the human is the land's master, coercing it into service, while for J the human is the land's servant, performing the duties demanded by its powers and processes."[19] As Hiebert sums up the contrast:

> Two distinct postures within creation are assumed by the human being in Priestly and Yahwistic perspectives. The Priestly human occupies a superior position within the created order. Created in God's image, humans are distinguished from the rest of creation and granted unique authority over it. They are to exercise this authority by populating the earth, ruling its animals, and subduing its land.... The human of Genesis 1 shares many of the characteristics of the priestly role itself. This was the role of a distinct, elite party in Israelite society, closely allied to royalty, that regarded itself as the mediator of divine rule to Israel and to creation itself....
>
> By contrast, the human being in the Yahwist's epic occupies a subordinate role within the created order. Created out of arable soil, the Yahwist's human is united with the rest of creation and placed in a subservient relationship to it. This subservience is expressed in the image of the soil as the beginning and end of human life and in the depiction of the cultivation of the soil as "serving" rather than "subduing." ... Basic to this image of the human is the ancient farmer's sense of dependence upon the soil, of the necessity of meeting its demands and cooperating with its processes, and of the ultimate lack of control over nature's own orders and powers.[20]

The Yahwist's sense of humility before and service to nature is recapitulated in the Book of Job. There nature mediates the sacred precisely because it is like God, sovereign, awesome, mysterious, and not reducible to the meanings and purposes that human beings give to it. It has its own meanings and directions that lie beyond our control, beyond our figuring and comprehension. That is why it can serve as a pointer to the "otherness" or transcendence of God. Think of the great theophany — the God of the whirlwind — in chapters 38 to 41 of the Book of Job. The weather, the workings of the heavens, the strangeness of animals remind us that God's universe is not created to fit the scale of our minds. Like the theology of the Yahwist, Job's Lord

---

19. Ibid., 157.
20. Ibid., 158–59.

of the whirlwind calls us to humility and joy before the wonder, the sheer strangeness and wildness, of created things, which God created for reasons that far exceed human designs.

> By what paths is the heat spread abroad
> or the east wind carried far and wide over the earth?

> Who has cut channels for the downpour
> and cleared a passage for the thunderstorm,
> for rain to fall on land where no man lives
> and on the desert wilderness,
> clothing lands waste and derelict with green
> and making grass to grow on thirsty ground? . . .

> Did you proclaim the rules that govern the heavens,
> or determine the laws of nature on the earth?
> Can you command the dense clouds
> to cover with their weight of waters? . . .

> Do you hunt her prey for the lioness
> and satisfy the hunger of young lions,
> as they crouch in the lair
> or lie in wait in the covert?
> Who provides the raven with its quarry
> when its fledglings croak for lack of food?
> Do you know when the mountain goats are born
> or attend the wild doe when she is in labor? . . .

> Who has let the wild ass of Syria range at will
> and given the wild ass of Arabia its freedom? . . .

> Does the wild ox consent to serve you,
> does it spend the night in your stall? . . .

> Did you give the horse his strength? . . .

> Do you instruct the vulture to fly high
> and build its nest aloft? . . .

> Can you pull the whale with a gaff
> or can you slip a noose round its tongue?
> (Job 38:24–39:27)

The Book of Job celebrates whatever is wild. God rejoices in whales, rejoices in all wildness, in whatever humans cannot trap or hook or tame.

T W O

Nature Symbolic of Promise

Can you draw out Leviathan with a fishhook,
Or press down his tongue with a chord?
Can you put a rope in his nose,
Or pierce his jaw with a hook?
Will he make many supplications to you?
Will he speak to you soft words?
Will he make a covenant with you to take him for your servant
  forever?   —Job 41:1–4

From the very beginning till now the entire creation, as we know,
has been groaning in one great act of giving birth.
                                                  —Romans 8:23

In defending the biblical outlook against its environmentalist detractors, as I have been doing, my intentions are modest. I do not wish to argue that the Bible offers us an entirely adequate ecological vision for our time. The environmental challenge that the late Carl Sagan and others articulate is something new, a phenomenon of the post-industrial world, and there is little likelihood that the Bible, inspired as it is but a document nonetheless from the ancient agricultural world, could provide us with all the answers that we need. On the other hand, the Bible offers far more resources for an ecological ethic than Lynn White and many other critics once supposed. And certainly the Bible can serve this foundational purpose far better than many other later developments in the Western Christian tradition, developments that took a markedly dualistic and earth-escaping form, and that are thus hostile to the material world and an environmental ethic. One thinks of various earth-despising gnostic tendencies within Christianity, or even of certain neo-Platonic elements that separate matter and spirit, soul and body.

When it comes to the attitude toward the physical world, the Christian tradition is more ambivalent than the Hebrew Bible is. Christianity has always been juggling a heritage composed of a synthesis of ancient Near Eastern, Hebrew, Greek, and Christian ideas. The transposition of Jewish monotheism into the doctrine of the Trinity — that is, the belief in One God in three ways — tries to bridge the gap between divine transcendence "outside" the material world and the divine presence "in" creation and history. Christian cosmology thereby seeks to encompass two different concepts of the divine-cosmos relation, on the one hand seeing God as wholly other, eternal and self-subsistent Being over against nondivine, dependent created being, and on the other hand seeing God as incarnate in Jesus of Nazareth and immanent as Holy Spirit in all creation.[1] As Alfred North Whitehead once put it, in deciding for the direct immanence of God in the person of Christ and in the world generally, the great fourth-century theologians of Alexandria and Antioch "have the distinction of being the only thinkers who in a fundamental metaphysical doctrine improved upon Plato."[2]

Taking off from this sense of divine immanence, both St. Augustine and Francis of Assisi imagine creation itself as a rich and variegated expression of God's overflowing goodness. Yet the Christian tradition as a whole is ambivalent. "The Christian contemplating the world," remarked the great theological historian M. D. Chenu, "is torn by a double attraction: to attain God through the world, the order of which reveals the Creator, or to renounce the world, from which God is radically distinct."[3] For example, consider how theologian Rosemary Ruether describes the Western ascetic tradition.

> For those seeking an ecological ethic for a new era . . . the heritage of Christian asceticism is Janus-faced. One side of this tradition, with its hostility to women, sexuality, and the body, and its contempt for the material world in favor of life after death, reinforces the pattern of neglect of and flight from the earth. But asceticism can also be understood, not as rejection of the body and the earth, but rather as a rejection of exploitation and excess, and thus as a return to egalitarian simple living in harmony with other humans and with nature.[4]

In his classic study of the neo-Platonic tradition in Western history, *The Great Chain of Being*, Arthur Lovejoy highlighted this tension in a slightly different but illuminating way. He remarks that there were two antithetical notions of transcendence, in effect two different Gods, in-

---

1. See Rosemary Ruether, *Gaia and God: An Ecofeminist Theology of Earth Healing* (San Francisco: HarperSanFrancisco, 1992), 26–31, 126–42, 184–94.
2. Alfred North Whitehead, *Adventures of Ideas* (New York: Macmillan, 1933), 214–15.
3. M. D. Chenu, *Nature, Man, and Society in the Twelfth Century: Essays on New Theological Perspectives in the Latin West*, ed. and trans. Jerome Taylor and Lester K. Little (Chicago: University of Chicago Press, 1968), 36.
4. Ruether, *Gaia and God*, 188.

volved in the development of Christian doctrine, the one an apotheosis of unity, self-sufficiency, and quietude; the other a celebration of diversity, self-transcendence, and fertility (goodness overflows, is diffusive of itself). The former God sponsored the principle of world-denial, and the latter sponsored the principle of world-affirmation. One God bids us to rise above the world and leave it behind; the other bids us to recognize our solidarity with the whole world and embrace it. Behind these two notions of the divine, Lovejoy observed, stood the two major Greek philosophical traditions: the world-transcending, self-sufficient Unmoved Mover of Aristotle's *Metaphysics,* as opposed to the overflowing, world-affirming Goodness of Plato's *Timaeus.*[5]

The ambivalence of the God-cosmos relation within historical Christianity is also mirrored in differing notions of the soul. Within the Hebrew tradition the soul had been understood as the life principle of the body, with future life taking the form of a resurrected body in a renovated earth. From this angle, human destiny is inseparable from the destiny of the whole earth or cosmos. This is the idea clearly reflected in St. Paul's Epistle to the Romans, chapter 8, where the whole cosmos is imaged as pregnant and groaning in the Spirit-driven throes of giving birth to a new heaven and new earth. At the same time, Christianity absorbed the Platonic notion of the soul as inherently immortal and having "fallen" through sin into gross mortal bodies. The soul-body split here leads to the conclusion that the essence of a human being consists of a transcendent, disembodied, immortal soul that can abandon its bodily life as accidental. Human destiny is thus severed from the fate of the physical world. Despite the fact that the church never entirely repudiated the Hebrew concepts of the resurrected body and a redeemed earth, the dominant Christian eschatology[6] has often been escapist; the human soul has been conceived as a thing apart, not sharing in the mortality of the rest of the earth's creatures.

Another way to look at this internal conflict is brought out by H. Paul Santmire. The question is how the idea of "transcending nature" is to be understood and how, historically, it has been understood in the West. Two major interpretations of transcendence are possible — one which Santmire calls the "spiritual tradition" and the other which he names the "ecological tradition" — and both lineages run through the entire Christian tradition of biblical interpretation. The spiritual

---

5. Arthur Lovejoy, *The Great Chain of Being: A Study in the History of an Idea* (New York: Harper & Brothers, 1936), 34ff., 84.

6. *Eschata* in Greek means ends or outcomes, and Christian eschatology has traditionally entailed reflection on the four "last things": death, judgment, hell, and heaven. In recent times eschatology has focused on hope in the promised reign of God in all human experience and in all creation.

tradition is marked by the root metaphor of ascent; humanity is called out of this world to commune with God above, as in the archetypal story of Moses ascending Mount Sinai or Aquinas's notion of the beatific vision in heaven. This is the tradition of the Gospel of John, the letter to the Hebrews, of Origen, Dante, Bonaventure, and Aquinas. It can lead to a spiritual devaluation of earth and an alienation of *Homo sapiens* from other life-forms. At the same time, one also has to recognize that rising above the earth has also led to the Western drive for justice, equality, compassion, and material improvement.

The ecological tradition, on the other hand, focuses on two other biblical root metaphors: that of migrating to the land of promise and that of the overflowing fecundity of God manifest in creation (the sacramental tradition). This is the tradition I shall stress in these pages. It is the tradition of the synoptic Gospels and St. Paul, of Irenaeus, Augustine, Francis of Assisi, and the American Puritans. It looks forward to a transfigured earth — the "new heaven and earth" of the Book of Revelation.[7]

Though the spirituality of ascent may be a perfectly legitimate path, then, it has its risks and dangers. Not only does it offer slim pickings for en ecological ethic; it can also father grand illusions. The point is that, like anything else human, the urge to transcendence is not an unalloyed good; it conceals certain built-in problems endemic to a perfervid otherworldliness or excess of supernaturalism. Here as elsewhere there can be too much of a good thing, a super-supernaturalism or false transcendence that turns the material world into the enemy and primary source of evil.

Can Christianity include nature within its moral circle? It depends on what stream within the larger tradition one latches on to. Unfortunately, the general rule of Western moral and social traditions, certainly since the seventeenth-century scientific revolution, has been that animals, trees, and the land do not have any moral standing in their own right. The human drama takes central place, and nature is seen as merely the stage on which this drama plays itself out. Consequently, a person's relations with nature tend to fall outside the sphere of moral right and wrong. This is exactly the outlook that is now being challenged so vigorously by environmentalists, raising the prospect of a major shift in the moral thinking of Western civilization: from anthropocentrism to a biocentric or ecocentric inclusiveness. Environmentalists challenge us to enlarge the circle of our moral concern to

---

7. H. Paul Santmire, *The Travail of Nature: The Ambiguous Ecological Promise of Christian Theology* (Philadelphia: Fortress Press, 1985), 17–29, 175–218.

include the land, air, water, forest, and all manner of life-forms. This nonhuman realm, they argue, makes moral claims upon us. But as we have just observed above, there is a whole stream of biblical Christian theology, stressing the eventual transformation of heaven and earth, that sees human destiny as inextricably linked to the destiny of the material world.

All the more reason, then, to return to the sources — and certain strengths in the biblical and Christian tradition that incorporate a positive attitude toward the earth.

Not Anthropocentrism but Theocentrism

For Judaism and Christianity, nature is a contingent, not an eternal, order. Things might not have turned out the way they have; in fact, given a doctrine of creation *ex nihilo* (from nothing), the universe as a whole is contingent: it need not have happened at all. This is equivalent to saying, as both Judaism and Christianity assert, that to divinize nature is idolatrous. Sagan & Co. may therefore be barking up the wrong tree to ask Jews and Christians to resacralize nature. For though the Bible finds all of God's creation "good," it is unalterably opposed to sacralizing nature, not because the Bible is anthropocentric but because it is unequivocally *theocentric*. That is the meaning of the first commandment: God alone is holy and worthy of worship. "I am the Lord your God who brought you out of Egypt, out of the land of slavery. You shall have no other god to set against me" (Exod. 20:2–3). To confess belief in the God of the Bible is, first of all, to fall on one's knees before the *mysterium tremendum*. It is also a performative act, for faith pledges to do something: "do justice, love mercy, and walk humbly with your God" (Mic. 6:8).

As the offspring of Judaism, authentic Christianity will be equally theocentric, and as such the heir to the Hebrew campaign against pagan animism, which was seen as idolatrous. Yes, "the heavens tell of the glory of God, the vault of heaven reveals his handiwork" (Ps. 19:1), but the created world, however awe-inspiring and beautiful, is not to be identified or confused with the Creator. To the biblical writers and redactors the heavens and the earth have no importance in themselves, as an object, say, of scientific interest, as they did for Greeks like Aristotle and as they do for us moderns. The principal function of creation is to proclaim the glory of God. Psalm 148 catches this spirit:

> Praise the Lord out of heaven;
> praise him in the heights. . . .

> Praise him sun and moon;
> praise him, all you shining stars;
> praise him, heaven of heavens,
> and you waters above the heavens....
>
> Praise the Lord from the earth,
> you water spouts and ocean depths;
> fire and hail, snow and ice,
> gales of wind, obeying his voice;
> all mountains and hills;
> all fruit trees and all cedars;
> wild beasts and cattle,
> creeping things and winged birds.
> (Ps. 148:1, 3–4, 7–10)

But to say that the heavens and the earth declare the glory of God was equivalently to declare that nature gives "hints and guesses" of God's promises. That is, nature itself is promissory, from beginning to end. Thus the archetypal statement of St. Paul in Romans 8:19–23: the universe as a whole is pregnant with promise.

> The whole creation is eagerly waiting for God to reveal his sons.
> ...From the very beginning till now the entire creation, as we know, has been groaning in one great act of giving birth.

Promise and the Land

The most fundamental theme throughout the Hebrew Bible is the covenant promise between God and the Israelites. But what is covenant about except the promise of land and the fecundity of the earth? Think of the call of Abraham:

> Leave your country, your family and your father's house, for the land I will show you.... So Abram went as Yahweh told him.... Abram passed through the land as far as Shechem's holy place, the Oak of Moreh. At the time the Canaanites were in the land. Yahweh appeared to Abram and said, "It is to your descendants that I will give this land." (Gen. 12:1, 4, 6–7)

> When the sun had set and darkness had fallen, there appeared a smoking furnace and a firebrand.... That day Yahweh made a Covenant with Abram in these terms: "To your descendants I give this land, from the wadi of Egypt to the Great River, the river Euphrates." (Gen. 15:17–18)

The call of the other patriarchs, and of Moses, echoes the same theme. Yahweh says to Moses:

> "I have seen the miserable state of my people in Egypt. I have heard their appeal to be free of their slave drivers. Yes, I am well aware of their sufferings. I mean to deliver them out of the hands of the Egyptians and bring them up out of the land to a land rich and broad, a land where milk and honey flow, the home of the Canaanites, the Hittites, the Amorites, the Perizzites, the Hivites and the Jebusites." (Exod. 3:7–8)

Indeed, there is no more root metaphor in the Bible than the metaphor of the promising journey: Moses leading the people of Israel toward the promised land (the exodus), or the return from exile to that promised land:

> For the Lord your God is bringing you into a good land, a land of brooks and water, of fountains and springs, flowing forth in valleys and hills, a land of wheat and barley, of vines and fig trees and pomegranates, a land of olive trees and honey, a land in which you will eat bread without scarcity, in which you will lack nothing, a land whose stones are iron, and out of whose hills you can dig copper. (Deut. 8:8–9)

In this way, the abundance of the land is the sign of God's overflowing blessing. Consider, above all, the Psalms of praise, notably Psalm 104:

> I will bless you, O Lord God!
> You fill the world with awe,
> You dress yourself in light,
> In rich, majestic light.
>
> You stretched the sky like a tent,
> Built your house beyond the rain.
> You ride upon the clouds,
> The wind becomes your wings,
> The storm becomes your herald,
> Your servants, bolts of light....
>
> God, how fertile your genius!
> You shape each thing,
> You fill the world
> With what you do....
>
> Let God's glory endure
> And the Lord delight in creating.

> One look from God, earth quivers;
> One touch, and mountains erupt.
>
> I will sing to my God
> Make music for the Lord
> As long as I live.
> Let my song give joy to God
> Who is joy to me.
> (Ps. 104:1–4, 24, 31–34)

At the same time, the blessings of a fruitful land function as the sign of what is to come in the future:

> Behold, I am doing a new thing; now it springs forth, do you not perceive it? I will make a way in the wilderness and rivers in the desert. The wild beasts will honor me, the jackals and the ostriches; for I give water in the wilderness, rivers in the desert, to give drink to my chosen people, the people whom I formed for myself that they might declare my praise. (Isa. 43:19–21)

The centrality of the land has not always been acknowledged by Christian biblical scholars, who have tended to stress the mighty acts of God in human history as opposed to God's activity in nature. "Preoccupation with existentialist decisions and transforming events," writes Walter Brueggemann, "has distracted us from seeing that this God is committed to his land and that his promise for his people is always his land."[8] Indeed, it is from its sense of the fecundity and blessing of the earth that Israel arrived at a broader sense of the goodness of the land and earth as a whole, as in the cadence of Genesis 1: "and God saw that it was good."

Transcendence and Negation

If the created world of nature is fundamentally good, however, the Bible takes a much tougher stand toward social organization and power arrangements. The power of the written word, in the use the Hebrews made of it, says the Sorbonne's Olivier Revault D'Allonnes, lies in the "effective power of negation, of denial." In this regard, Abraham is not only the father of the Jews, but of all free people. "Free men, like nomads," remarks D'Allonnes, "are those who do not know where they are going." Writes D'Allonnes:

---

8. Walter Brueggemann, *The Land: Place as Gift, Promise, and Challenge in Biblical Faith* (Philadelphia: Fortress Press, 1977), 6.

[Abraham] is the sedentary man who becomes a nomad, the man of the city who leaves it for the wide open spaces. Why? To escape what Brecht will call the Jungle of Cities, to be no longer an extra cog in the machine, in short to say no and by this very movement to set himself up and affirm himself in his subjectivity. That is what it is to be a man: to refuse. The animal, the slave, the senseless ones accept, continue, reproduce. They have no inwardness, that is to say *no place of refusal,* of negation, of criticism.... Abraham, whose final name comprises the same consonants as the name of the Hebrews, is probably the first free man of biblical antiquity, because he is the first to say no to the world and therefore yes to God.... Totally calm, Abraham leaves a city situated at a precise point in space, he leaves places like his native land, his home, as well as everything attached to it, to go to live thenceforth where the Eternal leads him; he does not abandon himself, he entrusts himself to absolute difference, to the succession where all becomes possible. In short, he leaves space for time, that is to say slavery for liberty. This tenth generation descendent of Shem was rightly recognized as the father of the Jews, and of all free men.[9]

It goes without saying, remarks D'Allonnes, that successive generations have tried to cover up or mask this seditious message.

The patriarchs Isaac and Jacob depended on a promise like their father Abraham's. As did Moses. And the other prophets. And herein lie the incomparable critical power of Jewish thought and its most important contribution to Western culture. The prophets did not allow themselves to be taken in by the world, to be sedentarized or completely assimilated. They are constantly probing the problematic of their societies, the concrete historical situation, the foreign affairs of the mighty and the politics of everyday life. (By tradition, the faithful Jew instinctively has what C. Wright Mills once called a "sociological imagination," viewing all social arrangements as contingent and changeable.) Why? If D'Allonnes has it right it is because those wedded to the biblical, prophetic tradition have at their mental command two contrasting postulates: an absolute beyond history, the unconditional divine will and promise of a world of justice in the certain but indefinite future; and an acute sense that everything immersed in time and history is relative, nonobligatory, and inconclusive. Hence they are unlikely to

---

9. Olivier Revault D'Allonnes, *Musical Variations on Jewish Thought* (New York: George Braziller, 1984), 68–69.

be bewitched by any ruling custom or dominant social paradigm. For the Jew, transcendence provides leverage for moving the world.

> Jewish thought is thus constituted and reinforced around two terms, one of which, in truth, is always missing: that is God, or the absolute, or the Messiah, or justice realized. The other term, which is the actual given, is completely relative, made completely relative by the first and, so to speak, returned to its proper place. The absolute functions as a relativizing factor of the other term.
>
> The characteristic by which Jewish thought is infallibly recognized is that it immediately grasps every object as non-obligatory and inconclusive in itself, as an object whose worth is set by its counterpoint....Non-Jewish consciousness falls into the trap of believing in things as they seem to be, always with some small aspect of the absolute, a gloss of eternity or of necessity, of universal truth. It too often lacks that irreplaceable sense of the relativity of things which total immersion in temporality lends to thought.[10]

If time is everything, as Genesis implies, then everything in it is situated and relative; nothing is eternal, nothing is given as is in an unambiguous, necessary, and immutable manner.

> To affirm the City of God, to write and describe the reign of justice, is certainly a falsehood, because that reign and that city are illusory, because the world is full of injustice and impiety. But this is done essentially in order to oppose to this unjust world a radical, absolute, unconditional refusal, a refusal which appears in its most pathetic form in Job and in Amos: if the world cannot be just, then let it vanish. A refusal which, in countless varied forms, from Jeremiah to Marx and from the *anavim* [the poor] to Marcuse, constitutes the rallying point of all who maintain an ideal, a hope, and who, as a result, are thereby attached, whether or not they want to be, whether or not they know it, to Israelite thought.[11]

For the prophets and the Jewish tradition, then, dominant social paradigms or the way in which the world currently works can never be decisive. That means that an industrial system that abuses the environment is not written into the natural order of things or on tablets of stone. The status quo will always be relative or contingent, not necessary. Imagination of the City of God takes precedence over the simply

---

10. Ibid., 64.
11. Ibid., 67–68.

factual; what must be takes priority over what is. In short, the biblical universe has to have a place in it not only for redundancy and the law of large numbers overwhelming minorities, but also a place for minorities, even minorities of one, who are determined to subvert or smash the ruling order. There has to be time and space, that is to say, not only for the indicative mood of what is everlastingly the case, but also for the subjunctive and imperative moods of what might be, could be, and must be — the reign of God — against all the odds.

We thus come to this startling axiom: that the claim of otherworldly justice or the kingdom of God, transcendence in the Hebrew sense, provides the crucial fulcrum for moving the world of space and time. Without transcendence, the world is locked down, settled, immobilized, rooted in place. Without it, there is no leverage on the world, no space to dream in, to conjecture, to imagine what might be, could be, must be. Transcendence is the brewing place of possibility, of a future different from the past. It gives purchase to hope.

Nature as Sacrament

Nature, as we said, is not God. Yet what many people seem to overlook are the implications of the Christian doctrine of God's immanence in creation. Christianity comes within inches of pantheism, and nothing brings this out more clearly than a look at medieval sacramental theology. Putting this theology together with its Ptolemaic astronomy, the medievals derived a cosmology, a view of the whole of nature and our place within nature. It was, as we said above, a mix of biblical and Greek ideas, reflecting the continuing influence of Plato and Aristotle as well as Scripture. In Ian G. Barbour's Gifford Lectures of 1989–90, it is schematized as follows:

- Nature was imagined as a fixed order, without internal change; there was directionality in human history, but the basic forms were thought to be immutable.

- Nature was teleological (purposeful). Every creature expressed both the divine purposes and its own in-built goals — and was explained in terms of such purposes (or final causes).

- Nature was substantive; the components were separate mental and material substances. A substance was taken to be independent and externally related, requiring nothing but itself (and God) in order to be.

- The cosmos was hierarchical, with each lower form serving the higher (God/man/woman/animal/plant). Nature was a single coherent whole, a graded but unified order, with all parts working together for God's purposes according to the divine plan. The institutions of church and society were also held to be fixed and hierarchical, integrated into the total cosmic order. The scheme was basically anthropocentric in holding that all creatures on earth were created for the benefit of humanity; and a sharp distinction was assumed between humanity and all other creatures. The earth was the center of the cosmos, surrounded by celestial spheres and the eternal heavens.[12]

The interpretive categories of the medieval cosmology were dualistic, with fundamental contrasts between soul and body, between immaterial spirit and transitory matter, and between the perfect eternal forms and their imperfect embodiments in the material world. The purpose of the material order was to serve the spiritual, and the goal of this life was to prepare for the next life after death. There are problems here: the otherworldly perspective, the dualism, the contempt for this world may undermine the kind of ecological ethic we seek. Nonetheless, nature has a value here that an industrial and technological culture often refuses.

The Christian culture of the medieval period, following Augustine of Hippo, likened nature to a book, a semiotic system, a set of signs signifying and transmitting the energies of what Aristotle called the *nous poetikos*, the prime Poet-Maker of the cosmos. Thus there are two books of revelation: the Bible and nature. The paradigmatic Christian text along this line, the source for a long lineage of Christian "natural theology" (i.e., signs in nature that God exists), is St. Paul's Epistle to the Romans. "God's invisible attributes," Paul wrote, "that is to say his everlasting power and deity, have been made visible, ever since the world began, to the eye of reason, in the things he has made" (Rom. 1:20). Once again, the feeling of the numinous, of the presence of the holy, may be experienced *in* or *through* nature, but should not be ascribed to nature. In this symbolic sense, but this sense only, nature mediates the sacred.

The universe, then, was presumed to be full of signs of God's promise and grace. It was, as the medievals put it, "sacramental." The term "sacrament" derived from the Roman soldier's solemn promise to serve the emperor. When Christians adopted the word for their rites of initi-

---

12. Adapted from Ian G. Barbour, *Religion in an Age of Science* (San Francisco: HarperSanFrancisco, 1990), 1:218–19.

ation and blessing, it came to mean the human act of giving a sensible sign (pouring water, rubbing ashes on the forehead, lighting a candle, burning incense, signing the cross, and so forth) that confers God's promise and grace.

Behind the use of earth, air, fire, and water in Christian ritual, however, lies a cosmological assertion inherited from the very meaning of the word "nature" (*physis* in Greek, *natura* in Latin) in ancient Mediterranean culture. The word meant "giving birth." And so, by extension, the primordial sacrament was seen as dynamic and generative nature itself, the visible manifestation or "sign" of the super-eminently bountiful Creator. God's energy, glory, favor, and promise were sensed (especially by contemplative monks and nuns) as flowing throughout the whole of creation much the way the sun's radiance pours down upon earth. (The very word "Catholic" refers to this, the Greek words *kata* and *holos* literally meaning "throughout the whole.") And it is to this rampant energy that the church and its saints are to testify.

The sacramentality of the natural world — that is, its promising character — is captured perfectly in Gerard Manley Hopkins's poem "God's Grandeur":

> The world is charged with the grandeur of God.
> It will flame out, like shining from shook foil;
> It gathers to a greatness, like ooze of oil
> Crushed....
> There lives the dearest freshness deep down things.... [13]

To Hopkins, as to the premodern sensibility of an Aquinas or Duns Scotus, nature has its own autonomy and (secondary) causality. But nature also serves as theophany, a revelation of the Holy One. As Vanderbilt University's Sallie McFague points out, the strength of this tradition consists in the fact that it epitomizes the sensibility that finds God in all things and all things as full of the glory of God:

> In spite of its limitations, traditional sacramentalism is an important perspective, for it is the major way Christianity has preserved and developed an appreciation for nature. It has encouraged Christians to look at the world as valuable — indeed, as holy — and has served as a counterforce to two other perspectives on nature within Christian history, one that divorces it totally from God through secularizing it and one that dominates and exploits it. Traditional sacramentalism has, in its own way, supported the

---

13. *A Hopkins Reader*, rev. and enlarged, ed. John Pick (New York: Doubleday Image Books, 1966), 47–48.

principle...that the presence of God is not limited to particular times or places but is coextensive with reality, with all that is. It has been one of the few traditions within Christianity that has encouraged both a spatial and a historical perspective; that is, Christian sacramentalism has included nature as a concern of God and a way to God rather than limiting divine activity to human history.[14]

The medieval cosmology consisted of a vast hierarchy or chain of being emanating from the creative power of the divine architect. Each creature in this vast array was seen as being sustained moment by moment by the Creator and as containing the imprint of its Creator. Creation, that is, manifested the *vestigia dei* (the imprints of God) and, accordingly, from a human perspective, could be understood as a ladder of ascent to God. As in St. Bonaventure's vision of the created world in the *Itinerarium mentis in Deum:*

All the creatures of the sense world lead the mind of the contemplative and wise man to the eternal God. For these creatures are shadows, echoes and pictures of that first, most powerful, most wise and most perfect Principle, of that eternal Source, Light and Fullness, of that efficient, exemplary and ordering Art. They are vestiges, representations, spectacles proposed to us and signs divinely given so that we can see God. These creatures, I say, are exemplars or rather exemplifications presented to souls still untrained and immersed in sensible things so that through sensible things which they see they will be carried over to intelligible things which they do not see as through signs to what is signified. The creatures of the sense world signify the invisible attributes of God, partly because God is the origin, exemplar and end of every creature, and every effect is the sign of its cause, the exemplification of its exemplar and the path to the end, to which it leads.[15]

The sacramentality of nature is rendered by Thomas of Celano, Francis of Assisi's early biographer, in this way:

Who could ever express the deep affection he bore for all things that belong to God? Or who would be able to tell all the sweet tenderness he enjoyed while contemplating in creatures the wisdom, power, and goodness of the Creator? From this reflection

---

14. Sallie McFague, *The Body of God: An Ecological Theology* (Minneapolis: Fortress Press, 1993), 184.

15. Bonaventure, *The Soul's Journey into God,* trans. and introduction Ewart Cousins (New York: Paulist Press, 1978), 75–76.

he often overflowed with amazing, unspeakable joy, as he looked at the sun, gazed at the moon, or observed the stars in the sky. . . .

Even for worms he had a warm love, since he had read this text about the Savior: I am a worm and not a man. That is why he used to pick them up from the road and put them in a safe place so that they would not be crushed by the footsteps of passersby.

What shall I say about the other lesser creatures? In the winter he had honey or the best wine put out for the bees so that they would not perish from the cold. He used to extol the artistry of their work and their remarkable ingenuity, giving glory to the Lord. With such an outpouring, he often used up an entire day or more in praise of them and other creatures. . . .

How great do you think was the delight the beauty of flowers brought to his soul whenever he saw their lovely form and noticed their sweet fragrance? . . . Whenever he found an abundance of flowers, he used to preach to them and invite them to praise the Lord, just as if they were endowed with reason. Fields and vineyards, rocks and woods, and all the beauties of the field, flowing springs and blooming gardens, earth and fire, air and wind: all these he urged to love God and to willing service. Finally, he used to call all creatures "brother" and "sister" and in a wonderful way, unknown to others, he could discern the secrets of the heart of creatures like someone already passed into the freedom of the glory of the children of God.[16]

This sense of finding God in all things is not confined to the Catholic sacramental tradition of the thirteenth century. It is equally prominent in eighteenth-century American Puritans. Jonathan Edwards (1703–58), for instance, describes his own early "awakening" to the presence of God as occurring while walking alone in his father's pasture in Connecticut. There, while looking up at the sky and the clouds, "there came into my mind so sweet a sense of the glorious majesty and grace of God, that I know not how to express." He continues:

After this my sense of divine things gradually increased. . . . The appearance of everything was altered; there seemed to be, as it were, a calm, sweet cast, or appearance of divine glory, in almost everything. God's excellency, his wisdom, his purity and love, seemed to appear in every thing; in the sun, moon, and stars; in

---

16. *Francis of Assisi: Early Documents*, ed. Regis J. Armstrong, O.F.M.Cap., J. A. Wayne Hellmann, O.F.M.Conv., William J. Short, O.F.M. (New York: New City Press, 1999), 1:250–51. See also Edward A. Armstrong, *St. Francis, Nature Mystic: The Derivation and Significance of the Nature Stories in the Franciscan Legend* (Berkeley: University of California Press, 1973).

the clouds, and blue sky; in the grass, flowers, trees; in the water, and all nature; which used greatly to fix my mind. I often used to sit and view the moon for continuance; and in the day, spent much time in viewing the clouds and the sky, to behold the sweet glory of God in these things; in the mean time, singing forth, with a low voice my contemplations of the Creator and Redeemer. And scarce anything, among all the works of nature, was so sweet to me as thunder and lightning; formerly, nothing had been so terrible to me.... I felt God, so to speak, at the first appearance of a thunder storm.[17]

Francis of Assisi and Jonathan Edwards were biocentrists.

Needless to say, the health of the earth is integral to its power to convey a message of promise and hope. If the sun is hazy or blocked by smog, if the water is unclean, the air poisonous, the wind full of dust and smoke, the soil eroded or desiccated, and biological diversity consumed by the fires burning up the rain forests, the sacramental "light" of nature grows dim. To degrade the earth is to interfere with the message of its Creator. "We should be clear about what happens," says eco-theologian Father Thomas Berry, "when we destroy the living forms of this planet. The first consequence is that we destroy modes of the divine presence. If we have a wonderful sense of the divine, it is because we live amid such awesome magnificence." In more ways than we can count, the richness of our cultural lives hinges on the context, the fact that we are surrounded by the riches of nature. Berry continues:

If we have a refinement of emotion and sensitivity, it is because of the delicacy, the fragrance, and indescribable beauty of song and music and rhythmic movement in the world about us. If we grow in our life vigor, it is because the earthly community challenges us, forces us to struggle to survive, but in the end reveals itself as a benign providence. But however benign, it must provide that absorbing drama of existence whereby we can experience the thrill of being alive in a fascinating and unending sequence of adventures.[18]

In other words, as Berry puts it, "this universe itself, but especially the planet Earth, needs to be experienced as the primary mode of divine presence, just as it is the primary educator, primary healer, primary

---

17. Cited in Louis Dupré and James A. Wiseman, O.S.B., *Light from Light: An Anthology of Christian Mysticism* (New York and Mahwah, N.J.: Paulist Press, 1988), 377.
18. Thomas Berry, *Dream of the Earth* (San Francisco: Sierra Club, 1988), 11.

commercial establishment, and primary lawgiver for all that exists within this life community."[19]

From an ecological perspective, however, the great weakness of sacramentalism lies in what we might call its theocentric utilitarianism. That is, in the sacramental vision, material things are understood instrumentally, as a means of attaining ecstatic spiritual states. The things of earth are not appreciated in their own right as having intrinsic value, but are seen as pointers or stepping stones in a person's pilgrimage back to God. Nature's value, then, lies in its symbolism, its capacity to serve as a medium of communication with God. This constitutes a problem for a spirituality of ascent, but not for what Santmire called the ecological tradition, which emphasizes that contemplation of God brings us back to earth. For God's promise encompasses all creation and intends nothing less than the transformation of all the earth.

The deeper challenge to sacramentalism in our day, however, may not lie in its utilitarianism, but in the signs that nature gives now, as we now understand it scientifically. Does nature give signs of promise as it once did? What signals are given by the big bang? By the double helix of DNA molecules? By the Darwinian competition for existence? By the certainty that the sun will eventually run out of fuel, turning earth into a cinder floating lifelessly in empty space? What do such phenomena have to say about the Creator? About the nature of the universe as a whole? Given the presuppositions of a premodern outlook, it may once have been somewhat easier to perceive the providence and benevolence of the Creator through nature than it is today. I am not sure, since premoderns were if anything more vulnerable to natural disasters than we are. In any case, if a sacramental understanding of the cosmos is to survive today, it will be necessary to update it in terms of contemporary science. One has to ask what signs are being given by the big bang, by dark matter, black holes, thermodynamics, and the prospect that the sun will burn out in the space of the next 5 billion years. I will return to such questions below, in chapter 9.

Sacrament as Human Deed

There are two kinds of sacrament here, which are often confused. The first is God's act: the ongoing act of creation itself (why there is something rather than nothing) that is manifest throughout the sensible world. The second is the human act, in imitation of or collaboration with the divine creativity, of making a sign of promise. (Whitehead

---

19. Ibid., 120.

talked of this in terms of responding to the divine "lure," where God is the source of all becoming and possibility in the cosmos.) What I shall call the cosmological or first sense of the word refers to nature's graceful signs, its spendthrift, life-giving abundance, contemplated and acknowledged with gratitude in moments of Sabbath "rest." This is the sense of sacrament that I have just referred to above, the idea that we can experience God's promises in and through nature. It is an experience of something beyond our control, what nature does to manifest the numinous.

The second sacramental sense is a response to the first, cosmological sacramentality, and involves human agency, productive work, the making of promising signs. Such signs take exemplary shape in ritual action (e.g., baptism and Eucharist) but should not be confined to ritual. Promise can as easily be embodied in building a house, making good beer, designing a city, or running a bank. In a medieval context, the common understanding was that humans were called to a partnership with the Creator in the task of completing creation: by clearing a forest, quarrying the stone for a cathedral, plowing and planting fields, building canals and cities. In other words, this second sense of sacrament involves what is called stewardship or, as we saw in chapter 1, the service of nature.

Whatever one calls it, this second sense of sacrament will not, perhaps, be welcomed by all environmentalists. Followers of the Earth First! school, who think of human beings as a "cancer" in the anatomy of nature and consequently view almost any technological intervention as negative, will not take to this idea. They demand that nature be left alone, untouched and untouchable by interfering human hands. If humans intervene in nature, they believe, they are bound to mess things up.

The Bible is fully aware that even good intentions, not to mention bad, have unforeseen consequences. A good deal of human work, as the Bible reminds us, is wasted or perverted energy, making war, supporting a parasitic overseer class, building monuments to paranoid tyrants, and the like. Genuine creative work, founded on both human need for food and shelter and on the desire to contribute to something larger than ourselves, is directed toward transforming nature into a world of human meaning and function. The Bible thereby gives no permission to abuse, much less to destroy, nature. Humankind, as the Priestly author of Genesis has it, is the custodian or steward of creation, whose creative work is to restore nature, so far as possible, to its paradisal condition. As the Bible has it, the animal world is to be changed into a pastoral environment of flocks and herds; the vegetable world is to be transformed into a cultivated land of harvests and vineyards and gardens; and the mineral world into cities and buildings and highways.

A sacramental consciousness in this second sense does not look backward to what is settled and always the same, as the natural sciences generally do. It focuses on the present and the future and asks: What are we making of the world of fossil fuels, silicon, metals, rain forests, and grains — and what, energized by God's promise in all these things, shall we make of them? Sacramental consciousness cannot, therefore, be Luddite. It will not go about smashing machines as evil; it requires technology to do its job. You don't build a culture of promise without planners and laborers, without scientists and engineers. The assumption is that nature is fertile, full of possibility, and that we are here to make something beautiful of it. This is our service to nature, to the soil from which we spring.

PART II

THE DEVELOPMENT
OF SCIENTIFIC MATERIALISM

The sacramental consciousness we have just examined was largely displaced by the objectivizing and mathematizing consciousness that arrived with the seventeenth-century scientific revolution. With this shift we move from a qualitative sky (akin to ourselves) to a quantitative sky, sheer empty, alien space. In a nutshell, it is the difference between a universe to which we belong and a universe that shuts us out to wander homeless. As an old and embittered Mark Twain once remarked: "Nothing exists save empty space and you."

The vision of a sacramental world survived this changeover, but as a minority, dissenting stream within Western consciousness. One can still recognize its power in what historians speak of as the "arcadian" tradition of nature writers, from Henry David Thoreau and John Muir forward to Gary Snyder, Annie Dillard, Diane Ackerman, and Barry Lopez in our own time. When you hear Muir exclaiming, after his first summer in California's high Sierras in 1869, that "all the wilderness seems to be full of tricks and plans to drive and draw us up into God's Light," you know that the consciousness that marked Francis of Assisi is still very much alive.

Yet, for the last several hundred years this kind of consciousness has been on the defensive. To put it mildly, sacramental consciousness no longer controls public policy. Hard-nosed scientific consciousness now plays that role. Indeed, when contemporary environmentalists decry Western dualism as underlying the environmental crisis, they implicitly refer to the kind of consciousness that arose in the West in the sixteenth

41

and seventeenth centuries with the scientific revolution and the rise, in the eighteenth and nineteenth centuries, of industrialism. The upshot was a separation from nature that over time degenerated into an adversarial relationship. This is another reminder that the environmental crisis, as a problem that we have brought on ourselves and our planet, is the unforeseen consequence of doing what we have done best. That is, it is due to our greatest achievements: our science and technology, our hugely productive capitalist economy, our triumphant individualism, and the cultural assumptions and thinking that lie behind (and legitimize) these achievements. The ecocrisis of our time allows us to see that these triumphs and the leading ideas behind them have exacted a steep cost.

This chapter and the following one are diagnostic, deconstructive, and, as it were, disillusioning. I want to look more closely at the genesis of our ecological problem, and to that end I will examine the role of science — science as an agent of cultural formation. Lynn White had it mostly wrong. Our real environmental problems start not with Abraham and Moses but with the new scientific consciousness of the seventeenth century. Classical Newtonian science, I will argue, has given rise to the philosophy of what Alfred North Whitehead called "scientific materialism," the idea that all reality, including mental reality, is finally reducible to meaningless matter in motion.[1] When nature is conceived in this way, in effect as a machine, it can have no moral standing. And hence can make no moral claim upon us. Our serious environmental problems really begin here.

The mechanistic paradigm that arose out of classic Newtonian physics meant that nature was devoid of moral status. It divorced human beings from nature and generated an attitude of neutrality toward the biophysical world that all too commonly translated into indifference, alienation, or open hostility (i.e., nature as something to be conquered). It was a mindset ideally suited to an emerging culture of industrial capitalism — what might be called economic materialism — which would proceed to exploit the natural world as if its resources were unlimited. The worldview of scientific materialism may be described as follows:

- Nature can be summarized in the image of a machine.

- In contrast to the static medieval view, change is given greater scope; but change is basically the rearrangement of unchanging components, the fundamental particles of nature. These particles

---

1. Whitehead, *Science and the Modern World* (New York: Macmillan, 1926), 25–26.

are still thought to be fixed, with no genuine novelty or historical development allowed.

- Nature is deterministic rather than (as in the medieval conception) teleological. Mechanical causes, not purposes, determine all natural events, and explanation consists in the specification of such causes. Assuming a complete knowledge of current states (or initial conditions), the future, therefore, could be predicted.

- The basic reality of nature consists in the separate fundamental atoms or particles. The theory of knowledge is classical realism: the object can be known as it is in itself apart from the observer. This atomism was paralleled by an individualistic view of society (developed, for example, in ideas of economic competition and social contract theories of government).

- The approach to nature was reductionistic and mechanistic rather than hierarchical. The physical mechanisms and laws were thought to determine all events (except, perhaps, those in the human mind).

- Newton accepted the Cartesian dualism of mind and body; God and human minds constituted the great exceptions in a mechanistic world. Even though the earth was no longer at the center of the cosmic system, human rationality was seen as the mark of our uniqueness. But the leaders of the eighteenth-century Enlightenment believed that humanity was also a part of the all-encompassing world machine, whose operation could be explained without reference to God. This materialistic world held no place for consciousness or inwardness except as subjective illusions. Since nature is a machine, it is an object that can be exploited for human uses.[2]

Allied to this mechanistic worldview is the cognate doctrine of "scientism," the notion that the scientific method provides the only reliable source of knowledge.

Scientific materialism empties nature of value, except as resource for human manipulation, and is thus intimately connected to economic materialism. What scientific materialism gives us is an empty, meaningless mass of atoms upon which humans can readily impose their meanings. What it offers, in other words, is a quintessentially anthropocentric outlook. Nature takes on a single meaning, that of

---

2. Adapted from Ian G. Barbour, *Religion in an Age of Science* (San Francisco: HarperSanFrancisco, 1990), 1:220.

"resource" or "raw material" for human exploitation and use. Science may occasionally have known better, but all too often over the last three hundred years science itself has served as a willing confederate of this utilitarian, exploitative outlook. In appealing to church, temple, and synagogue to supply moral fervor for the environmental movement, Carl Sagan and his cohorts seem to acknowledge this, saying in effect that a strictly scientific understanding of the material world fails to provide a motive for wanting to protect and preserve its integrity and wholeness.

What our ecological age requires, I will argue, is a way of thinking, a philosophy or cosmology, that recognizes the objective value of the natural world prior to any projections of ours. Scientific materialism does not provide this.

THREE

Imperial Ecology and the Death of Nature

Classical physics is a science of dead things and a strategy of the kill.... The world is in order according to this mathematical physics. The laws are the same everywhere.... There is nothing to be learned, to be discovered, to be invented, in this repetitive world, which falls in parallel lines of identity.

— MICHEL SERRES, *Hermes*

There are no limits to the carrying capacity of the earth that are likely to bind at any time in the foreseeable future. The idea that we should put limits on growth because of some natural limit is a profound error.

— LAWRENCE SUMMERS, U.S. Secretary of the Treasury under President Clinton

If until very recently modern Christianity has very little to boast about when it comes to caring for the planet, science is not in an altogether different position. For when confronted with something as large and complex as even regional, much less global, ecosystems and the question of whether human action is now damaging them in perhaps irreversible ways, science has its own severely troubled history to remember. The Sagan group congratulates itself by claiming that many of its members have "long engaged in combating the environmental crisis," and this was certainly true of Sagan himself. But what is the overall record of science in this regard? Has it always been on the side of the angels, saving wilderness areas and defending rainforest biodiversity? Not at all. Like the churches, science is a latecomer to ecological awakening. Modern science and technology are part of a modernizing movement whose dominant motive, from the very start in the seventeenth century, has been exploitative.

The Sagan group explicitly acknowledged that science and technology by themselves were not equal to the task of dealing with the current ecological challenge. Religion is brought in precisely to supply what science is powerless to provide: moral fervor and commitment. What these scientists do not publicly advert to is the darker side of their own history, that science has contributed greatly to the degradation of the natural world. Like religion, science is part of the ecological problem. Scientists have been sorcerer's apprentices, aides and accomplices in the Promethean efforts of industry — which in great part funds science and sets down the research program — to tear up the earth, to remake it in our own doubtful image and for our own often narrow interests. Since the very outset of the scientific revolution in the seventeenth century, much of the scientific community has proven more homocentric and aggressively utilitarian than any churchman ever dreamed of being. (This is why "deep ecologists" are so critical of contemporary science, particularly in its servitude to the military-industrial complex.) Nature, from this scientific angle, is commonly viewed as a great machine, a stockpile of raw material to fuel industrial growth and development — and nothing more. Let us examine the development of this conception.

Literacy and Detachment from the Earth

The sacramental consciousness we referred to in the last chapter was unable to withstand the cultural assaults of a detached, scientific view of nature and an all-powerful extractive capitalism. For a sacramental consciousness began to wane in the West with the fifteenth-century invention of the printing press and the seventeenth-century scientific revolution. The close of the fifteenth century was a defining moment for Western Europe — and it is difficult to say which was the bigger event, Columbus's discovery of "the new world" or Gutenberg's invention of the printing press. Western consciousness was profoundly altered by both events. But my vote is that Gutenberg's invention had a more profound impact on human consciousness.[1] From the very first, of course, beginning around 2000 B.C.E., literacy had given eyesight a certain priority over the other senses when it came to intellectual analysis. But until Gutenberg, literacy had remained an elite phenomenon. The beginnings of mass literacy, however, which the printing of books made possible, greatly intensified the dominance of vision, the distancing, objectivizing sense, and spatial analysis thereby came to the fore. (Even time was spacialized into "lengths" and "distances.") We were no longer mortised into nature, as an oral culture was. Womb-like na-

---

1. See Walter J. Ong, S.J., *The Presence of the Word: Some Prolegomena for Cultural and Religious History* (Minneapolis: University of Minnesota Press, [1967] 1981).

ture vanishes; we now stand "outside" it—in effect, as a spectator. For a huge public, print enabled a new kind of detachment from nature. Indeed, its effect enables us to read the whole history of consciousness as the gradual emancipation of humans from an embeddedness in nature.

The oral person automatically feels centered by the surrounding sense of sound. He or she also feels that nature speaks, that nature is vocal and full of creative and destructive energy. The oral person had no way of stopping the world, much less of separating himself or herself from the rush and tangle of events. In contrast, the literate person can stop the world and get off it—by immobilizing events onto a page, where they can be carefully mapped and studied. Nature is thereby stilled, frozen, as it were, in a succession of still shots. No longer wrapped up in the noisy immediacy of existential affairs, the literate person acquires psychological distance—and space for reflection and studied choice. Where the oral person is always involved in personal and social interaction, the literate person can become an observer, a spectator and outsider—wrapped up in his or her own thoughts. Correlatively, as rural populations moved to an urban, artificial environment, nature lost its tactile nearness and "good vibes." It ceased to be a matter of touch, taste, hearing, and smell, and became a matter of seeing what was spread out before us as in linear print upon an inert page. The clear advantage and gain was that nature could now be stilled, dissected, and analyzed to an extent never previously possible or imaginable. That is, modern science became possible. But paradoxically the very object of science became remote. We transferred nature from a lived experience of energy into nature laid out on a page and fragmentized into its parts.

As we move away from immersion in nature, we gain freedom; we also lose something. The spread of literacy is a story of emerging freedom and, at the same time, a story of the loss of that surplus of meaning such as we find in ancient saga and myth—in Homer's *Iliad,* in Norse saga, in the Bible. Looking back, it sometimes appears that the arcadian state of hunter-gatherer societies possessed certain clear advantages over the wonderworks and gadgets of modern industrial society. We move from ancient fusion states of psychic and spiritual depth to visual surfaces. That is, we are reduced to seeing the play of light on shallow surfaces.

Correspondingly, the root metaphor of our relationship to nature changes: We no longer rest in nature as in amniotic fluid but "bestride the world as if on a stage." A new sense of power and mobility is evident, with attendant warnings from poets like John Donne that even though we stand out in a new way, "no man is an island." The warning would be unnecessary unless Donne's urban audience was beginning to feel islanded: cut off, isolated, and set apart.

Mass literacy and books meant that consciousness was distanced from nature, and thus free in a new way. The Cartesian ego was born. One no longer did one's thinking in the thick social context of an oral society. We were no longer part of things as we once had been. One shut oneself up in an ivory tower and did one's thinking alone, as Descartes did. In effect, the Western world textualized nature, reducing it to the image of linear, leaden type — so many ingot letters of an alphabet that we can master and play with technologically.

With the voyages of discovery throughout the "new world," of course, knowledge of the diversity of nature increased exponentially. At the same time, because fewer people were tied to the soil, nature lost its original sense of being a generative, birth-giving matrix. It became an object, raw material, resources to be converted into a commodity, in sum, a dead thing. Even animals, Descartes thought, were no more than machines. This prepared the way for Isaac Newton's iron laws of motion and gravity. Indeed, it paved the way for Immanuel Kant's sense that the numinous depths of things are inaccessible to us, that all a sight-dominated being can get at is the way light plays upon the surfaces of things. That is, all we can know about are phenomena, not *noumena*, or the inner sanctum of things.

Imperial Ecology

What environmental historian Donald Worster calls the tradition of "imperial ecology" was brought to us by two revolutionary prophets of the seventeenth century, René Descartes (1596–1650) and Francis Bacon (1561–1626).[2]

Francis Bacon, lord chancellor of England and herald of the conquest of nature, was the more colorful figure of the two. Loren Eiseley called him the "man who saw through time," in the sense that he was the visionary and propagandist for the dawning age of reason, the modern age.[3] If the nature of paleolithic cultures had been a living whole governed by spiritual forces, and the nature of the agricultural revolution was a garden to be cultivated, the nature of the scientific and industrial revolutions consisted of the "parts" of a mechanical apparatus

---

2. Donald Worster, *Nature's Economy: A History of Ecological Ideas*, 2d ed. (Cambridge: Cambridge University Press, [1977] 1994), 29; also 26–55.

3. Loren Eiseley, *The Man Who Saw through Time* (New York: Charles Scribner's Sons, [1961] 1973).

that could be constantly "remade" by human reason and imagination. We are entering the world of *homo faber* — man the maker.

At one stroke Bacon revolutionized the West's relation to the natural world by envisioning that through science we could restore the earth to its "perfect and original condition" — a new paradisal garden, a new Jerusalem. In this regard, Bacon picks up the apocalyptic tradition of the fourteenth-century Joachim of Floris and the radical Franciscans, who looked forward to an "age of the Spirit" that would restore Edenic bliss to humankind. Bacon saw that science and the practical arts, or what we would call technology, are the means to this eschatological end. For Bacon, neither the aboriginal Paleolithic idea of harmony with nature nor the classical ideal of nature as a bountiful world that sustained humankind was any longer acceptable. Bacon's ideal was nothing less than the complete mastery of nature. It was a radically modern idea — the notion that the world was not a fixed stage, that everything in the world could be refashioned to human purposes through science.

Using metaphors taken from the practice of interrogating and torturing witches, Bacon proclaimed that nature "exhibits herself more clearly under the trials and vexations of art [mechanical devices] than when left to herself." In the search for truth, nature's "holes and corners" were to be entered and penetrated. Nature was to be "bound into service," made a "slave," and "put under constraint." She was to be "dissected" and "forced out of her natural state and squeezed and moulded" so that "human knowledge and human power meet as one." The new science, Bacon prophesied, would produce a "blessed race of heroes and supermen."

Descartes shattered what was left of the holism of the medieval worldview by sharply dividing the realm of mind (*res cogitans*) from the realm of matter (*res extensa*). Gone was that quasi-animistic creative matrix, the organic whole, the diverse array of omens and signs which Aquinas and Bonaventure had known as nature and in which their minds felt at home. Nature, Descartes declared, was nothing but a machine, a clockworks, that could be understood by analyzing its constituent parts. It had nothing in common with mind.

Descartes's philosophy of science, unlike Bacon's, was in important respects Platonic. To understand nature was to discover functional relationships between abstractly conceived processes and objects that could be expressed mathematically. In this sense science is not reducible to empirical observation, as Bacon tended to believe; in only an indirect way is science about the world we see around us. The Cartesian tradition of science has only contempt for those content to describe qualitative relationships, say in the natural history of the whale or the mountain gorilla. The idea, rather, is to bring natural processes within the scope of conceptual, mathematical understanding — and thus formulate laws that will ultimately serve human interests. The aim of modern science, he argued in the *Discourse on Method,* is to

> know the power and action of fire, water, air, the stars, the heavens and all the other bodies in our environment, as distinctly as we know the various crafts of our artisans; and we could use this knowledge — as the artisans use theirs — for all the purposes for which it is appropriate, and thus make ourselves, as it were, the lords and masters of nature. (VI.62)

For Descartes, the paradigmatic example of material substance was a piece of wax, the traditional symbol of malleability.

In the interest of completeness one also ought to mention the post-Cartesian development represented by the nineteenth-century German philosopher G. W. F. Hegel (1770–1831), also followed by Karl Marx. Hegel gave a more anthropocentric and historicizing spin to things. His idea was that nature consisted of a kind of "negativity" that has to be overcome by being humanized by art. In this perspective, natural beauty is depreciated, at least in comparison to works of art in which nature is properly transformed and rendered less strange. Nature deserves appreciation, Hegel believed, only when it is converted from wilderness into a farm, a garden, or a city.

Thus within modern Western thought we have two leading traditions: the Cartesian-Baconian, in which matter is inert, passive, and the human relationship to it is that of absolute despot, reshaping and reforming what has no power of resistance or agency; and the Hegelian, in which nature exists only in potency, as something which it is the human task to actualize through art, science, philosophy, and technology. The human project, according to Hegel, is to convert raw nature into a mirror in which we can see our own faces, and thus understand the movement of *Geist,* or spirit-in-the-world. In the Hegelian view, the human role in history is to complete the unfolding of the universe, not by simply living in nature, but by actually fulfilling its historical destiny to become spiritualized. In some respects, this Hegelian approach resembles the sacramental dynamic we sketched out in chapter 2.

Enter Isaac Newton: The Death of Nature

The "superman" Bacon dreamed of appeared in the shape of Isaac Newton (1642–1727). What, then, did Newton accomplish? What sign does his universe offer us? Above all, Newton embodied the distinctive mentality of the modern age, which Whitehead sums up as a "vehement and passionate interest in the relation of general principles to irreducible and stubborn facts."[4] All over the world and at all times there have been practical people absorbed by "stubborn facts," says Whitehead; and equally, all over the world and at all times there have been people of philosophic temperament who have delighted in articulating general principles. "It is this union of passionate interest in the detailed facts with equal devotion to abstract generalisation which forms the novelty in our present society." No longer are the "detailed facts" of interest for what they symbolize about a transcendent world, as in the medieval frame of things; no, one is interested in the occurrences of life "for their own sake." The new scientific attitude of the seventeenth century not only expressed a Baconian interest in mastery and control of the natural world; it also exhibited an element of disinterested attention to other species and things. As such, it represented a widening of the human horizon of understanding and concern.

Newton's laws of motion are an enormous achievement. They enabled us to close the gap that had previously existed in medieval cosmology between the supposedly immutable celestial spheres and the changeable and corruptible sublunar sphere of earth. From now on, both the heavens and the earth are ruled by the same laws. The laws of motion are familiar:

1. Every body continues in its state of rest or uniform motion in a straight line unless it is compelled to change that state by forces impressed on it.

2. The change of motion is proportional to the motive force impressed; and is made in the direction of the right line in which that force is impressed.

3. To every action there is always an equal reaction: or, the mutual actions of two bodies upon each other are always equal, and directed to opposite parts.

From these basic principles, Newton derived the motions of the planets, the comets, the moon, and the sea. And within this same framework, Johannes Kepler's earlier laws concerning planetary orbits appeared naturally as a consequence of supposing that the gravitational force between any two bodies is directly proportional to the product of their

---

4. Alfred North Whitehead, *Science and the Modern World* (New York: Macmillan, 1926), 4. See also Frank E. Manuel, *A Portrait of Isaac Newton* (Cambridge, Mass.: Harvard University Press, 1968).

masses and inversely proportional to the square of the distance between them (the law of gravity). If Descartes embodied the new detached ego of the modern West, Newton gave us its objective correlate: an objective world of deterministic law.

In no way did Newton's "mechanical philosophy" alienate him from a religious view of the cosmos. He remained a lifelong member of the Church of England and was sincerely devout (though his theology was secretly Unitarian). Like all the other great "natural philosophers" of the seventeenth century (Galileo, Descartes, Dalton, Leibniz, Pascal, et al.), Newton never thought of his theories as undermining the love and worship of God. Quite the opposite, the deterministic laws of gravity and motion were understood as proceeding from the fiat of God's omnipotent will. And these clocklike regularities — what were they except the bona fides of a timeless and trustworthy deity? Like his scientific peers, Newton conceived it to be his religious duty to unravel the wonders of God's creation for his fellows. For this whole generation of scientists, in fact, religion and science were complementary. "This most beautiful system of Sun, planets, and comets," wrote Newton, "could only proceed from the counsel and dominion of an intelligent and powerful Being."

Nonetheless, to my way of thinking the environmental crisis of our time begins here — in a way, with the denigration of matter. Up until this moment, the image of nature as a machine had the authority of Galileo, Bacon, and Descartes, but lacked a definitive proof. Newton provided that. In effect, his *Principia Mathematica* convinced Western Europeans that the state of nature was that of martial law. Everything that existed had its fixed place in an absolute container space. And within this container space atoms lined up in strict military file. Nature's eros and ambiguity, its randomness and unpredictability, so familiar to the ancients, are simply ignored or repressed. Turbulence and fluctuation become invisible. What was once thought of as nature's internal creativity is nullified. The impulses to move or change come from outside the system in question.

How did this come about? Nothing shows it better than the puzzle of Newtonian dynamical motion. Newton formulated immutable laws for what physicists call "integral systems," stable, closed systems that do not interact with their environment or undergo abrupt shocks and turbulence — the kinds of system that one finds mostly in a laboratory and not in the messy, real world. Every instant of such a system, like that of an automaton or a pendulum, is the integral repetition of the proceeding pattern or cycle. The start of the process is identical with its end, and the whole process can be reversed without changing anything.

The Newtonian method was to posit an inert body in isolation, endowed with rectilinear and uniform motion (the so-called initial conditions). One then calculated the modification of this linear movement from place to place (the trajectory) as determined by external forces (wind, waterpower, horsepower, gravity, muscle, etc.). The point was to deduce the truth concerning all other possible states of the system — the distribution of masses in space and their velocities, for instance — from the initial conditions. The classic Newtonian focus thus stood in utter opposition to that of his great German rival, G. W. Leibniz, whose approach to matter emphasized bodies in relationship (monads that were internally related to everything else in the cosmos).

Newton's disciple Pierre Simon de Laplace (1749–1827) would later argue that the universe is completely determined — and we no longer require the "hypothesis" of God. Things run by themselves. In principle, if you could ascertain the position and velocity of everything in the universe at any given time, you could predict (and retrodict) the past and future of the whole world for all time. (Physicists could then retire, their task complete.) In the big picture, the future is preordained and no different than the past. The time variable in classical equations is irrelevant, a mere extrinsic parameter. All motion is conceived as being perfectly symmetrical and therefore reversible. It makes no difference whether time runs forward or backward. As Alexandre Koyré once dryly remarked, Newtonian dynamical motion is "a motion unrelated to time or, more strangely, a motion which proceeds in an atemporal time — a notion as paradoxical as that of change without change."[5]

In this respect, classical physics denies our ordinary experience of time, which so clearly signals that the past is done, the future not yet — and the two are distinguishable, not to be identified with each other. The past is closed, settled; the future open, undetermined. So far as the inverse square law of gravity is concerned, however, a film of gravitational motion can run backward without affecting the calculation, and this oddity is taken by many physicists as a definitive clue to the nature of reality. The past and future are accordingly taken to be indistinguishable. In short, nature is stuck in the same groove and simply repeats itself, going nowhere. The story it tells is that of "eternal return." As Alfred North Whitehead once put it, to the viewpoint of the mechanistic materialism of the seventeenth century, nature is a "dull affair, soundless, scentless, colourless; merely the hurrying of material, end-

---

5. Alexandre Koyré, *Newtonian Studies* (Cambridge, Mass.: Harvard University Press, 1965), 11, 3–24.

lessly, meaninglessly."[6] Or, as Michel Serres, a contemporary French philosopher of science, has it,

> Classical physics is a science of dead things and a strategy of the kill.... The world is in order according to this mathematical physics. The laws are the same everywhere.... There is nothing to be learned, to be discovered, to be invented, in this repetitive world, which falls in parallel lines of identity. Nothing new under the sun of identity. It is information-free, complete redundance.... There is death forever. Nature is put to death or is not allowed to be born. And the science of all this is nothing, can be summed up as nothing. Stable, unchanging, redundant, it recopies the same writing in the same atomic letters.[7]

In short, nature in this sense allows for no genesis, no becoming, no novelty. What sign does Newtonian nature give? What is its sacramental or symbolic sense? The sign of death. It represents a world that is going nowhere, that is guaranteed to dash any conceivable promise. As one can imagine, benevolent and not-so-benevolent eighteenth-century despots found such ideas highly congenial. And nineteenth-century Russian nihilists would find their hopelessness stamped and sealed with approval by the very stars and atoms.

The timelessness of classical physics thus runs not only counter to the time-centeredness of Western Judeo-Christian culture, but counter to the evolutionary outlook that Darwin would introduce. In the Newtonian perspective, the genetic "chance variation" at the root of neo-Darwinian theory is a cosmic anomaly, an aberration limited to the strange conditions of planet earth. The surprise here is that many modern-day physicists continue to see things this way, in effect attributing our sense of irreversible time to mere subjective illusion. Take Einstein, for example. Shortly before his own death in 1955, in a letter to the bereaved widow of his friend Michele Angelo Besso, Einstein wrote that death was not the last word. "For us convinced physicists," he said, "the distinction between past, present and future is only an illusion, however persistent."[8]

---

6. Whitehead, *Science and the Modern World*, 80.

7. Michel Serres, *Hermes: Literature, Science, and Philosophy*, ed. Josué V. Harari and David F. Bell (Baltimore: Johns Hopkins University Press, 1982), 100.

8. *Albert Einstein, Correspondance, 1903–1955*, ed. and trans. Pierre Speziali (Paris: Hermann, 1972), 638.

Classical Physics and Economic Materialism

My argument here is not against the laws of classical physics per se. The problem has to do with the use of such laws as decisive clues to the nature of reality. Even at their own proper level as a representation of the nature of nature, I would argue that the laws of integral systems catch only part of the picture — an abstraction — and not the whole. There are, as I will indicate in chapters 9 and 10, other kinds of systems: open, nonlinear, complex systems that don't fit into the classical paradigm of a clock or pendulum. Until very recently, such systems have been virtually invisible to scientists, but all of a sudden over the space of the last few decades, in the form of chaos theory, such unpredictable systems are everywhere. I will come back to this in chapter 9.

Be that as it may, one reason that modern industrial economies run the way they do — assuming that nature will never run out of supplies and that growth will be endless — is that they borrow heavily from Newtonian mechanics. Consult the index of any basic economics textbook; you will not find references to what Wendell Berry calls the "Great Economy," the economy of the planet earth, into which our small human economies must fit as a subsystem. Nowhere to be found are terms like the "hydrological cycle" or "carbon cycles," much less entries for "environment," "natural resources," "depletion," "sustainable development," or "pollution." The basic laws of ecology are missing. For the founder of free market economics, Adam Smith (1723–90), and all his successors physical things consist of indestructible matter, and they assumed that with sufficient capital this stuff can be endlessly recycled into an infinite variety of useful and frivolous commodities. Nature resembles a machine made of replaceable parts, parts that can be assembled, disassembled, reassembled, exchanged, and substituted for. Little attention therefore need be paid to the varied details, needs, or dynamics of the earth's own economy, that basic economy that sustains the whole community of life over time.

Given sufficient capital, possible shortages and physical limits can be ignored. As ethicist Larry Rasmussen puts it,

> When this view prevails, as it still does in most capitalist practices, business is an open, linear system. With technology, resource extraction, and mobility, growth will always be possible, assuming capital. No inherent limits to expansion exist. Bizarre as it may seem, economic theory and practice do not conceive nature as

genuinely alive and finite here. Nor do they entertain the notion
that the earth is round and thus closed.[9]

Capitalist business still lives by "cowboy economics." It assumes that if
things run out here or there, there is always more free pasture over the
next hill. In this conception, earth is not round and limited, but flat and
endless in extension. "There are no limits to the carrying capacity of
the earth that are likely to bind at any time in the foreseeable future,"
claimed President Clinton's secretary of the treasury and former World
Bank official Lawrence Summers. "The idea that we should put limits
on growth because of some natural limit is a profound error."

Another reason for this expansionist vision is the source of value.
Until human beings acquire and transform the "raw material" of nature and make something of it, it has no value. Millions of years may
lie behind the creation of an acre of fertile topsoil, and millions more
behind the formation of the fossil fuels deep in earth's crust, but the
value here lies in human creativity and use. "Undeveloped" land is
simply "empty," and "raw" material is worth nothing. What is the
value of a *living* tree? Almost nothing. Its value is the price at which
dead lumber from it can be sold in a market. The myriad functions
of a tree for ecosystem maintenance — watershed protection, habitat
provision, soil stabilization — are ignored. Market prices don't incorporate the needs of other species, only the needs of human producers
and consumers of "finished" products.

Adam Smith and Karl Marx, much Catholic social teaching, and
management guru Peter Drucker are all agreed on this point. Before
an entrepreneur gets hold of them, plants are just weeds, says Drucker,
and every mineral is just another rock. Nature only begins to figure in
accounting procedures when human labor takes interest and subjects
it to a process of commodification. The question of earth's "carrying
capacity" — the maximum rate of resource consumption and waste
discharge that can be sustained without permanently damaging the
ecosystem upon which we are dependent — never comes up because
the notion of nature that we think with is of passive resources awaiting
human transformation.

The preservation of nature simply does not compute with the
assumptions of industrial capitalism (or industrial socialism either). Environmental historian Donald Worster sums up the problem this way:

---

9. Larry Rasmussen, *Earth Community, Earth Ethics* (Maryknoll, N.Y.: Orbis Books,
1996), 119.

Any suggestion that nature has an intrinsic order that must be preserved has been viewed by many industrial leaders as a serious threat. They have had another, rival order to create — an economic one. Industrialism has sought not the preservation but the total domination of the natural order and its radical transformation into consumer goods. The environment has been seen to exist mainly for the purpose of supplying an endless line of goods and absorbing the byproducts of waste and pollution. Whatever has not been produced by some industry and placed on the market for sale has had little value. It has been viewed, in the most negative word that industrial culture knows, as "useless." Since the only way industrialists can use nature is to disorganize it, in order to extract the specific commodities they value, typically they have regarded as most useless of all those very qualities of stability, harmony, symbiosis, and integration that characterize the living world in the composite. They have tended to devalue both the services that natural systems provide people, like forest regulating stream flow, and the aesthetic satisfaction that contemplating such order affords.[10]

The Clockmaker God

No one can deny that great nature is marked by patterns of redundancy and repetition. "Eternal return" is a major aspect of nature, and we can be grateful that this is so. The laws of classical physics (and their analogues in the other sciences) capture this stability, this determinism in things. Not everything is up for grabs, a contingent matter of chance or accident. Nature's very difference in this respect from fickle and changeable human beings, the fact that, unlike us, the physical world is so often dependably invariant, is a great blessing. We can count on certain very big structures in our environment remaining predictable, steadfast, and the same at least for a very long time, in some cases forever. If we want to send a *Voyager* satellite to photograph Saturn or Jupiter, we still have to rely on Newton's laws of motion and gravity — and they work brilliantly to get us there. In addition, for believers the very stability of nature can be seen as a sign of the dependability of the Creator.

In the minus department, however, is the fact that the ingenious Lawgiver who (at least for the theistic Newton) stands behind the laws

---

10. Donald Worster, *The Wealth of Nature: Environmental History and the Ecological Imagination* (New York: Oxford University Press, 1993), 179.

of classical physics is not the Holy One that Jews and Christians worship as immanent in all creation and "closer to us than we are to ourselves." Rather, it is the Absentee Landlord of deism. For once Newton's God creates the cosmic machine, it will run by itself, and God can retire like a spent rocket booster. What a Newtonian cosmology suggests is a Great Engineer who constructs the cosmic clockworks but thereafter retreats beyond the heavens, sealed off from creation and thus inevitably superfluous in history and daily life.

The otherness of God becomes a vicious joke. For object-thinking insinuates itself into our everyday theology, and God is imagined as another object "out there," usually way out there. In short, God becomes another kind of object, an utterly remote and largely otiose "thing," envisioned as some kind of spy satellite circling the earth. And we have no way of reaching him. For in the classical scientific dispensation, nature is dead, speechless, Whitehead's "dull affair . . . the hurrying of material, endlessly, meaninglessly." An inert, mechanistic landscape can no longer serve as a medium of communication between ourselves and the Creator. Nature ceases to be semiotic, gives no signs, as the medieval material world did; rather, it is a silent expanse that signifies nothing. As far as we humans are concerned, nature shuts us out; all analogy or kinship is broken, and we are shut up inside our skins. In such a world, one can no longer contemplate the elements, the stars, or any other feature of nature, as Francis of Assisi and Jonathan Edwards did, and expect to taste and touch the Spirit immanent in all things. It's as if the radio frequency that we once used to communicate with the Master of the Universe had gone dead. Nature has ceased to be the medium of the sacred.

FOUR

The Competitive Ethos Triumphant

The world is not to be narrowed till it will go into the under-standing ... but the understanding is to be expanded and opened till it can take in the image of the world.

— FRANCIS BACON, *The Parasceue*

We have changed the very chemistry of the planet, we have altered the biosystem, we have changed the topography and even the geological structure of the planet, structures and functions that have taken hundreds of millions and even billions of years to bring into existence. Such an order of change in its nature and in its order of magnitude has never before entered into Earth history or into human consciousness.   — THOMAS BERRY, *Dream of Earth*

When Francis Bacon's dream of science transforming the earth was hitched up to the eighteenth-century industrial revolution that it eventually helped to produce, we had a powerful combination: the Western "genius" that has dominated and colonized the world for the last several centuries. As we have noted, Bacon's vision was not strictly secular; initially it was linked to Christian eschatology—a vision of the "kingdom come," the New Jerusalem. The dream was that industrial culture would supplant poverty, disease, and toil with an abundance that permits an enriched, expanded choice. And certainly for the expanding middle classes, industrialism delivered on this promise. The economic historian Shepherd Clough has summarized the overall performance of capitalism this way:

The historian of the mid-twentieth century who studies the economic development of Western culture of the last 150 years is struck at once by the enormous quantitative increase in the production of goods and services. Just how great the increase was is difficult to state in precise terms, but...what evidence we have indicates more than a doubling of French national income from 1850 to World War II, a quadrupling of that of Germany for the same period, a tripling of that of Italy from 1860 to 1938, and an eightfold increase in that of the United States from 1869–1878 to 1929–1938. Such increases made possible a rise in the population of Europe from some 187,693,000 people in 1800 to over 530,000,000 in 1938, and in the United States from 4,000,000 in 1790 to 140,000,000 in 1946. Over the entire period there was an increase in income per capita of some two to four times.[1]

Capitalism's successes are not in question. At least not by me. Most people (at least in the West) live longer, are materially better off, and enjoy more individual freedoms than their medieval progenitors did. But the question is whether we have traded overt forms of social domination and oppression for more subtle forms of control and alienation unique to the industrial world. Critics of urban societies point out that they have separated humans from nature, destroyed or weakened the bonds of traditional communities (neighborhood, kin), weakened our sense of civic community, and made us dependent on vast, impersonal systems (market economies, bureaucracies, etc.) that elicit neither loyalty nor comprehension.

The consequences for the environment have become apparent only in the twentieth century. Cognized as a giant mechanism, the universe and the earth become a huge resource base to be used, developed, and managed for human needs and desires. Environmentalists are hard put to oppose this utilitarianism; it is reinforced daily by the whole economic system and consequently is deeply embedded in the Western psyche. And in addition, when environmentalists ask us to extend our ethical concern to the ecosystem, they encounter staunch resistance from influential academic ethicists. The earth, we are authoritatively told, can make no moral claims upon us. For according to the dominant "social contract" theory of ethics championed by Harvard's John Rawls and others, for all practical purposes our duties are limited to other humans, and at that to sane, adult, responsible humans, who alone are capable of entering into free, reciprocal relations. Properly speaking, then, animals have no moral standing or "rights." Nor does an ecosystem or the biosphere.

---

1. Cited by Robert Heilbroner, *Visions of the Future: The Distant Past, Yesterday, Today, and Tomorrow* (New York: Oxford University Press, 1995), 58.

Ever since the eighteenth-century Enlightenment, all the terms that express that an obligation is serious or binding — duty, right, law, morality, obligation, justice — have been narrowed down to apply only in the context of a free contract between rational agents. Hence endangered whales, snail darters, and spotted owls are out of the picture, or at best put down as optional, unimportant considerations. But as British ethicist Mary Midgley points out, the theoretical model upon which social contract theory rests is drawn from seventeenth-century Newtonian physics.[2] For Enlightenment thinkers like John Locke (1632–1704) and David Hume (1711–76), human society was conceived as analogous to a collection of Newton's utterly separate, impenetrable particles of matter, which possessed no hooks or internal structure. Within this framework it was hard to understand how or why such atoms would combine or connect. Interdependence and relationship were puzzles.

The ancient Greek and biblical idea that human nature was essentially social had been forgotten or rejected, and in its place emerged the atomized individual, originally distinct and independent of every other individual, who combines with others and undertakes reciprocal duties only through his or her own choice and on the basis of private self-interest. On this model, all significant moral relations between individuals are perfectly symmetrical ones expressed by contract. Nonsymmetrical duties to the weak, the inarticulate, and the mute — to whomever or whatever cannot argue back — do not count. Right and duty stop at the border of the perfectly rational members of the human species.

What this does is isolate human beings from the rest of creation to which we belong and to which we are kin. We are split off, our animal and biochemical nature suppressed. In effect, duties to non-contractors — to other species on the food chain, to ecosystems, to the biosphere — are deemed of no consequence. They do not matter. What matters, what is glorified and endowed with all the transcendent value that once attached to God, is the human individual (and his or her consumer choice). Friedrich Nietzsche (1844–1900), who championed this new version of the Baconian "superman," merely took over from post-Reformation, individualist theology the assumption that the rest of creation counted only as a frame for human redemption. What we are looking at here is the other side of classic Newtonian science, its subjective correlate: the supremacy of expressive individualism.

2. See Mary Midgley, "Duties Concerning Islands," in *Environmental Ethics,* ed. Robert Elliot (New York: Oxford University Press, 1995), 90–91.

How the Industrial World Works

Unlike agriculturists, who learned that the natural world possessed an intrinsic order that had to be respected and preserved, industrial individualists not only tend the garden of the world; they seek above all to "remake" it. Qualities of stability, harmony, symbiosis, and integration tend to mean little or are overridden by constant innovation, constant change, and constant readjustment. As Karl Marx, one of the great admirers of industrial culture, expressed this in *The Communist Manifesto:*

> Constant revolutionizing of production, uninterrupted disturbance of all social conditions, everlasting uncertainty and agitation distinguish [this] epoch from all earlier ones. All fixed, fast-frozen relations, with their train of ancient and venerable prejudices and opinions, are swept away. All new-formed ones become antiquated before they can ossify. All that is solid melts into air, all that is holy is profaned.

Of course Marx was thinking of the impact of industrial capitalism on the social community, but his words apply equally to the natural order. The sense of an ecological whole that once see ned relatively permanent and solid has tended to dissolve — to melt into air.

Consider for a minute what sociologists refer to as the "dominant social paradigm" of a society, the implicit model of how the world works that is broadly shared by the people of a given society. It is the mental model that underlies a society's stated goals and ways of organizing itself. Scholars generally agree that the dominant social paradigm of free market industrial societies goes something like this:

- Low evaluation of "nature" for its own sake. The natural environment is valued as a resource to produce goods; humans dominate nature; and economic growth is more important than environmental protection.

- Compassion mainly for those near and dear. Other species are exploited for human needs; less concern shown for "other people"; more concern is shown for this generation of humans than for future ones.

- The assumption that maximizing wealth is important and risks are acceptable in doing so. Faith in science and high technology as beneficial; use of markets rather than regulation to allocate risks; risks are typically borne by individuals.

- The assumption of no physical (real) limits to growth: Problems with resource shortages and population growth can be overcome by human technological inventiveness.

- The assumption that modern society, culture, and politics are basically okay: No serious damage to nature by humans; emphasis on competition and democracy but also on efficiency, expert knowledge, hierarchies, and control by large-scale organizations; variations in ownership and control of the means of production; complex and fast lifestyles.[3]

In agricultural societies, commerce and culture were regulated almost entirely by natural energy flows, chiefly solar energy as captured by food, wood, and wind. By contrast, industrial societies were created through the use of fossil fuel energy stored deep in the crust of earth. This led to a fundamental shift in the human relationship to nature. Commerce and culture changed from working with natural forces to overcoming them for human ends. Both production processes and people could be separated from intrinsic ties to the land. In the place of such ties an artificial world would be created, with few constraints from the very nature on which humankind utterly depended. Industrial ecology had found a way, through stored energy and the processes of industrialization, commerce, and trade, to massively remake nature for the sake of human society. And it thus found a way to live against the grain of the rest of nature. From our point of view, this seemed (at first) like a very agreeable arrangement. From earth's point of view, the opposite was the case. To the earth, industrialization spells deforestation, soil erosion, and salinization; desertification; decrease of the genetic pool; higher levels of pollution and other waste; and the destruction of cultures that are alien to modernity. It looks like a succession of more and more damaging ways to meet the needs and wants of one inordinately aggressive species.

Industrial culture runs so deeply in the Western psyche that its anti-nature assumptions have become an unexamined part of the scientific subculture. Many of these assumptions are highly problematic, especially when considered in light of ecological degradation. Is the storehouse of nature really limitless? Do we — governments, corporations, private property owners — have an absolute right to reconfigure nature as we will (without environmental impact studies)? Is economic growth, driven in large part by population growth, the only thinkable

---

3. Adapted from Lester Milbrath, *Envisioning a Sustainable Society: Learning Our Way Out* (Albany: State University of New York Press, 1989), 119.

way to go? Are there no ecological limits that expansionist economic policies must deal with? Are science and technology neutral? Is it true that what can be done scientifically and technologically should be done? Do we have the kind of control over "unintended consequences" that we commonly assume? Is economic development congruent with ecological sanity? Most of these questions should be answered in the negative.

One may question whether it entirely makes sense to speak, as environmentalists increasingly do, of the "rights" of nature. But surely one can agree that an egoistic, short-sighted anthropocentrism is no longer morally or pragmatically viable in our world (if it ever was). And surely it no longer makes sense to think of nature as existing solely to satisfy human needs and whims. In some sense, we have to start thinking our way toward seeing the biophysical world as intrinsically valuable. At the very least, for the billions of years the cosmos was rolling on without a human presence, it was valued by God.

Arcadian Ecology

The imperial ecology of Francis Bacon has dominated the Western attitude toward nature for nearly four hundred years, until very recent times — arguably until the 1960s when, thanks to Rachel Carson, the environmental movement captured popular attention as it never had before. But from the very outset of the scientific revolution, Bacon's conquering attitude has had its critics. There was an alternative, dissenting view of nature which in some measure harked back to the sacred nature of archaic hunter-gatherer society. Donald Worster calls this the "arcadian" ecological tradition, and as founding father of this lineage of respect for undisturbed nature he singles out the late eighteenth-century parson-naturalist Gilbert White (1720–93).[4] White's fame rests on a single book, *The Natural History of Selborne,* a study of the seasons, plants, and wildlife of his rural Hampshire parish some fifty miles southwest of London. The book, a collection of letters to fellow naturalists published in 1789, was largely ignored for fifty years after White's death. At the time England had no patience for a rural minister's preoccupations with earthworms, wrens, and swallows; it was too obsessed with the enclosure of farm lands, the new factory system in Manchester, and James Watts's new steam engine. But by 1830, helped along by the Romantic movement's critical re-

---

4. Donald Worster, *Nature's Economy: A History of Ecological Ideas,* 2d ed. (Cambridge: Cambridge University Press, [1977] 1994), 3–25.

action to mechanistic science and crass industrialization, a "Selborne cult" began to develop. The work has since become one of the most revered books in the English language, appearing in over a hundred editions by the mid–twentieth century.

Like those of many of the amateur field naturalists of his time, White's observations of the flora and fauna of his parish were diffuse, ranging over taxonomy, animal behavior, and the study of seasonal change.[5] Among other things, he was the first to distinguish the three species of leaf warblers, as well as identifying the harvest mouse and a large nocturnal bat. With exhaustive precision he recorded the comings and goings of swallows and martins. He found that swallows propagate on the wing, as well as eat, drink, and bathe in their flight. And he closely followed the early morning prowls of his garden tortoise, Timothy, "intent on sexual attachments, which transport him beyond his usual gravity and induce him to forget for a time his ordinary solemn deportment."

White's field studies went considerably beyond mere random observation and entertainment. The power of his appeal lay in the idyllic image he presented of the preindustrial countryside in which humankind seemed part of a stable natural order sustained by the ceaseless activity of other species. While the truth was that Hampshire was an artificial order, modified by human diligence over a thousand years or more, it did constitute a rural order that a later generation, surrounded by the "Satanic mills" of industrialism, would look back to with fond nostalgia. Even as White wrote, Selborne was facing increasing assault from the forces that his contemporary, cleric Thomas Malthus, was writing about: the more efficient farming methods being devised to feed the growing population of the world's first industrial nation. But where Malthus saw nothing but competition and struggle for survival, White saw collaboration and unity.

White's program was nothing less than to see how many creatures the Selborne district contained and to understand how they were all united in an interrelated system, an ecological whole. Even lowly species, he realized, played an important role in maintaining the stability of the ecosystem.

The most insignificant insects and reptiles are of much more consequence, and have much more influence in the economy of

5. Most scientists of this period, known as "natural philosophers," were amateurs. Although a rudimentary scientific community began to appear in the eighteenth century, it was only in the nineteenth century that the professional scientist in the modern sense took center stage. The word "scientist" itself was coined by the British mathematician William Whewell only in 1840.

nature, than the incurious are aware of; and are mighty in their effect, from the minuteness, which renders them less an object of attention; and from their numbers and fecundity. Earthworms, though in appearance a small and despicable link in the chain of nature, if lost would make a formidable chasm.

The earthworm, White went on, provides a food supply for diverse species of birds, which in turn are fare for foxes and men. Further, by loosening the soil, the lowly worm helps aerate and manure the farmer's fields — another "extraordinary provision of nature." White's religious beliefs formed a vital part of his rare sympathy and admiration for all living things. He was drawn to an ecological perspective by a deep reverence for the divine providence that had devised this beautiful, majestic whole. In turn, the ingenious interrelationships in nature testified to the benevolence of the Creator. Science and faith formed parts of an integral outlook.

White's view of nature highlighted its benevolence; he devoted little attention to the more violent side that Charles Darwin would later emphasize. White could also be strongly utilitarian in his science. In his strolls about his parish he never lost sight of utility, always turning to account what he learned about frosts or aphids or earthworms. On the basis of such study, he believed, the microcosm of Selborne could be better managed. Nature had been created, he was sure, for human benefit. Yet what White is most remembered for today is his evocation of arcadian harmony with nature. At the very least, we find a biocentric attitude, one that embraces all living things in its affection. As Donald Worster puts it,

> The Selborne that emerges in the letters is a personal realization of the ancient arcadian dream of reanimating man's loyalties to the earth and its vital energies.... [T]he overwhelming impression in this arcadian writing... is of a man eager to accept all nature into his parish sympathies. That desire is what the rediscovery of pagan literature [especially Virgil's *Eclogues* and *Georgics*] in the eighteenth century was primarily about: a longing to reestablish an inner sense of harmony between man and nature through an outer physical reconciliation.[6]

The rise of the natural history essay in the latter half of the nineteenth century, says Worster, was an "essential legacy of the Selborne cult." Thus when we think of nature writers, from the Romantic poets

---

6. Worster, *Nature's Economy*, 9–10.

like Blake and Wordsworth who objected to the new industrial society and the new methods of scientific analysis, on up to Henry Thoreau, John Muir, Aldo Leopold, Rachel Carson, and their successors from Annie Dillard and Diane Ackerman to Edward Abbey, Barry Lopez, and Wendell Berry, who champion a holistic approach to nature, we are dealing with the arcadian lineage of Gilbert White. But it is also the reemergence of what we have spoken of as the sacramental consciousness.

Listen, for instance, to John Muir (1838–1914), naturalist and founder of the Sierra Club, speaking of the "hospitable, Godful wilderness" to which he found himself so mightily attracted. He sounds like Francis of Assisi enraptured by the presence of God in the natural world. "One is constantly reminded," says Muir,

> of the infinite lavishness and fertility of Nature — inexhaustible abundance amid what seems enormous waste. And yet when we look into any of her operations that lie within reach of our minds, we learn that not one particle of her material is wasted or worn out. It is eternally flowing from use to use, beauty yet to higher beauty; and we soon cease to lament waste and death, and rather rejoice and exult in the imperishable wealth of the universe, and faithfully watch and wait the reappearance of everything that melts and fades and dies about us, feeling sure that its next appearance will be better and more beautiful than the last.[7]

Though raised a strict evangelical Presbyterian, Muir, like many Americans since, found his church in nature. Looking out upon the Sierra's Cathedral Peak, Muir acknowledges that "this I may say is the first time I have been to church in California, led here at last, every door graciously opened for the poor lonely worshiper. In our best times everything turns into religion, all the world seems a church and the mountains altars."[8]

The Harsh Lesson of the Galapagos

The single most important figure in the history of ecology over the past two or three centuries, however, is neither Bacon nor Gilbert White. It is Charles Darwin (1809–82). No one else has contributed more to the development of ecology as a flourishing field of science, and no other individual has had a greater influence on Western culture's perception

---

7. John Muir, "My First Summer in the Sierra," in *Nature Writings* (New York: Library of America, 1997), 296.
8. Ibid., 301.

of nature. With Darwin we pass from Gilbert White's essentially benign view of nature to the more troubled and conflicted vision of a fiercely competitive "struggle for existence." As Donald Worster puts it, "Ecology after Darwin came to be, as much or more than economics, the dismal science."[9]

When the young Charles Darwin left England aboard the H.M.S. *Beagle* in 1831, there was ferment in the air. Geologists like Charles Lyell (1797–1875) had begun to see the earth as a dynamic body, its structure constantly reformed by volcanoes and sediments and re-shaped by winds and rivers and inundating and retreating seas. The traditional biblical view of a landscape created by God and fixed for all eternity was giving way. In the broadest way, change, not permanence, seemed to be the way of the world. It was evolving. Yet when Darwin embarked on his great journey, he left as a Romantic, a convinced disciple of the Gilbert White school. Bound for a five-year trip around the world, Darwin brought with him, along with the first edition of Lyell's *Principles of Geology,* a copy of Alexander von Humboldt's *Personal Narrative* describing his travels in Latin America during the years 1799 to 1804. The book was a stirring, highly colored, romantic record of the sublime landscapes von Humboldt, the premier scientist of his day, had explored, from the island of Tenerife to the headwaters of the Orinoco to Mount Chimborazo in Ecuador. Von Humboldt (1769–1859) had managed to integrate all the science of his time — geology, climatology, physics, natural history, and economics — and see it as so many steps ascending to a Romantic worship of nature.

Darwin never completely lost the biocentric attitude that he learned from White and von Humboldt, and by including humankind as one species among others within natural history, he broke decisively with the Cartesian separation of mind and matter and took a step back toward medieval organicism. But the voyage of the *Beagle* deprived him of any idyllic notion he once had that nature was inevitably friendly to humankind.

What particularly disabused Darwin of this belief was the visit to the Galapagos, a cluster of craters and solidified lava flows, supporting a weird crop of cacti and low shrubs under a blistering equatorial sun some six hundred miles west of Ecuador. When Darwin arrived on these shores in September of 1835 as his ship's naturalist, he'd been charting the coastal waters of South America for four years, making scientific expeditions over its interior plains and into the Andean mountains and collecting rocks, plants, and animals to send back to London

9. Worster, *Nature's Economy,* 114.

and Cambridge. Now he encountered a landscape unlike anything he had seen before. Nature here was bleak, depraved, and hostile.

The fifteen islands, he observed, had been thrust out of the seabed in a series of recent volcanic eruptions. It was like visiting Hades, the kingdom of Pluto: "A broken field of black basaltic lava," wrote Darwin, "thrown into the most rugged waves, and crossed by great fissures, is every where covered by stunted, sun-burnt brushwood, which shows little sign of life."[10] Arriving aboard a whaling ship some six years later, Herman Melville had a similar reaction. That isolated archipelago, he later wrote, had left him with recurrent nightmares — as if he had "slept upon evilly enchanted ground." Observing Rock Redondo, a natural tower rising 250 feet high straight from the sea and the nesting site for thousands of sea birds, Melville remembered the "demonic din." This was no place for a robin or canary, says Melville; it was the home of wild, fierce birds that had never seen a tree, much less warbled a springtime melody from a maple branch. "In no world but a fallen one," he wrote, "could such lands exist."

Despite the bleak appearances, Darwin found strange life on these moon-like desert landscapes: great orange centipedes, albatrosses, sea lions, blue-footed boobies, giant land turtles and iguanas, and most interesting, twenty-six kinds of land birds, including thirteen species of finches that differed not only from their mainland relatives but from one another in appearance, distribution, and eating habits. Some lived on the ground by crushing hard seeds with their nutcracker beaks. Others dwelt in trees farther inland, eating insects with their much sharper, slender bills, while still others resembled parrots and ate fruit. Could God have contrived all these marvelous adaptations whole-cloth from the beginning of time? "Seeing this gradation and diversity of structure in one small, intimately related group of birds," Darwin wrote, "one might really fancy that from an original paucity of birds in this archipelago, one species had been taken and modified for different ends."

Leaving the Galapagos in October of 1835, bound for the hospitable shores of Gauguin's Tahiti and Australia, Darwin departed with the questions about variation and adaptation that would lead him to his theory of evolution by natural selection. Could the conventional natural history of Linnaeus and William Paley — the idea of fixed species — encompass the wild diversity and adaptation that Darwin had seen with his own eyes? Or did the Galapagos demand another kind of expla-

---

10. The citations of Darwin and Melville are drawn from Worster's chapter "Fallen Nature," in *Nature's Economy*, 115–29.

nation? But beyond these scientific questions, says Donald Worster, "Darwin also carried away, in his imagination if not in his nostrils, the odor of sulfur and brimstone.... Nature, it was now starkly clear, had its more hideous face, blighted and polluted by its own forces, rivaling the new industrial environment in its desolation."[11]

In the second half of the nineteenth century, the very sense of humanity's alienation from nature that Romanticism had resisted began to surge back into prominence, aided and abetted by Darwin's vision of nature as antagonistic, malignant, and fearful. The discovery of the Galapagos, at least as represented by Darwin and Melville, reintroduced the Anglo-American mind to a potent counterforce to the arcadian vision of White and Thoreau. A more hopeful attitude toward nature, which Thoreau had accented, lost intellectual respectability and thus influence. The pendulum swung the other way, to a more pessimistic view of nature. "Before long," writes Donald Worster, "it would be commonplace that species were the product of blind physical laws, operating without regard for human moral values. The conviction would spread, with substantial scientific and literary support, that nature could no longer be viewed as a solicitous mother, worthy of her children's love and concern."[12]

Are Ecologists the Good Guys?

The use of the word "ecology" is a recent event. The German Darwinian biologist Ernst Haeckel coined the term "ecology" (from the Greek *oikos*, meaning household) in 1866. "By ecology," he said,

> we mean the body of knowledge concerning the economy of nature — the investigation of the total relations of the animal both to its organic and its inorganic environment; including above all, its friendly and inimical relation with those animals and plants with which it comes directly or indirectly into contact — in a word, ecology is the study of all the complex interrelations referred to by Darwin as the conditions of the struggle for existence.[13]

Harvard entomologist Edward O. Wilson offers a more succinct definition: "the scientific study of the interaction of organisms with their

---

11. Worster, *Nature's Economy*, 119–20.
12. Ibid., 122.
13. Cited in Robert E. Ricklefs, *The Economy of Nature*, 2d ed. (New York: W. H. Freeman, 1990), 1.

environment, including the physical environment and other organisms living in it."[14]

Are ecologists the good guys (and gals), always on the right side of ecological questions? That we are prone to make the mistake of thinking so is the result of confusing the advocates with the egg-heads, the science of ecology with environmental activists who advocate the protection of our environment (whales, snail darters, spotted owls, rainforests, rivers, wilderness, etc.) in the political forum. The two represent very different mental traditions. Ecologists descend from the lineage of Darwin, Newton, and Galileo. The environmentalists descend from evangelical preachers, abolitionists, suffragettes, civil rights activists, and radical "left wing" Protestantism in general.

One must remind oneself that from its beginnings as a scientific discipline in the last decade of the nineteenth century, the main function of university-based ecology has been to help government and industry in the "scientific management" of natural resources. The science of ecology, that is, is there to minimize the damage of exploitation, not to question the logic or wisdom of that exploitation. Indeed, that's the service Aldo Leopold (1886–1948) performed for most of his life as a wildlife specialist and forest manager in the American southwest. One of the founders of the Wilderness Society in 1935 and canonized saint of the environmental movement, Leopold also directed Wisconsin's department of forestry. Let's be blunt: For the greater part of his career, in other words, he was an employee of the lumber industry.

At least up until the 1960s, when Rachel Carson's attack on DDT in *Silent Spring* (1962) suddenly galvanized a whole nation (and the number of ecologists doubled in a decade), theoretical ecology had been the tool, the means, through which our industrial culture pursued its unquestioned goals: the maximum utilization of earth's supposedly limitless supply of matter-energy. From this angle, the only value the Adirondacks or the Colorado River have is the value the almighty market places on them as potential commodities. To think of all ecologists as tree-hugging environmentalists is an illusion. Being a scientific ecologist is not necessarily the same thing as being an environmental activist. Some ecologists are environmental activists; many are not.

Ecology is not a unified discipline. It is a collection of distinct research programs — in plant ecology, animal ecology, oceanography, field studies, systems ecology, and so forth. And the debates about the relative importance of cooperation and competition, or how nature is to be pictured (as a living organism, a machine, or analogous to

---

14. Edward O. Wilson, *The Diversity of Life* (New York: W. W. Norton, 1992), 396.

an economic system), have been fierce. While a holistic approach was prominent in the "dust bowl" years of the 1930s, the scene following World War II has been increasingly fragmented.

It hasn't always been so. Throughout the early part of this century the dominant notion of ecological order was associated with the "dynamic ecology" of the Nebraska ecologist Frederick Clements. Clements was mainly concerned with the process of vegetational succession, the sequence of plant communities that appear and succeed each other over a period of time on any given piece of soil. In the natural course of things, Clements argued, the landscape reaches a "final climax" stage of stability, which he did not hesitate to call a "superorganism." By that term he meant an assemblage of plants that had achieved a close integration of parts, a self-sustaining capability, that resembled the unity of a single animal or plant. In some special sense, it had become a live, coherent being, not a collection of atomistic individuals, and exercised some degree of control over the nonliving world around it, as organisms do. Clements's ideas translated rather readily into public policy. The lesson was that since organic nature tended toward a stable climax state, so far as possible human beings ought to respect and preserve that state.

In the 1940s, however, scientists began to use a new vocabulary of description, speaking of "energy flows," "trophic levels," and "ecosystem." Perhaps the most influential exponent of this approach was Eugene P. Odum from North Carolina and Georgia, who found in his saltwater marshes, tidal estuaries, and cotton fields the pulsating energy of the sun that drove the whole animate world of plants and animals. In 1953 Eugene Odum published what was arguably one of the most influential works of ecology ever written, *The Fundamentals of Ecology.* The earth, he and his collaborators taught, is organized into an interlocking system of ecosystems. Ecosystems manifest a steady tendency toward an ideal order or norm marked by a shift from competition in the early stages to increased interrelatedness and cooperation in later stages. The stages are traceable, and when ecosystems mature they achieve a state of relative "homeostasis," or equilibrium. Homeostasis perdures until damage interrupts or breaks the established pattern.

The chief sources of such damage, Odum believed, were human beings, more particularly modern human beings who treat nature as if it were nothing but a "supply depot" rather than the home (*oikos*) in which we all must live. Since the 1970s, however, Odum's concept of a normative equilibrium state for ecosystems has been thrown into doubt; the dominant thinking today is that change goes on constantly without ever reaching an ideal state of stability. Consequently it is increasingly difficult, if not impossible, for ecologists to advise policy-makers on what the "carrying capacity" or "sustainable yield" from any ecosystem might ideally be. Instead of being a study of stable states, contemporary ecology has become a study of disturbance, disharmony, and chaos.

The kind of holism Friedrich von Humboldt once represented in science has thus suffered steady decline in recent decades. The scientific reaction to atmospheric chemist James Lovelock is a case in point. In the 1970s Lovelock came up with the "Gaia hypothesis," the theory that the biosphere, organic life itself, not only created earth's atmosphere but also regulates it, keeping it favorable to life. Life, argued Lovelock and his collaborator, microbiologist Lynn Margulis, creates the conditions for its own existence, regulating temperature, the chemical composition of the atmosphere, and the salinity of oceans. Living and nonliving systems, it turns out, are tightly interlinked and cooperate in keeping our planet hospitable to life. Drawing on geology, microbiology, and atmospheric chemistry, the theory pulled together an impressive array of evidence and received an enormous popular response, especially among environmentalists. But at first the response of Lovelock's scientific colleagues, when they did not scoff at the idea, was notably chilly. In scientific and funding circles, organic models of nature are decidedly "out."

In order to qualify for membership in the scientific club, ecology in recent decades has cast aside the image of holistic nature and committed itself more firmly than ever to materialistic models based on the concept of exploitation and the Darwinian struggle for existence. And there lies the heart of the problem. For as historian Peter J. Bowler puts it, "The image of Nature as a machine that can be tinkered with at our pleasure is a potent symbol of the exploitative view of humankind's relationship to the rest of the universe."[15] The irony of the situation is striking.

To an outsider it does indeed seem strange that, at the time when there is an increasing call for humankind to respect the global environment or face extinction, the science of ecology has moved firmly away from the organic model of Nature that seems most likely to encourage the right kind of behavior. Radical environmentalists actively encourage the view that the earth should be treated as an organic, feminine system that nurtures all life including our own. As concern for the environment grows among

---

15. Peter J. Bowler, *The Environmental Sciences* (New York: W. W. Norton, 1993), 430.

the general public, this world view is likely to expand its influence. Yet paradoxically science itself has committed itself ever more strongly to a model of Nature based on individual struggle, a devil-take-the-hindmost philosophy that offers little support for harmonious inter-species relationships and openly endorses competition as the mechanism of progress within species.[16]

The fact that through the ministrations of science human beings today have achieved the technological power to destroy the habitable earth, and that in some respects we are now doing so at a rapid rate, is something entirely new and unprecedented in the history of the planet. As "ecologian" Father Thomas Berry claims,

We have changed the very chemistry of the planet, we have altered the biosystem, we have changed the topography and even the geological structure of the planet, structures and functions that have taken hundreds of millions and even billions of years to bring into existence. Such an order of change in its nature and in its order of magnitude has never before entered into Earth history or into human consciousness.[17]

Given the magnitude of the problem and its lack of historical precedent, it is no surprise that neither science nor religion has been quite up to the challenge. Nuclear weapons, global warming, ozone depletion, pollution, deforestation, and genetic destruction — taken singly or together, they are all too much, both for our philosophies and for the institutions that were built for a different and smaller world.

---

16. Ibid., 547.
17. Thomas Berry, *The Dream of the Earth* (San Francisco: Sierra Club, 1988), xiii.

PART III

STATE OF THE EARTH

Transcendence in the Judeo-Christian perspective is not an idle aestheticism. As I tried to show in chapters 1 and 2, if it is authentic, contemplating the kingdom of God has an impact on the world, makes a difference, does work. Historically, it has taken us in at least two very different directions: on the one hand, to a spirituality of ascent that teaches contempt for the world and concentrates the mind on life after death; and on the other, to a spirituality that finds God's goodness and promise poured out into the world. In the latter case, God is found in all things, and transcendence consequently does not mean escape from the earth. As an example of this point, bacteriologist René Dubos was in the habit of pointing, not to Francis of Assisi, but to Benedict of Nursia's (ca. 480–547) "theology of the earth." Spreading throughout medieval Europe, Benedict's diligent monks tended the earth, drained swamps, cleared forests, improved fields, and tended their gardens. Dubos found them exemplifying the best of Christian stewardship and displaying an "ethical attitude" toward the biophysical world.

For the Benedictine tradition, serving and glorifying God meant (and still means) stewardship, caring for the gift, the promise that God has given into our trust — the very bounty and fruitfulness of the earth. No, from this perspective, transcendence does not mean escape from the earth. It means that from the visionary heights of a Mt. Sinai, as it were, we look back down upon the state of the earth and see things critically, as the Hebrew prophets saw them. For the prophets, human sin had ecological effects. It constituted a blight upon the land. Thus the prophet Hosea:

The land mourns,
  and everything that dwells in it languishes:
the beasts of the field,
  the birds of the air,
  and even the fish of the sea perish. (Hos. 4:3)

The biblical tradition, as we saw in chapter 2, enables one to say no to one's culture. It also asks us to understand what has gone wrong — why the land mourns today. It may also help us recognize that the march of modernity, as we indicated in the last section, has not always meant progress. Modernity also means amnesia and loss of an earlier wisdom.

For instance, the hierarchical "great chain of being" thinking that Christianity inherited from Platonism had certain advantages over individualistic social contract ethics. It enabled believers, at least up until the seventeenth century, to think of their moral obligations as extending beyond the human, to the various orders of reality, animate and inanimate, in which they were implicated. Well up into Renaissance times, that is to say, people understood themselves not primarily as individuals, but as members of groups, families, tribes, species, the animal world, and nature-in-the-large, and accordingly conceived of their moral relations to these various wholes of which they formed a part. All creatures, in Thomas Aquinas's great vision of the analogy of being, had existence insofar as they participated to one degree or another in the very being of God. With the coming of the scientific revolution and modern individualism, this broad sense of kinship and moral obligation shrank appreciably, as we have seen, restricted now to the human complement.

In the next three chapters, I want to examine some of the consequences of this narrowing of our moral horizons. I will try to assess the state of the earth and come to some preliminary conclusion about the institutional or structural arrangements that contribute to ecological breakdown.

Have we in fact been making something beautiful of nature? Or have we been sowing ruin? Is it true, as some would allege, that we are risking ecological meltdown? Does the very mention of the word "environment" require us to speak of "crisis"? There was a time, a short time ago, when polluted rivers were breaking into flame, when almost no informed citizen doubted that we were in environmental trouble. But clean-up costs money, cuts into the profit line, and by the late 1970s when it became apparent that the environmental movement was no passing fad, American corporations took to the offensive with political lobbying, public relations campaigns, punitive litigation, and research studies, all of it designed to refute or discredit the claims of environmentalists and regulatory agencies. By the 1980s and 1990s, a well coordinated counter-movement was underway. In 1990 corporate anti-environmental political lobbying and public relations efforts in the United States were estimated to amount to $500 million annually. Industries formed coalitions with pro-environment-sounding names — the National Wetlands Coalition (oil drillers and real estate developers), the U.S. Council on Energy Awareness (the nuclear power industry), the Alliance for America (timber cutters, oil drillers, ranchers, miners) — aimed at destroying environmentalism "by taking away their money and their members." The airwaves are consequently filled with information and disinformation overload.

So we have to examine the factual question: Is there an environmental crisis? A crisis, let us say, is a rapidly deteriorating situation that, if left unattended, will lead to disaster in the near future. Are we in crisis? Or have environmentalists been scaring us into precipitous and costly remedies for dangers that don't exist?

Certainly there are many distinguished voices raising the alarm. The U.S. environmental situation, Vice President Al Gore insists, is "extremely grave — the worst crisis our country has ever faced." Worse than the Civil War? Than the Great Depression? George Mitchell, the former majority leader of the Senate, tells us that environmental abuse risks "turning the world into a lifeless desert." Gaylord Nelson, who as a Senator in 1970 originated Earth Day and is now a lawyer for the Wilderness Society, declared in 1990 that current ecological problems "are a greater risk to the Earth's life-sustaining systems than a nuclear war."[1] Are such statements to be believed? Or is this all hype and scare tactics?

An examination of the vital signs of the earth, we will find, gives no basis for complacency. On a variety of fronts — soil, water, forest, biodiversity, energy, waste disposal, and carbon emissions — we are headed for crisis in the twenty-first century. What are the dynamics in our culture and the social arrangements that drive us to an unsustainable economy within the "Great Economy" of nature? In the next three chapters, I first will examine the reasons for thinking that modern industrial society continues to abuse the planet; second, we will take a look at some of the institutional economic and political arrangements that facilitate such destruction.

---

1. Cited by Gregg Easterbrook, *A Moment on Earth: The Coming Age of Environmental Optimism* (New York: Penguin Books, 1995), xiii.

What is our moral responsibility in light of the analysis in this section? Basically, I am saying that the facts speak for themselves: we are not doing justice to the earth. At a minimum, a utilitarian calculus should lead us to take prudent remedial action, be it in the form of recycling, clean technology, and/or institutional reform. It is in our enlightened self-interest to conserve, preserve, and restore the well-being of the Great Economy of nature that supports us. At the same time, it seems to me that for religious believers, the motives for action may be even stronger, based on the perceived intrinsic value of the natural world to God and our responsibility to glorify God by how we care for creation.

FIVE

Is There
an Environmental Crisis?

The ecological perspective begins with a view of the whole, an understanding of how the various parts of nature interact in patterns that tend toward balance and persist over time. But this perspective cannot treat the earth as something separate from human civilization; we are part of the whole too, and looking at it means also looking at ourselves. And if we do not see that...we are, in effect, a natural force just like the winds and the tides, then we will not be able to see how dangerously we are threatening to push the earth out of balance.   — AL GORE, *Earth in Balance*

However the deed was done, once genus *Homo sapiens* was called forth into being, the wholly spontaneous ordering of the environment ended. And unless there is an extinction of intellect, wholly spontaneous nature will never return. Nature is not diminished by this.   — GREGG EASTERBROOK, *A Moment on the Earth*

It is a century now since Darwin.... We know now what was unknown to all the proceeding caravan of generations: that men are only fellow-voyagers with other creatures in the odyssey of evolution. This new knowledge should have given us, by this time, a sense of kinship with fellow creatures; a wish to live and let live; a sense of wonder over the magnitude and duration of the biotic enterprise.   — ALDO LEOPOLD, *Sand County Almanac*

The almost inevitable onset of global warming in this century, writes Bill McKibben, will spell the "end of nature" as we have known it. Not the end of wind and sun and photosynthesis, but the end of a whole "set of human ideas about nature and our place in it." McKibben enlarges on the point.

The idea of nature will not survive the new global pollution — the carbon dioxide and the CFCs [chlorofluorocarbons] and the like. This new rupture with nature is different not only in scope but also in kind. . . . We have changed the atmosphere, and thus we are changing the weather. By changing the weather, we make every spot on earth man-made and artificial. We have deprived nature of its independence, and that is fatal to its meaning. Nature's independence is its meaning; without it there is nothing but us.[1]

In the late 1980s, David Foreman, head of the ecological-sabotage organization Earth First!, was in the habit of calling human beings "a cancer on the Earth." Is this the truth, or just blatant misanthropy?

The Case against Environmental Hype

In 1995 Gregg Easterbrook, a former *Newsweek* writer and now an editor at the *New Republic,* challenged the apocalyptic strain of environmentalists in his book *A Moment on Earth: The Coming Age of Environmental Optimism.*[2] Easterbrook claimed to be a friend of environmentalism. But with such friends, who needs enemies? "Ecological consciousness," he maintained, "is a leading force for good in world affairs." The particular target of his scorn was the scare tactics of environmentalist-doomsayers. He distinguished himself over against these pessimists as an "ecorealist," someone who realized how much progress we have made and was not afraid to say so. Easterbrook accused people like Paul Ehrlich, Al Gore, Carolyn Merchant, Thomas Berry, Herman Daly, Jeremy Rifkin, and Bill McKibben of stressing the bad news and systematically suppressing any good news about improvements in our environmental situation.

"Environmentalists, who are surely on the right side of history," wrote Easterbrook, "are increasingly on the wrong side of the present, risking their credibility by proclaiming emergencies that do not exist."[3] The prospect, for instance, that the continued burning of fossil fuels will heat up the globe by an average of four to eight degrees Fahrenheit in the next century, Easterbrook allows, is "the most disturbing ecological prospect of our moment on Earth."[4] But, he argues, environmentalists exaggerate the dangers here. The movement fails to count up its remarkable successes over the past three decades.

---

1. Bill McKibben, *The End of Nature* (New York: Doubleday Anchor Books, 1990), 58.
2. Gregg Easterbrook, *A Moment on Earth: The Coming Age of Environmental Optimism* (New York: Penguin Books, 1995).
3. Ibid., xvi.
4. Ibid., 278.

Take smog, for example. In the 1980s, ambient smog in the United States declined a composite 16 percent, even as economic output expanded and the number of automobiles increased rapidly. At the beginning of the 1980s major cities reported about six hundred air-quality-alert days each year. By the end of the decade, that figure was cut in half, down to three hundred days. Air pollution from lead, by far the most dangerous atmospheric poison, declined by 89 percent; carbon monoxide went down 31 percent; and sulfur dioxide, the main component of acid rain, was down 27 percent. In brief, American air was much less dirty in 1990 than it was in 1980.

According to Easterbrook, this positive trend in air quality is matched in almost every other area as well. At least in the United States, he says, the trend lines have been positive in recent years: in water pollution, ocean pollution, toxic discharges, acid rain emissions, soil loss, radiation exposure, species protection, and recycling. "Enviros won the last 20 years of political battles by a wide margin," argues Easterbrook, "but you'd never know it from their public statements. That their cause has become mainstream makes many environmentalists nervous."[5]

In contrast to the doomsayers, Easterbrook spells out an ecological impulse grounded in what he calls the more sober rationality of "ecorealism." Nature, he argues, is much tougher and more resilient than enviros commonly lead us to believe. Some of the more sensible principles of ecorealism are as follows:

- Skeptical debate is good for the environmental movement. The public need not be brainwashed into believing in ecological protection, since a clean environment is in everyone's interest. Thus the environmental movement must learn to entertain skeptical debate in a reasoned manner or it will discredit itself, as all close-minded political movements eventually discredit themselves.

- Weapons aside, technology is not growing more dangerous and wasteful. It grows cleaner and more resource-efficient.

- As positive as trends are in the first world, they are negative in the third. One reason the West must shake off instant doomsday thinking about the United States and Western Europe is so that resources can be diverted to ecological protection in the developing world.

- It is pointless for men and women to debate what the "correct" reality for nature might have been before people arrived on the

---

5. Ibid., 381.

scene. There has never been and can never be any fixed, correct environmental reality. There are only moments on the earth, moments that may be good or bad.

- All environmental errors are reversible save one: extinction. Therefore the prevention of extinction is a priority.

- However the deed was done, once genus *Homo sapiens* was called forth into being, the wholly spontaneous ordering of the environment ended. And unless there is an extinction of intellect, wholly spontaneous nature will never return. Nature is not diminished by this. A fairly straightforward reading of natural history suggests that evolution spent 3.8 billion years working assiduously to bring about the demise of the wholly spontaneous order, via the creation of intellect.

- In principle the human population is no enemy of nature.

- Nature is not ending, nor is human damage to the environment "unprecedented." Nature has repelled forces of magnitude many times greater than the worst human malfeasance. Nature, says Easterbrook, "makes pollutants, poisons, and suffering on a scale so far unapproached by men and women except during periods of warfare." While World War I took 14 million lives over four years, he points out, in the two years after the war ended the Spanish flu took 20 million lives.

- Nature is not ponderously slow. It's just old. Old and slow are quite different concepts. That the living world can adjust with surprising alacrity is the reason nature has been able to get old. Most natural recoveries from ecological duress happen with amazing speed.

- If nature's adjustment to the human presence began thousands of years ago, perhaps it will soon be complete. Far from reeling helplessly before a human onslaught, nature may be on the verge of reasserting itself.

- Nature still rules much more of the earth than does genus *Homo*. To the statistical majority of nature's creatures the arrival of men and women goes unnoticed.

- To people the distinction between artificial and natural means a great deal. To nature it means nothing at all.

- The fundamental force of nature is not an amoral struggle between hunter and hunted. Most living things center their existence on cooperation and coexistence, the sort of behavior women and men should emulate. This is one reason nature will soon be viewed again in the way it was by the thinkers of the Enlightenment — as a trove of wisdom and an exemplar for society.

- Nature, limited by spontaneous interactions among elements randomly disturbed, may have an upper-bound limit on its potential to foster life and evolve. Yet nature appears to enjoy fostering life and evolving. So perhaps nature hoped to acquire new sets of abilities, such as action by design. Therefore maybe nature needs us.[6]

That Easterbrook's critique of environmental alarmism drew sharp cries of protest probably indicates that he'd struck a raw nerve — and a good deal of unpalatable truth. For one thing, it does the movement no good to exaggerate the extent of environmental damage or threat. Easterbrook is right: crying wolf too often undermines the movement's credibility. Second, big nature, as he points out, is doubtless less fragile and tougher than many environmentalists assume. Biological life has survived ice ages, cosmic and solar radiation, volcanism, the reversal of the magnetic poles, the rearrangement of continents, the transformation of plains and mountain ranges, fluctuations in the ocean currents and jet streams, the vacillation of sea levels, and collisions with asteroids and comets bearing more force than nuclear bombs. "Were the environment fragile it would have expired many eons before the advent of the industrial affronts of the dreaming ape," writes Easterbrook. "Human assaults on the environment, though mischievous, are pinpricks compared to forces of the magnitude nature is accustomed to resisting."[7]

Easterbrook's book also has the virtue of highlighting a little-known feature of much environmentalist writing and rhetoric. The pessimism of many of these writers is rooted in a dualistic vision of nature and humanity that borders on the Manichaean. The two are seen as utterly separate (as in McKibben's vision of the "independence" of nature) and inexorably hostile. Spontaneous nature, the autonomous self-alignment of the physical and biological worlds, is regarded as innocent and essentially good, whereas human beings are regarded as a foreign intrusion or an evil curse upon the earth. What we are often exposed to in environmentalist writing, then, combines Rousseauian romanticism with everyday misanthropy. No one will deny that human interven-

---

6. Ibid., 647–51.
7. Ibid., 25.

tions in nature have often been destructive — witness the demise of ancient city states in the Tigris-Euphrates valley from over-irrigation and the salinization of the soil, or the death of the great Mayan culture in Central America for similar reasons. But to maintain that humans are somehow "unnatural" by nature and must pursue an adversarial relationship to nature is to cook the books in favor of misanthropy. It is to inflate nature's goodness on the one side and to exaggerate human evil on the other. It makes it appear that the battle to save the environment was lost some seven thousand years ago as soon as human beings began to take up systematic agriculture.

Yet Easterbrook's critique is itself skewed. First, his picture of the current situation can be optimistic because he concentrates his attention on progress in the United States, while almost wholly ignoring the bleak situation in the developing nations of Africa, Latin America, and south and southeast Asia. Second, his attack on environmental catastrophism skews the analysis. Real environmental problems are minimized and shorn of any urgency. Nowhere is this more evident than in the chapter on global warming. At the start of that chapter, Easterbrook briefly acknowledges that an "artificial greenhouse effect is the most disturbing ecological prospect of our moment on the Earth," and he offers that it is a prospect "against which women and men are well advised to take immediate steps." But nowhere does Easterbrook make a concerted case for these steps, and the point is quickly lost in the following thirty-eight pages, which make the case that scientific models of climatic change are uncertain, that Mt. Pinatubo's eruption in 1991 put much more carbon dioxide in the air than industry and automobiles do, and, in any case, warming might improve the agricultural production of Canada and Siberia. Easterbrook is so busy beating up environmentalists for the exaggerations of their "worst case" scenarios that the reader finally forgets the last line of this chapter, which asserts that "any reasonable policy that reduces the odds of climate change is more than worth the price."[8]

Reading Earth's Vital Signs:
Soil and Food Production, Water, Forests, Biodiversity

So we return to the question of the health of our planet. Are we in serious trouble, in crisis mode? Are we approaching the limits of the planet's carrying capacity? Disaster may not be as imminent as some environmentalists would have it, but it does lie around the corner if we

8. Ibid., 316.

don't take concerted action now. Complacency is hardly warranted. A survey of the condition of the planet's resources — soil, water, biotic diversity, and energy resources — suggests that despite certain improvements in the first world, the global situation merits serious concern.[9] Some regions are worse off than others (indeed, already in crisis). Concerted local and global action is called for.

It is true, as Gregg Easterbrook and others have noted recently, that the forest cover of the northeastern United States has increased since the 1920s. In the mid–nineteenth century, Vermont, Massachusetts, and Connecticut were 35 percent woodland; today, with a tripling of population, they are 59 percent woodland. Maine was then 74 percent forested; it is now 90 percent. New Hampshire, once 50 percent woodland, is now 86 percent forest-covered. Western Europe reflects similar figures, having 30 percent more woodland now than fifty years ago. Western agriculture also claims less land than it used to. In the 1930s, U.S. production of wheat, corn, and cotton amounted to 210 million metric tons from 77 million acres. By the late 1980s, the U.S. produced 600 million metric tons from 72 million acres. Crop yields trebled. Between 1980 and 1990, production of cotton, corn, and wheat rose by 20 to 40 percent while the total land in use declined by 56 million acres. What Easterbrook downplays, however, is that the increase in crop yields and the decline in land use in the 1980s, relative to the 1930s, was accomplished only by far greater inputs of fossil fuel energy, artificial fertilizer, and use of mechanized equipment.

Soil and Food Production

In the less affluent world, however, the story is generally grim. While more land has been brought into agricultural production — much of it fragile and marginal land — and while irrigation, fertilizers, and new seed hybrids (the "green revolution") have steadily increased total food production in recent decades, per capita food production has declined in the 1980s. Yes, the new "industrial agriculture" has expanded the food supply remarkably, but it has also led to the abandonment of traditional methods of soil preservation: terracing, contour plowing, crop rotation, fallow years, the use of manure, herd migration, and shifting agriculture. Continuous cropping of monocultures and overgrazing have resulted in an overall decline in the quality of the soil. Among major food producers, the United States alone is making

---

9. Many of the facts and figures in the following survey come from Charles L. Harper, *Environment and Society: Human Perspectives on Environmental Issues* (Upper Saddle River, N.J.: Prentice Hall, 1996), 71–104, 165–91, 199–221. See also Paul Kennedy, *Preparing for the Twenty-First Century* (New York: Vintage Books, 1993), 21–46, 65–81, 95–121.

progress in reducing soil erosion. (Still, agronomists report crop losses between 15 and 30 percent due to soil degrading in North America.) A 1992 UN study of worldwide soil health concluded that over the last forty-five years 11 percent of the earth's arable land has suffered severe degradation (an area the size of India and China combined). In all, this UN study reported, 17 percent of the planet's vegetated area had been degraded by overgrazing, harmful agriculture, industrial and urban pollution, or deforestation.

The consequences of overharvesting and poor resource management are not limited to the land. The world's fish catch peaked in the 1970s and has steadily declined since then. The total catch in the North Atlantic fishing banks, for example, has declined 32 percent since the 1970s — to a great extent as a result of high-tech fishing methods such as huge drag nets.

Simply put, the strategies and technologies that have served to keep food production growing more rapidly than population (adding more land, new genetic hybrids, increasing fertilizers, pesticides, herbicides, and irrigation) have apparently reached their limit. Good grain-producing land, irrigated land, forested areas, and grazing land are not expected to increase much in the near future. For the world as a whole, food production per capita has been declining for some years. From 1984 to 1990, the annual growth of grain production was 1 percent, while population growth was nearly 2 percent. This comparison is more ominous than it looks, because 1984 and 1990 were bumper-crop years, when per-hectare yields of wheat, rice, and corn set new records in all major grain-producing regions. In 1993–94 world grain production declined by 12 percent, and seafood by 9 percent. The evidence suggests that we have passed critical thresholds in the production of food.

Water

Clean, fresh water, the lifeblood of the biosphere and the most critical resource for agriculture — and equally essential for industrial and household use — promises to be in short supply on a global basis in the near future. Global water demand has tripled since 1950, and the consequences are apparent in falling water tables, shrinking lakes and wetlands, and dwindling streams and rivers. With the growth of irrigation, groundwater is being pumped out more rapidly than recharge rates, so that water tables have declined severely in South India, China, and the great Ogallala Aquifer in the American Great Plains. According to the UN, twenty-six countries with a population of 232 million people are now rated as water-scarce. Water conflicts bode ill for the future — between India and Pakistan over water-rich Kashmir, between Israel and Syria over the Jordan river basin, among Ethiopia, Sudan, and Egypt over the headwaters of the Nile, and among Turkey, Syria, and Iraq over the headwaters of the Euphrates. By the year 2025, over 1 billion people in Africa and southern and western Asia will live under conditions of extreme water scarcity.

Forests

Worldwide, forests are in severe retreat. The loss is gravely significant in that trees create and hold soil, control floods, maintain water tables, keep rivers and seacoasts free of silt, and recycle gases (especially carbon dioxide and oxygen) that maintain the chemical balance of the atmosphere. And most underappreciated, "old-growth" forests provide the habitat for living species that are to be found nowhere else. Since the beginning of agriculture seven thousand years ago, one-third of the world's forests have been destroyed, and the pace of destruction has accelerated since the 1960s. Few virgin or old-growth forests are left anywhere on the planet.

A combination of forces — multinational companies seeking profits, governments desperate to pay off international debts, landowners and ranchers wanting farm and grazing land, and peasants wanting firewood — conspires to eradicate tropical rain forests at an alarming pace. India and Sri Lanka have almost no forests left, and they are swiftly being clear-cut in Indonesia, Malaysia, Thailand, and the Philippines. The Atlantic coast forests of Brazil are 95 percent gone, while in the Amazon basin, 5,355 square miles are being cut, bulldozed, or burned each year. In 1990, 880 million hectares of tropical forest were cut, of which nearly half, some 330 million hectares, were in Brazil alone. At current rates of cutting, the planet's rainforests will be gone within the next twenty to ninety years.

Of the thirty-three developing nations that once exported tropical hardwoods, the World Bank figured that only ten would be able to do so by the year 2000. And what makes this all the more distressing is the unlikelihood of any quick recovery. For when cleared of tree cover, heavy tropical rains leach and erode the existing soil of nutrients, making agriculture unsustainable and forest regrowth long and difficult. For all practical purposes, rainforests constitute finite, nonrenewable resources.

Over the decades, woodcutters on the slopes of the Himalayas in Nepal have downed so many trees that the spring snow melt erodes topsoil and causes floods downstream in Bangladesh and India. In the Czech and Slovak Republics, 71 percent of the trees are damaged or killed by acid rain produced by industrial pollution. Sixty percent of the planet's great conifer forests on the Pacific Northwest coast in the U.S. and Canada, stretching from the Olympic peninsula in Washington State to the Tongas forest in Alaska, have been felled for lumber.

Biodiversity

Roughly 1.4 million species have been identified on the earth, though scientists suspect the total number may lie between ten and 100 million species. Biodiversity, not space travel, is the great unexplored frontier of the future. Ninety percent of the species of plants, animals, and microorganisms lack a specific name. They are all family, our distant kin. All higher eukaryotic organisms (those with nucleated cells), from flowering plants to insects to ourselves, descend from a single ancestral population of organisms that lived some 1.8 billion years ago. Our kinship with all living creatures is stamped in our genetic code, on the elementary features of our cell structure.

We have co-evolved with all these living things. "For more than 99 percent of human history," writes Harvard entomologist Edward O. Wilson, "people have lived in hunter-gatherer bands intimately involved with other organisms.... In short, the brain evolved in a biocentric world, not a machine-regulated one."[10] We are thus hardwired to feel kin to all life-forms (biophilia, he calls it). It's why, he argues, we fear snakes, why more children and adults in the U.S. and Canada visit zoos than attend all professional sports combined, and why the wealthy continue to seek to dwell amid parkland or on promontories above water.

Shall we grant "rights" to our kinfolk? Do we have obligations to nonhuman life? At a minimum, have they been committed to our care by a caring Creator? A total of 42,580 vertebrate species have been named — among them some 6,300 reptiles, 9,040 birds, 4,000 mammals. In contrast, some 990,000 species of invertebrates have been identified, 290,00 of them beetles alone (seven times the number of all vertebrates). Recent estimates of the number of invertebrate species go as high as 10 million or more. In two hundred kilograms of animal tissue found in a hectare of Brazilian forest floor, 93 percent of it consisted of invertebrates. And these creatures perform indispensable duties. Leafcutter ants in Central and South America, for example, keep the forest alive by processing most dead vegetation and returning nutrients to the soil, without which plant life could not thrive.

---

10. Edward O. Wilson, *In Search of Nature* (Washington, D.C.: Island Press, 1996), 166.

As Edward O. Wilson says, the real movers and shakers of the earth are the invertebrates, which arrived on the planet some 600 million years ago, about 100 million years ahead of vertebrates.[11] We need invertebrates; they don't need us. If our species were to disappear from the planet, things would go on with little visible change. But if invertebrates were to disappear, the human species would probably last only a few months, and most fish, amphibians, birds, and mammals would go extinct with them, because without invertebrates fungi would perish, the soil would rot, and dead vegetation would pile up and dry up, killing off the nutrient cycles upon which plant and animal life depends. Within a few decades the earth would return to its barren state of 2 billion years ago, composed of 1 percent bacteria, algae, and a few other simple multicellular plants. It is at our peril that we fail to recognize the unpaid public services that these bugs perform for the living world. As Wilson says, they "run the world."

Along with coastal wetlands, marshes, and mangrove swamps, the rainforests represent the planet's great genetic storehouses. Organisms more complex than bacteria contain between 1 and 10 billion nucleotide letters, sculpted by natural selection, mutation, and recombination beyond knowing — information the equivalent of a whole set of the *Encyclopaedia Britannica*. On at least five different occasions during the 4.5-billion-year history of the planet, the earth has suffered spasms of extinctions that took 10 million years to repair. But now, with the loss of rainforests, we are threatened with another mass extinction. Though they take up only 5 percent of the earth's surface, rainforests contain an estimated 50 percent of the known species of plants and animals, and at the current rate of forest and wetland destruction, at least fifty to a hundred species vanish each day — forever. E. O. Wilson conservatively estimates the loss at thirty thousand species a year, seventy-four a day, three every hour. All told, the UN estimates that 25 percent of living species may become extinct in the next twenty-five years. The current human-produced extinction spasm threatens to be the greatest since the end of the Mesozoic era some 65 million years ago, when the dinosaurs departed.[12]

Why should we care? The utilitarian argument is all too obvious. Preserving this great genetic treasury lies in our self-interest. The actual or potential value of forest products — oils, gums, latexes, flavorings, alcohols, spices, resins, fannins, steroids, waxes, acids, phenols, rattans, bamboo, balsam, pesticides, and dyes — is incalculable. Further,

---

11. Ibid., 141–61.
12. Edward O. Wilson, *The Diversity of Life* (New York: W. W. Norton, 1993).

forests are the repositories of restorative agents for soil and water, as well as being the storehouses of natural foods like the recently discovered "winged bean" from New Guinea, which grows rapidly, is completely edible (roots, seeds, leaves, stems, and flowers), and has the nutritional value of the soybean. Forests are also the source of an array of disease-resistant grains and natural drugs. In 1970, when 70 percent of U.S. seed corn owing its ancestry to six inbred lines fell victim to a leaf fungus, spreading from the Great Lakes to the Gulf of Mexico, the damage was halted with the aid of a blight-resistant germ plasma derived from a wild variety of corn. As for medicines, alkaloid-bearing plants and other plant species protect against a variety of diseases, including cancer.

Finally, biodiversity is the key to the maintenance of the world as we know it. The maintenance of the ecosystems on which all life, including human life, depends hinges on a diversity of species occupying different niches. Biodiversity maintains food chains, regulates the water supply, controls pests and pathogens, and regulates the climate. Each living thing contains 1 to 10 billion bits of information in its genetic code, acquired by an astronomical number of mutations and episodes of natural selection over millions of years. It is this process that has enabled life to adapt to an incredible diversity of environmental circumstances. It constitutes nature's strength and resilience in the face of major changes, whereas an increasingly homogeneous biosphere will be highly vulnerable to even minor changes.

If species diversity continues its steep decline, as it is currently doing, natural speciation will not refill the gap left by extinction — at least not in any meaningful human time scale. When the dinosaurs became extinct 65 million years ago, it took 5 to 10 million years before biodiversity returned to the previous levels. Biodiversity — the available gene pool — is effectively irreplaceable. Once lost, for all practical purposes it cannot be regained.

Before the scientific and industrial revolutions, we could use the excuse that preserving biodiversity was beyond our powers, nature's or God's concern, not ours. The responsibility now lies at our doorstep. Ethicist Holmes Rolston III raises the challenge clearly. In the final analysis, the utilitarian argument is inadequate; it does justice neither to other species, our fellow-citizens on the planet, nor to our own better selves. Our social contract needs expanding.

> Several billion years worth of creative toil, several million species of teeming life, have been handed over to the care of this late-coming species in which mind has flowered and morals have

emerged. Ought not those of this sole moral species do something less self-interested than to count all the produce of an evolutionary ecosystem as rivets in their spaceship, resources in their larder, laboratory materials, recreation for their ride?

We are suffering, says Rolston, from an "endangered ethic," an obsolete, too narrow ethic formed in Newtonian times.

The contemporary ethical systems seem misfits in the role most recently demanded of them. There is something overspecialized about an ethic, held by the dominant class of *Homo sapiens,* that regards the welfare of only one of several million species as an object of duty. If this requires a paradigm change about the sorts of things to which duty can attach, so much the worse for those ethics no longer functioning in, nor suited to, their changing environment. The anthropocentrism associated with them was fiction anyway. There is something Newtonian, not yet Einsteinian, besides something morally naive, about living in a reference frame where one species takes itself as absolute and values everything else relative to its utility.[13]

Somehow, we are caught in a vast cultural lag. Ethically, we have not caught up with our physics!

---

13. Holmes Rolston III, "Duties to Endangered Species," in *Environmental Ethics,* ed. Robert Elliot (New York: Oxford University Press, 1995), 75.

Pushing the Limits

Industrial economists cannot measure the economy by the health of nature, for they regard nature as simply a source of "raw materials." They cannot measure it by the health of people, for they regard people as "labor" (that is, as tools or machine parts) or as "consumers." They can measure the health of the economy only in sums of money. — WENDELL BERRY, *Home Economics*

The sky is not falling; the sky is filling up, changing its composition. As we only have one sky, this is a serious problem. — BILL McKIBBEN, *The Comforting Whirlwind*

Is economic growth the solution to our problem or is it at the heart of our problem? What economists, corporate CEOs, and politicians have trouble facing is that while the global economy grows, the planet itself is not growing; it has fixed limits. No one wishes to look at the stubborn truth that a triumphantly productive world, even while it produces affluence, is "hurtling toward a wall, an unidentified point in time when economic expansion would collectively collide with the physical capacity of the ecosystem."[1] No, no one can say exactly when this collision will actually occur. Humans are enormously inventive and we may yet alter our patterns of consumption or our birth rates, all of which may postpone the inevitable. But the wall exists and may be approaching much faster than anyone imagines.

Built-in Blindness to Limits

Talk of an overstressed planet is common these days. Yet no real reform of the global economic architecture is occurring. For when it comes to belief systems and operative structures, an expansionist economics remains firmly in place. NAFTA (North American Free Trade

---

1. William Greider, *One World, Ready or Not: The Manic Logic of Global Capitalism* (New York: Simon & Schuster, 1997), 455.

Agreement), the GATT treaty (the 160 nations joined by the General Agreement on Tariffs and Trade), and the establishment in 1995 of the World Trade Organization (W.T.O.) are all built on the prescription that "more" is better. Environmental concern is either a luxury or a formula for going out of business. The W.T.O. has been quick to annul local environmental restrictions when they conflict with the openness of unrestricted markets. (Recently they overrode the European ban on hormone-treated meat, U.S. laws to protect dolphins, and a Massachusetts boycott of Burmese products.) Even the United Nations Brundtland Commission, appointed to prepare for the Rio de Janeiro Earth Summit on Environment and Development in 1992, argued that a sustainable world must involve "more rapid economic growth in both industrial and developing countries." Though it exhibited an acute awareness of how poverty contributed to environmental damage and called for a concerted effort to reduce social inequities, the Brundtland Commission envisioned a five- to ten-fold increase in world industrial output by the time world population stabilizes in the twenty-first century.

Part of our blindness about economic growth stems from the fact that we have been fooling ourselves with misleading accounting procedures — mainly the Gross National Product (GNP). As I pointed out above, in chapters 3 and 4, mainstream economists do not regard the market system of production and consumption as a subsystem within the global or local ecosystem. They treat it as a self-contained arrangement separate from its external, natural surroundings and fail to ask how it depends on this larger context. Consequently the data on accumulated capital conceal the destruction of assets in the process of producing goods that are designed for built-in obsolescence. To be sure, economists grant that nature serves as a source of raw materials and as a sink for wastes, but they typically refuse to draw the obvious inference: that this means that we can't afford to overburden the ecosystem. That is to say they refuse to see that there's a scale limit on the human economy which we ignore at our peril. Again, they see nature as limitless and as a source to be drawn upon endlessly.

Former World Bank economist Herman Daly and theologian John B. Cobb Jr. aim to correct our blindness in this respect by devising a different way of measuring prosperity, one that takes into account what mainstream economists leave out of the picture.[2] Their Index of Sustainable Economic Welfare measures losses and the costs of produc-

---

2. Herman E. Daly and John B. Cobb Jr., *For the Common Good: Redirecting the Economy toward Community, the Environment, and a Sustainable Future* (Boston: Beacon Press, 1989), 401–55.

tion that corporations normally "externalize" — the costs of air and water pollution, the destruction of wetlands, the deterioration of farmland and long-term environmental damage such as ozone depletion and the consumption of nonrenewable resources. Adding in environmental health risks, auto accidents, and foreign debt also changes the picture. The standard GNP accounting declares that since the mid-1970s, U.S. income per capita has gone up in real value by 25 percent. Daly acknowledged great progress in the areas that Gregg Easterbrook has highlighted — the costs of pollution have gone way down — but his Index of Sustainable Economic Welfare calculated that economic well-being in sustainable terms has actually been declining since 1976, receding to levels of the mid-1960s. Where the GNP counts gain, a more realistic measurement counts loss of headway.

Can economic growth be made compatible with saving the planet? Probably not. But if we distinguish between growth and development and define development as meaning qualitative improvement without quantitative growth beyond the point where the ecosystem cannot regenerate, then there is no reason to think that the desire for qualitative improvement could not drive the economy as well as mere accumulation of more stuff. This doesn't have to be a prescription for "zero growth" or a state of permanent depression either, as CEOs fear. What is demanded is a redesign of the manufacturing process so that, so far as possible, there's a zero growth in energy and material inputs or throughputs in the system, and thus both greater efficiency and minimization of waste. Instead of being an open pass-through system, manufacturing would be a closed loop. Waste material would be recovered and put into some new type of factory that transforms waste into new materials — in the way in which scrap paper and scrap metal are currently being recycled for new products. In other words, alongside of what some have called a "plus factory," we require a "minus" or "inverse factory" that does the dirty work of recovering and converting waste materials.[3] At the moment, however, we are a long way from a production system that works in this way.

Energy Consumption

How close are we to pressing up against the biophysical limits of the planet? The answer: Close enough that within the next fifty years our children and grandchildren may well curse us, their parents and grandparents, for our unwillingness either to pay the true costs of using up

---

3. See Greider, *One World, Ready or Not,* 449–51.

the planet's resources or to change our profligate habits of consuming. One way to grasp the limits we are up against is to examine our uses of the stored energy capital of the planet, built up over millions of years. The ultimate source of all the planet's activity is the radiant energy of the sun. Autotrophic green plants (i.e., self-nourishing ones) transform solar energy into complex carbohydrate chemical forms by the process of photosynthesis, which are then consumed and converted into kinetic energy through the respiration processes of other species. Energy flows through the planetary ecosystem as a second species consumes the first, a third consumes the second, and so on up the chain. As the process proceeds, energy tends to degenerate, to become progressively more disorganized, to be dissipated in the form of heat which cannot be further used for kinetic energy or to sustain respiration. This is to say that the recycling of energy is subject to the second law of thermodynamics, or the law of entropy. And to acknowledge this law means that our fuel supplies are ultimately exhaustible.

Ecologists define the net primary production (NPP) of the biosphere as the total of energy that green plants snatch from sunlight and fix into living tissues, which is the basis of all food chains. The NPP is the energy flow that powers all of nature, including ourselves, on this planet. Several years ago, ecologists at Stanford University tried to measure how much of this photosynthetic product human beings used.[4] Their astounding conclusion was that we already absorb 25 percent of the earth's product as a whole and 40 percent of the photosynthetic product of the land. Humans directly consumed only 3 percent of the land-based NPP (through food, animal feed, and firewood). But indirectly, another 36 percent was consumed in crop wastes, forest burning and clearing, desert creation, and the conversion of natural areas into human settlements.

If this 40 percent figure is anywhere near correct — and GNP utterly ignores any such calculation — then the obvious and disturbing question to ask is, what will be the impact of the next doubling of the world's population and economic production? What will the planet be like when we are appropriating 80 percent of NPP? Will we find ourselves dwelling in a tight little island, wholly manicured and under human control, with no wilderness and no space for expansion or room for mistakes? Is this a viable biosphere? No one really knows.

Most of our current energy needs, of course, are supplied from vegetation long buried in the earth's crust — in the form of oil, natural

---

4. See Peter M. Vitousek et al., "Human Appropriation of the Products of Photosynthesis," *BioScience* 36 (1986): 368.

gas, and coal. In 1990 these fossil fuels accounted for between 80 and 88 percent of total world energy flows. All other sources of energy — hydropower, solar, wind, nuclear, traditional fuels (wood, dung, plant refuse) — together comprised the remainder. In the years since the pessimistic projections of the early 1970s, estimates of known oil reserves have doubled, and energy analysts now agree that for the time being the supply of fuels is not an issue. Known reserves of crude oil will last until sometime in the middle of this century, and natural gas will last at least that long, maybe longer. More, the world's supply of coal is projected to last for two hundred to a thousand years. There is no immediate energy crisis.

Yet there is a chronic, long-term problem. We are running out of cheap oil. Most analysts figure that current consumption rates of oil will deplete the easily affordable reserves somewhere between the years 2030 and 2072. To maintain the present rate of oil use means that every ten years we must discover as much oil as there is in Saudi Arabia (which holds 25 percent of the world's known reserves). Very few think that is feasible. Most experts expect little of the world's affordable oil to be left after 2059. That is why energy companies are already diversifying and working on alternative sources of energy.

In 1990 the world's 5.3 billion people consumed 13.7 terawatts of energy (a terawatt being equivalent to the energy of 5 billion barrels of oil). But that figure conceals the enormous disparities between consumption rates among nations. In 1990 the industrialized nations, with about one-fifth of the world's population, consumed almost three-fourths of the world's energy. The United Sates alone, with only 6 percent of the world's people, consumed 30 percent of the world's energy. A typical upper middle-class American family household consumes as much energy as does a whole village in Bangladesh or Ethiopia.

If we assume that world population may stabilize in the next century at somewhere between 9 and 14 billion people — and we also assume great progress in third world development and energy efficiency — then 9 billion people might consume 27 terawatts, and 14 billion would consume 42 terawatts. Even this lower figure would double the 1990 world energy consumption, and the higher figure would triple it. Can we expect to achieve these figures at a tolerable cost? If growing numbers of Chinese, Indians, Indonesians, and Malaysians become energy consumers at anything close to current Western levels, the planet's energy and mineral supplies will be rapidly depleted, and the resulting environmental consequences in land and water degradation, toxic wastes, and the release of heat-trapping greenhouse gases would likely add up to a very real crisis.

For the moment, however, the energy problem may have less to do with supplies than with the disposal of industrial waste, both solid and gaseous. In short, sink problems.

Pollution and Other Garbage

Environmental problems are not limited to overuse or poor management of physical and biological resources but also involve "effluents" — pollution and wastes — that stem from human social and economic activity. "Acid rain," produced by auto and industrial emissions, has damaged or killed forests in Appalachia, the New England States, Canada, and the Black Forest of Germany, Poland, and Central Europe. In the former Czechoslovakia, 70 percent of the rivers are severely polluted; in Poland, half the cities and 35 percent of industries do not even treat wastes; and in Russia, the air in 103 cities (with some 50 million people) exceeds minimum health standards by ten to fifty times. In Eastern Europe and Russia, these conditions have produced shortened life expectancy, soaring cancer rates, and a host of other maladies. While oil spills like that of the tanker *Exxon Valdez* in pristine Prince William Sound in Alaska in 1989 get all the headlines, the fact is that 50 to 90 percent of oil pollution in the seas comes from the land, when waste oil is dumped by individuals, cities, and industries into streams that eventually empty into the ocean.

In the United States, 50 percent of the groundwater is polluted by some combination of seepage from underground storage tanks, hazardous wastes, and sewage and landfill drainage, or from accumulated nitrates, pesticides, and herbicides from farming. In Long Island, New York, 23 percent of 330 wells tested were contaminated with Aldicarb, a pesticide used on potato fields. In Nebraska, the wells of forty-two counties turned out to be contaminated by farm run-off, one out of seven of them with the herbicide Atrazine (which has been linked to lymphatic tumors and cancers). Kansas has recently threatened to sue Nebraska because of high Atrazine levels in the Blue River, which flows into the drinking water reservoirs of Manhattan, Lawrence, Topeka, and Kansas City.

Solid waste — 75 percent of it from mining and oil and gas refining, 13 percent from agriculture, 9.5 percent from industry, and 1.5 percent municipal garbage — has become a major problem. We threw away enough aluminum in 1990 to rebuild the entire commercial airline fleet every three months. We also tossed out enough disposable plates and cups to serve a meal to everyone in the world six times a year, and enough glass bottles to fill the 1,350-foot-high New York World Trade

Center every two weeks. In 1993 the United States recycled only 11 percent of its trash.

Municipal landfills are overflowing (70 percent of them reached capacity by 2000), and local communities resist building more landfills and dumps in their back yards. Consider the celebrated case in 1987, when a big barge from Long Island carrying 3,190 tons of municipal garbage meandered south, attempting unsuccessfully to unload its cargo in North Carolina, Florida, Louisiana, the Bahamas, Mexico, and Honduras. After a six-thousand-mile trip lasting 164 days, it returned to New York and sat in the harbor for three months before the solid waste was finally incinerated in Brooklyn.

But in comparison to sanitary, state-of-the-art first world landfills and incineration, the third world garbage disposal scene is an utter nightmare. Burgeoning cities like Mexico City, Manila, Caracas, Port-au-Prince, and Lagos are inundated with mountainous dumps, untreated by any sanitary methods, full of infectious disease and toxic chemicals — and lived off by an army of rag pickers and scavengers.

Global Warming

More disturbing still is what industrial and automobile emissions are doing to the air we breathe — and to the weather. Many experts now believe that we are imperiling our ecological niche with the threat of global warming. Over the past century, the vaporous by-products of industrial culture, in the form of greenhouse gases such as carbon dioxide, methane, and nitrous oxides, have trapped enough heat in the atmosphere to raise earth's average surface temperature a half a degree Celsius (one degree Fahrenheit). If the trend continues, it could change climate patterns worldwide, thawing glaciers, boosting the sea level, scorching plains into deserts, and shifting vegetation zones.[5]

Without our atmosphere, average global temperature would be about minus 18 degrees Celsius (minus 0.4 degrees Fahrenheit) instead of the present 59 degrees F. All the incoming sunlight would strike earth's surface, causing it to emit infrared waves like a gigantic radiator. That heat would simply travel unimpeded back out into empty space. Because of the atmosphere, however, only a fraction of that heat is reflected back into space. The rest is trapped in the lower air layers, which contain a number of gases — water vapor, CO_2,

---

5. For a balanced overview of the climate debate, see Curt Suplee, "Untangling the Science of Climate," *National Geographic* 193, no. 5 (May 1998): 44–49. Also Jonathan Weiner, *The Next Hundred Years: Shaping the Fate of Our Living Earth* (New York: Bantam Books, 1990), 26–112.

methane, and others — that absorb outgoing infrared radiation. As those gases heat up, some of the heat radiates back to the surface (the greenhouse effect). Human beings have little direct control over the predominant greenhouse gas, water vapor, but we do have some control over other greenhouse gases, which intensify the greenhouse effect, for instance, carbon dioxide (produced by burning fossil fuels), methane (from rice fields, decomposing garbage, cattle ranching, etc.), nitrous oxide (from agriculture and industry), and various solvents and refrigerants like chlorofluorocarbons, or CFCs, which are now banned by international treaty because of their damaging effect on the earth's protective ozone layer.

In 1992 when the nations of the world met in Rio de Janeiro to devise collective measures to meet environmental problems, mainstream scientists could not agree whether man-made emissions had contributed to the rise in global temperature that began in the late nineteenth century. As a result of this lack of scientific agreement only voluntary targets for reductions in emissions were adopted. At Rio, the U.S. vowed to try to stabilize carbon emissions at 1990 levels by the year 2000. Instead we've gone on an unprecedented binge. In 1997 our fuel use shot up 3.5 percent, the biggest annual increase on record. By 2000 we were burning 15 percent more fossil fuel than we did in 1990 and thus spewing out 15 percent more heat-trapping greenhouse gases.

Since 1992, however, the scientific consensus has firmed up dramatically. In 1995 and again in 2000, the twenty-five hundred scientists involved in the UN Intergovernmental Panel on Climate Change (IPCC) concluded that man-made emissions were a critical factor in global warming. The language of both the 1995 and 2000 reports was cautious: "The balance of evidence," said the 1995 finding, "suggests a discernible human influence on global climate." The amount of that influence, the group noted, is unknown because of "uncertainties in key factors," including the degree to which clouds and the oceans affect the rate of temperature change. The role of clouds and airborne suspended particles called aerosols is difficult to factor into the computer simulations that scientists use to project future climate patterns. Oceans, which serve as a vast sink for carbon dioxide, present a similar problem. Human activity, we know, releases approximately 7 billion metric tons of carbon dioxide into the atmosphere every year, adding to the 750 billion tons that is already there. Yet only about half our emissions, some 3 billion tons, remains in the air. The rest is absorbed by terrestrial and marine plants, buried in ocean sediments, taken in by seawater, or otherwise sequestered. Of that "missing" amount of carbon, the oceans apparently remove at least a billion tons from the atmosphere each year.

But scientists don't understand precisely how the oceans interact with the air to remove CO_2. How much more carbon can the seas hold, and what level of global warming would it take to alter their capacity? And to what extent will the oceans' ability to soak up and store heat delay or avert climate change? It may take a decade or more of additional research to resolve these and other uncertainties. Meanwhile, although the specific consequences of human activity remain unclear, much is known. Says Dr. Benjamin D. Santer of the Lawrence Livermore National Laboratory and the chief author of the panel's chapter on detection of human influence on the climate, "The question is not whether, but rather to what extent" greenhouse gases are influencing the climate.

The IPCC estimates that rising CO_2 emissions, mostly from burning coal, oil, and gas, account for about 60 percent of the global warming observed since 1850. Carbon dioxide concentration in the atmosphere has been increasing about 0.3 percent a year, and it is now about 30 percent higher than it was before the industrial revolution began. If current rates continue, it will rise to at least twice preindustrial levels by about 2060 and by the end of the next century could be four times as high. This is particularly troublesome because CO_2 has a lifespan of more than a hundred years in the atmosphere, compared with eight days for water vapor. Methane persists in the atmosphere for nearly a decade and is now 2.5 times as prevalent as it was in the eighteenth century. Unless current rates of combustion can be reduced, the IPCC panel warned, over the next century average global temperatures will probably rise between 1.8 and 6.3 degrees Fahrenheit. A rise of 2 to 6 degrees may not sound like much, but it is. With a rise of a half degree of warming, the average global temperature would approach the highest level in the ten thousand years since the last ice age. The temperature was only 5 to 9 degrees colder in the depths of the last ice age, and the "little ice age," an anomalous cold snap that peaked from 1570 to 1730 and forced European farmers to abandon their fields, was caused by a drop in average temperature of only a half degree Celsius.

From now on, say scientists, when you look out the window at the weather, part of what you see will have been produced by ourselves. And within the next fifty years, we're going to be responsible for even more of the weather. Among other effects, a warming atmosphere sucks up more water from the oceans and in general makes more moisture available to developing storms. Global warming, in other words, may be revving up the planet's rainmaking machine. A rainier world, on the other hand, may also portend more heat waves in summer, such as the deadly Midwest heat wave of the summer of 1995. The uncertainties no longer pertain to whether our factories and car exhausts are having this warming effect. The uncertainties have to do with exactly when it will kick in, to what extent oceans and clouds may delay the impact, and who the winners and losers will be.

Doubtless there will be winners. High concentrations of CO_2 in the air can have a fertilizing effect on plants, which is why some commercial greenhouses increase the CO_2 level to three times the level outside. Earlier and longer growing seasons might also be most welcome in Canada and northern Russia. But the environmental and economic dislocations elsewhere might very well be calamitous. Temperature changes in the middle level of the scale the IPCC envisions (say a rise of 3.5 degrees) could cause a twenty-inch rise in sea levels that would flood coastal lowlands and tropical islands, increase storms and desertification, and damage forests and croplands in current temperate zones. Tropical diseases would also spread northward. If the temperature climbs as expected, affluent nations may be able to buy themselves out of the problem. Developing nations will not have this option and will be the worst losers. Vast areas of China, Bangladesh, and Egypt, not to mention the island nations of the Pacific and Indian Oceans, will disappear underwater. Wet areas already subject to erosion will grow wetter; dry areas are projected to grow even dryer.

There is little ground for believing that climate change will come gradually, so as to facilitate adaptation. The historical evidence from boring into Arctic ice cores is that climate change can occur abruptly, in the space of decades or even years. Perhaps the most feared change of this sort would be an abrupt collapse of the huge Atlantic "conveyor belt" that brings warm water north from the Equator, keeping Europe several degrees warmer than it would otherwise be. What if human-induced global warming altered the delicate temperature difference between the flows and at the same time caused increased rainfall over the oceans, diluting the salinity of the northward flow? The whole system could simply shut down, as ocean-sediment evidence suggests it has several times in the past. The effect? Much of northern Europe would be uninhabitable.

Preventive Action?

Should we take preventive action now, as many physical and environmental scientists advocate? Or should we adopt a wait-and-see attitude, as many economists and industrialists say? To allow populations and carbon emissions to continue to rise at current rates — until, say, computer climate modeling becomes a more certain science in another two decades — is to take a huge gamble and risk catastrophe. The prudent course would be to take early action to prevent the worst possible outcomes. If we act and the threat is real, we win. If the threat is not real, we lose only our insurance premiums. But if the threat is real and we do nothing until it is too late, we risk losing on a monumental scale.

The remedies — investing in cleaner fuels, cleaner cars, and new technologies — will be costly, and for this reason both developing nations and industry in affluent nations have resisted strong measures. The third world is fighting desperately for the right to pollute as freely as the first world once did. But the point is that without taking draconian measures, many of the costs would quickly pay for themselves in terms of increased efficiencies. And the programs that we would undertake to deal with global warming — reducing energy inefficiency and the wasteful consumption of nonrenewable resources and promoting reforestation, sustainable agriculture, soil conservation, land reform, and the alleviation of poverty — are projects that ought to be launched in any case and in their own right.

At the December 1998 UN meeting in Kyoto to endorse a new international climate treaty, industrialized nations promised to reduce carbon emissions by an average of 5 percent below 1990 levels between 2008 and 2012. Big developing nations like India and China refused any reductions in emissions, and the United States, the world's biggest producer of carbon dioxide emissions, delayed signing till the follow-up Buenos Aires conference in November of 1999. The signing, which the Clinton administration had long promised, reestablishes a leadership role for the United States in this critical area, even though ratification by the Senate is doubtful until countries like Brazil, China, and India come aboard.

What we need to do, in the words of Robert Watson, the World Bank's climate guru, is to "structurally decarbonize" the economy so that by the middle of the next century fossil fuels will have all but disappeared. The U.S. energy industry has been conducting a vigorous campaign of resistance to this idea. Our big oil companies, it would seem, would have us live in the specious present, as if there will be no next generation. It is encouraging, then, to learn that not every transnational corporation thinks this way. British Petroleum, Royal Dutch Shell, Boeing, Monsanto, General Motors, and United Technologies have all announced that they will reduce emissions, and by greater amounts than required, even before the Kyoto treaty is formally ratified. Before most companies will join in this movement, governments of the industrial powers will need to give industry the financial, political, and social incentives to choose renewable power sources over coal and oil.

Gregg Easterbrook is right to say that environmentalism is today a mainstream movement and a political "success" story in the United States and Western Europe. Between 1966 and 1990, Congress approved more than fifty-five pieces of environmental legislation, which even the Reagan administration was unable to erase. There is evidence that in the popular mind the once dominant industrial paradigm, with its low regard for nature and its obsession with economic growth, is presently giving way to a new ecological paradigm, involving an acceptance of limits on economic growth and the importance of maintaining the balance of nature.[6] But if things are looking up in certain locales, why, as we have just seen, are things still in such bad shape, promising worse to come? Or, to put it another way, if we have made as much headway as Gregg Easterbrook claims, what is it about the dynamics of Western culture that makes the going so very slow? What is it about our frame of mind and our institutions that, for all the progress we have made, still ensures that unsustainable practice has the upper hand?

---

6. See Charles L. Harper, *Environment and Society* (Upper Saddle River, N.J.: Prentice Hall, 1996), 323–24.

SEVEN

The Dynamics of Unsustainability

Like the rich man in the parable, the industrialist thinks to escape the persistent obligations of the human condition by means of "much goods laid up for many years" — by means, in other words, of quantities: resources, supplies, stockpiles, funds, reserves. But this is a grossly oversimplifying dream and, thus, a dangerous one.... The topsoil exists as such because it is ceaselessly transforming death into life, ceaselessly supplying food and water to all that lives in it and from it; otherwise, "All flesh shall perish together, and man shall turn again to dust." If we are to live well on and from our land, we must live by faith in the ceaselessness of these processes and by faith in our own willingness and ability to collaborate with them.

— WENDELL BERRY, *Home Economics*

Environmental damage is nothing new. It has been with us for a very long time, beginning somewhere just east of Eden. The question we now come to, in light of the situation described in the last two chapters, is this: How to live in a sustainable relationship with the rest of the earth? Or to put it more poetically, how do we learn to tread more lightly upon the earth? We cannot exist without modifying and borrowing from the ecosystems around us — for food, clothing, shelter, energy, and other material goods. But how do we do so without "overshoot," that is, without overloading our ecosystem's carrying capacity? The current buzzword in environmentalist circles is "sustainability," the capacity of natural and social systems to survive and thrive together.

How is a "sustainable society" defined? It is one that does not exceed its environmental carrying capacity. For ecologists, carrying capacity is described as "the population of a given species that can be supported indefinitely in a defined habitat without permanently damaging the ecosystem upon which it is dependent." The problem here, as we shall see in a moment, is that when modern urbanites (like myself) are in the process of exceeding carrying capacity, it is usually not at all visible out the window of either glass office towers or suburban enclaves. Affluent cities and nations do not draw simply from their local ecosystems. They expropriate the carrying capacity of ecosystems at great distances, all over the globe. A city the size of Chicago, with a population of 2.9 million, consumes as much as the 97 million people of Bangladesh do. And, in order to sustain its lavish lifestyle, Chicago must reach around the earth. The environmental costs of maintaining such high-living cities are rarely seen by those, like me, who benefit from living in them.

The more troublesome term is "sustainable development," that is, the belief that we can continue to push for a high rate of economic growth and at the same time protect and preserve the environment. At the moment, sustainable development is the most widely recommended antidote to the global social, economic, and ecological crises. Does it make sense? Only in the abstract. In the concrete it often spells ruination.

Scientific Uncertainty

When contemporary environmentalism first emerged in the 1960s and '70s, its goal — to save the living world around us from destructive technology, overpopulation, and overconsumption — was a lot clearer than the somewhat muddled picture today. The strategies were also clearer. One had to entertain the radical thought that there had to be limits: to population, to technology, to the ideology of growth and appetite. Underlying this sense of limits was the heretical judgment that the progressive secular and materialistic philosophy on which modern life rests was deeply flawed, and finally self-defeating. It was putting the whole fabric of life in jeopardy. And thus the only sure way to the environmental goal was to challenge that philosophy at its foundation and find a new one based on simplicity and spiritual richness. In some sense one had to be a "deep ecologist," that is, a critic of the whole ideology of modernity.

At least two things have blunted that original clarity of thrust. First, the seductive notion of sustainable development and, second, an over-estimation of what ecological science could do for us. The idea of sustainable development lures us into thinking that we can have our cake and eat it, that we can continue business as usual, without undue sacrifice or accommodation to nature's limits. The supposition is that ecologists will be able to tell us exactly when and where ecosystems are undergoing severe stress from human demands. But this overlooks the major changes that have occurred in the field of ecology in recent decades. Today's ecologists have turned agnostic about nature's order, and at the same time they have become less disapproving of human manipulation of the environment for economic purposes.

It used to be that ecologists were confident they could specify a given ecosystem's ideal state of equilibrium, or homeostasis — and thus give an accurate picture of its carrying capacity. Or, to put it another way, an ecologist was supposed to be able to tell when soils, forests, fisheries, and waters were being overstressed, when they would rebound from stress, how they could avoid collapse and maintain output, and so on. There was an ideal balance or order out there in nature, and the ecologist could advise us on how to sustain or achieve it.

Beginning in the 1970s, ecology went off on a search for new ways to describe forests, grasslands, oceans, and all the other biomes of the planet, and subsequently it began to be afflicted by what Donald Worster calls a "new permissiveness." Virtually all notions of stability, equilibrium, balance, and order vanished. No integrated community, no enduring system of relationships, no deep interdependence appears. Nor is there any way of specifying a normal "yield" or "output" from any natural system. Sure, the sun appears regularly and the four seasons come and go, but if you look at populations of plants or animals in any area that we might call wild or pristine, you will find no regularity, no constancy, no order at all. Here is how Daniel Botkin, a leading California ecologist, describes the new ecology in his 1990 book *Discordant Harmonies:*

> Until the past few years, the predominant theories in ecology presumed...a very strict concept of a highly structured, ordered, and regulated, steady-state ecological system. Scientists know now that this view is wrong at local and regional levels...that is, at the levels of populations and ecosystems. Change now appears to be intrinsic and natural at many scales of time and space in the biosphere.[1]

In the absence of any clear idea of what a healthy ecosystem might be, one ends up with a utilitarian, economic, and anthropocentric definition of sustainability. "Sustainability," says Donald Worster, "is, by and large, an economic concept on which economists are clear and ecologists are muddled."[2]

---

1. Daniel B. Botkin, *Discordant Harmonies: A New Ecology for the Twenty-First Century* (New York: Oxford University Press, 1990), 10.
2. Donald Worster, *The Wealth of Nature: Environmental History and the Ecological Imagination* (New York: Oxford University Press, 1993), 153.

Sustainable development, argues Worster, is a deeply flawed idea. First, as even the Brundtland report makes clear, it relies on the view that the natural world exists primarily to serve the material demands of the human species. Nature holds no intrinsic meaning; it is nothing but a pool of resources to be exploited. Second, though the idea of sustainable development acknowledges some sort of limit on our material demands, the whole idea depends on the assumption that we can readily determine the carrying capacity of local and regional ecosystems. But in light of the new arguments suggesting how turbulent, complex, and unpredictable nature is, that assumption seems highly optimistic and unreliable. Ecologists are refusing to specify limits for us. Finally, the sustainability ideal rests on an uncritical acceptance of the worldview of progressive secular materialism and the institutions associated with it — capitalism, socialism, and industrialism. All of these escape criticism.

But this is unsupportable — or unsustainable. For, from all we have seen, it is precisely the structures of industrial capitalism that continue to do an injustice to the earth.

Fitting into the Great Economy

Why do unsustainable economic practices retain the upper hand in our society? The primary reason is this: Every human economy, as poet-farmer Wendell Berry puts it, is a mere subsystem in a larger whole, the "Great Economy" — the economy of nature. We must learn to fit harmoniously within the constraints of this greater whole. Remember, says Berry, only nature knows how to make water, air, forests, and topsoil. Long before humans arrived on the scene, nature had created the central goods of the biosphere: oceans and sky, sun and forests, photosynthesis and hydrological cycles, rivers and mountains, DNA and food chains. These wonders are a once-only endowment of earth, and when they run down or out we do not know how to regenerate them. No human inventiveness can restore an extinct species. "The most important truth about ourselves, our artifacts and our civilization," says Jeremy Rifkin, "is that it is all borrowed."[3] All the molecules of our bodies are only temporarily ours as they pass in and out, and back to the environment. We take from nature and transform things into useful objects, yet ultimately everything returns to nature after we have used it. All our activity, says Rifkin, is an economics of borrowing. We are indebted "to the core of our being."

---

3. Jeremy Rifkin, *Declaration of a Heretic* (Boston: Routledge and Kegan Paul, 1988), 97.

Our culture hasn't learned the lesson here: that nature establishes the primary values, and what we do is quite secondary, derivative, and artificial. We can only "add value" to natural things, by transforming trees, say, into board feet, board feet into furniture and housing and so forth. But all along we are dealing with materials and powers that we did not make, that were made by the Great Economy. To be sure, there is some latitude. We are uniquely inventive creatures, able to develop technologies and sociocultural environments that can to a degree transcend environmental limits. For instance, we find substitutes for some depleted resources: celluloid for elephant ivory, kerosene for whale oil, coal rather than wood, fiber optics instead of copper wire, electric cars instead of fuel-guzzlers. But finally we remain creatures, and that means that our economy is embedded in and dependent upon the broader webs of life in the geosphere and biosphere. Unless we choose to go the way of the ancient Babylonians and Mayans, we cannot push nature beyond its limits or violate its requirements for renewing and replenishing itself. Beyond the corporate bottom line lies nature's bottom line: the laws of ecology.

Does our throwaway economy act like a proper subsystem? Does it conform to nature's basic operating laws? Not in the least. First, nature works on current solar income. Sunlight is virtually the only input not already contained in the earth's closed system. Everything else belongs to a one-time endowment. That's why, in the second place, nature conserves, constantly recycles matter and energy. Waste from one life-form becomes food for another or builds essential habitat. Waste is minimized. Everything is reclaimed, reused, or recycled; otherwise nature doesn't produce it. Finally, nature depends and thrives on diversity and differences and perishes on uniformity. Nature is not mass-produced. Healthy systems are varied and specific to time and place. This is why biodiversity is crucial, for it means adaptability, evolution, and survival in unstable environments. A globalized system of mass production and one-time use runs against the grain of nature itself.

As we have noted above, and in chapters 3 and 4, industrial economics refuses to accept the limitations of our embeddedness in nature. Standard economic theory and business practices abstract human beings and commerce from the ecosphere. As ethicist Larry Rasmussen puts it, there is an "eerie otherworldliness" here, a kind of gnostic disregard of earth's rhythms and requirements.[4] Biological life is simply missing from the equations of economists.

---

4. Larry Rasmussen, *Earth Community, Earth Ethics* (Maryknoll, N.Y.: Orbis Books, 1996), 115.

What we require, argues economist Herman Daly, is something like the Plimsoll line drawn on commercial ships.[5] Cargo ships will carry all sorts of things, and the weight can be distributed in a variety of ways, but at some point added cargo will submerge the Plimsoll line on the hull, indicating that safe carrying capacity has been exceeded and the ship will sink. In effect, says Daly, economic theory and business practice operate without any Plimsoll line for the biospheric ship. Instead, as I have noted above, we live by an expansionist vision of limitless resources and never-ending growth — as if the earth were not round but flat and endless. As one economist phrases it, "The basic world view of conventional economics is one in which individual human consumers are the central figures. Their tastes and preferences are taken as given, and are the dominant determining force. The resource base is viewed as essentially limitless due to technical progress and infinite substitutability." For these reasons, our economy can ignore ecological laws and operate on a cowboy or frontier principle — at a time when the frontier has disappeared. Our blindness to ecological consequences is built-in to the system. As the World Council of Churches would put it, the "integrity of creation" is forgotten. That is, we disregard what theologians refer to as "the value of all creatures in themselves, for one another, and for God, and their interconnectedness in a diverse whole that has unique value for God."[6]

Driving Forces behind Environmental Damage

The changes taking place in the environment today differ from those of the past in two respects. One, the pace of change has dramatically accelerated, and, two, the most significant changes are now anthropogenic — produced by humans. As I noted in the Introduction, the principal driving forces behind such environmental changes come down to four: (1) growth in population; (2) institutional arrangements, mainly related to political and economic structures set up to spur economic growth; (3) cultural factors, including attitudes, belief systems, social paradigms, and views of nature; and (4) technological change.

- *Population size and growth:* The question here is fairly straight-forward: If environmental degradation is already apparent with today's 6 billion people, how will we accommodate the 11 to

---

5. Cited in ibid., 116.
6. See Jay McDaniel, "'Where Is the Holy Spirit Anyway?' Response to a Skeptical Environmentalist," *Ecumenical Review* 42, no. 2 (April 1990): 165.

14 billion expected in the next century without devastating the resource base of the planet?

• *Institutional arrangements:* In industrial economies, as I have already noted, the central dynamic is the pursuit of continuous economic expansion. Competition makes higher profitability a key to corporate survival, and firms must constantly grow to attract investors and increase profits. And the chief function of governments is to provide the political environment for such continuous growth. Both orthodox economic theory and socioeconomic policy at the national and international levels assume that unlimited economic expansion is desirable, possible, and necessary. Yet this ideology of growth depletes the stock of nonrenewable resources and often taxes the stock of renewable resources (fish, aquifers, forests) at a rate that far exceeds its replacement rate.

• *Cultural values and belief systems:* Belief systems legitimate and normalize the social arrangements and practices of societies. As I tried to point out in chapters 3 and 4, ever since the time of Newton, Western society has tended to view the physical world as inert, a meaningless scurrying of atoms whose only value consists of the values human beings "add" or impose through industrial processes. By itself, in other words, nature is simply "raw material," of no value until human labor transforms it into commodities useful to human society. Hence nature has no intrinsic value, only instrumental value. This is the last word in anthropocentrism — and issues an open invitation for exploitation and abuse.

Materialism exacerbates the problem. Consumerism, the incarnation of materialistic values, has elevated buying and shopping to a sacred ritual and civic duty in our society — precisely insofar as it maintains demand for ever-more goods and services, needed or not. Though every world religion, from Christianity to Hinduism, Buddhism, and Islam, denounces such materialism, these protests seem to have little effect.

• *Technology* enabling the human transformation of the environment: In market economies, technology has assumed a major role in improving productivity, mainly by removing human labor. Energy technology underlies all economic activity and growth, and more productive technology has offered new ways to exploit natural resources, hastening resource depletion and increasing pollutant emissions. Our faith in and use of technology has been a Faustian bargain, trading current gain against long-term welfare and survival.

Analysts have divided in stressing one or another of these four factors as either the source of impending catastrophe or as the way out of our troubles — and the arguments go way back, to Adam Smith and Thomas Malthus, to Condorcet and Karl Marx. A reminder about these early arguments between economistic and technocratic optimists on the one side and Malthusian and structuralist pessimists on the other side helps to put the current debate in perspective. The optimists view nature as a limitless cornucopia, whereas the pessimists, with a more tragic sense of life, envision scenarios of limits.

Malthusian, Structuralist, and Economistic Arguments

It is Adam Smith (1723–90), not Moses, says historian Donald Worster, whom we must understand "if we are to get down to the really important roots of the modern environmental crisis."[7] The secret of increasing wealth, concluded Smith in *The Wealth of Nations* (1776), lay in establishing a "system of natural liberty" in which "every man, as long as he does not violate the laws of justice, is left perfectly free to pursue his own interest in his own way, and to bring both his industry and capital into competition with those of any other man, or order of men." Smith was hardly oblivious of the dependence of human production and services upon the earth's biophysical resources. But he maintained that labor and not nature constituted "economic value." Hence all those services that nature supplies free of charge, and to which we have referred above — the air and water that sustain life, the process of photosynthesis in plants, energy cycles, food chains, nutrient cycles, regulation of water supply, pest and pathogen control, climate regulation — are passed over and rated as nothing. Nature has only instrumental or utilitarian value when human labor and industry "add value" to it. The nonhuman realm of "unimproved" land is "valueless" and lays no obligations on us.

Smith's view was that unregulated markets provided the best mechanism to determine the economic value of goods and services. In sharply distinguishing economic value from social or moral value, he began the tendency of classical Western economic thought to abstract economics from the rest of the social world. Taking his lead from the bustling

---

7. Worster, *The Wealth of Nature*, 214.

success of English traders, shopkeepers, and merchants, Smith was a grand optimist. He argued that the individual desire for profits would, through the "unseen hand of the market," produce the best possible economic and social world, allocating investment, labor, and technology in the most efficient ways. David Ricardo (1772–1823) wasn't so confident that all would turn out so well. Economic growth and the desire for profits, he thought, would lead people to bring even marginal resources, such as poor and infertile land, into production. The law of diminishing returns would set in, and in the long term only owners, not workers, stood to gain by the system.

An even more ominous analysis issued from Thomas Malthus (1776–1834), an Anglican clergyman, who was the first to raise the specter in his *Essay on Population* of 1798 that an exponential growth in population would outrun the capacity of British agriculture to produce enough food to feed the numbers. Malthus argued that after boom would come bust, that as rising wages and better living conditions led to population growth, farm production would not keep up, and this would inevitably lead to the checks of misery, famine, pestilence, war, and social chaos. Nothing doing, argued the Marquis de Condorcet (1743–94), a contemporary French political economist. Advances in scientific technology, Condorcet was sure, would more than offset population growth:

> New instruments, machines, and looms can add to man's strength
> ...[and]...improve at once the quality and accuracy of man's
> productions, and can diminish the time and labor that has to be
> expended on them....A very small amount of ground will be
> able to produce a great quantity of supplies...with less wastage
> of raw materials.[8]

Throughout the nineteenth century (at the very least), Condorcet's "technological fix" had the better of the argument. Technology did out-perform the four horsemen of the apocalypse.

Some fifty years after the exchange between Malthus and Condorcet, Karl Marx (1818–83) weighed in, and like Malthus and Ricardo he saw chaos at the end of the capitalist era. Condemning Malthus's theory as no more than a rationale for class exploitation, Marx focused on the social factors. The real cause of human misery and deprivation, he argued, was not overpopulation, but the concentration of economic resources and political power in the hands of capitalist owners. Marx

---

8. Cited in Charles L. Harper, *Environment and Society: Human Perspectives on Environmental Issues* (Upper Saddle River, N.J.: Prentice Hall, 1996), 165.

adumbrates what might be called the "structuralist argument," the thesis that, though population may aggravate every other aspect of the problem, the primary source of human misery and environmental deterioration can be traced to social institutions and structural arrangements. Paradoxically enough, the World Council of Churches and the pope agree with Marx on this point.

The Debate Continues

Few debates in the social and natural sciences have been as acrimonious as the one about the consequences of population growth. Neo-Malthusian ecologists like Paul Ehrlich (*The Population Bomb*, 1968) claim that population growth is perhaps the most significant underlying cause of both environmental damage and human misery. It drives the poor either to urban slums or to cultivate marginal, easily erodable lands with "slash and burn" methods. The economic gains of developing nations are typically undercut and stalled, goes the argument, by rapid population growth. At some point and in the long run, there are limits to the physical capacity of the planet to sustain growth, and if we are having trouble now, with 6 billion, one hesitates to imagine the planet's stress in the next century when the population is expected to double or triple. One can certainly agree up to a point: If not the principal cause of ecological and human woe, population exacerbates every other problem. Reducing fertility and birth rates — without resorting to coercive methods — surely seems to be in the interest of the planet.

Neo-Malthusian prophecies of doom, however, have not panned out, and neoclassical economists have had a great deal of sport at the expense of the Malthusians. In 1968 Paul Ehrlich trumpeted that "the battle to feed humanity is over. In the 1970s," he predicted, "the world will undergo famines — hundreds of millions are going to starve to death."[9] He had not foreseen the green revolution, the huge rise in worldwide agricultural production due to the new biotechnology. Similarly, in 1972, at the time of the OPEC crisis, the Club of Rome produced studies predicting that the world would run out of gas by 1992 and arable land by the year 2000, and that civilization would collapse in 2070. It is too early to say whether that last prophecy will prove true, but the others have not panned out. The expectation of permanent shortage and high oil prices has not materialized. Famines and widespread malnutrition did indeed mark the 1970s and '80s, es-

---

9. Cited in ibid., 166.

pecially in Africa, but nothing on the scale predicted by Ehrlich has occurred. Until very recently global food production has continued to outstrip population growth.[10] (As I noted above, this may be coming to an end.)

Structuralists typically argue that economic stagnation in the developing world is primarily the outcome of poverty, inequitable trade policies, political corruption, unjust land distribution, and poor resource management. According to this analysis, the neo-Malthusians simply have the causation wrong. Population growth is a serious issue, admits biologist Barry Commoner (a structuralist), but plans to control population in less developed nations by focusing on birth control, abortion, or sterilization, he argues, miss the point. They forget why, in the first place, poor people have large families. The reason is poverty itself, and what goes with it: poor health care and the prospect that few of one's children will survive. Until one gets at the social, political, and economic arrangements that support poverty, one hasn't gotten to the bottom of things. It seems to be a well-demonstrated fact: The best birth control lies in better economic and educational conditions for women. Furthermore, argues Commoner, neo-Malthusians put pressure in the wrong place. It is not indigenous people and subsistence farmers who are responsible for most of the world's deforestation, but first world demand — and the lumber companies, large cash-crop estates, and mining firms that serve these markets.[11]

In general, both mainstream Protestants allied in the World Council of Churches (WCC) and Roman Catholic social teaching favor the structuralist approach to this issue. What causes the farming of marginalized lands? asks a 1975 WCC statement on a "just, participatory, and sustainable society." Peasant farmers are driven to such lands, went the reply, when the better land is appropriated by elites to grow export crops for global agribusiness. Pope John Paul's New Year's message of 1990, "The Ecological Crisis: A Common Responsibility," gives a very similar analysis:

It must also be said that the proper ecological balance will not be found without directly addressing the structural forms of poverty that exist throughout the world. Rural poverty and unjust land

---

10. Amartya Sen, the winner of the 1998 Nobel Prize in economics, has cogently argued that famines (e.g., the Bangladesh famine of 1974) are not related to a shortage of food but to the inability of the rural poor to afford the price of available food. Growing population will be a "problem," not because of food shortages, but because so many people have insufficient economic power to obtain food by growing or buying it. See Amartya Sen, *Development as Freedom* (New York: Knopf, 1999).

11. See Barry Commoner, *Making Peace with the Planet* (New York: New Press, 1992), 141–68.

distribution in many countries, for example, have led to subsistence farming and to the exhaustion of the soil. Once their land yields no more, many farmers move on to clear new land, thus accelerating uncontrolled deforestation, or they settle in urban centers which lack the infrastructure to receive them. Likewise, some heavily indebted countries are destroying their natural heritage, at the price of irreparable ecological imbalances, in order to develop new products for export. In the face of such situations it would be wrong to assign responsibility to the poor alone for the negative environmental consequences of their actions. Rather, the poor, to whom the earth is entrusted no less than to others, must be enabled to find a way out of their poverty. This will require a courageous reform of structures, as well as new ways of relating among peoples and States.[12]

Most neoliberal economists strongly disagree. There is no need, they reply, for the "courageous reform of structures" that the pope calls for. Believing that nature's cornucopia cannot be exhausted, they simply deny that there is a demographic or environmental problem at all. What problem, they ask? To this day, economists like Julian Simon have discounted resource constraints and population pressures. These problems, they claim, can be understood as market failures. Arguing like Adam Smith and Condorcet did before them, neoclassical economists insist that there's nothing here that a combination of human inventiveness and/or fully functioning markets won't solve. When resources become scarce, the argument goes, well-functioning markets encourage us to protect them by raising the price or otherwise allocating them in the most efficient ways. Population growth and other resource problems thus will typically stimulate investment in increased efficiency, resource substitution, conservation, and innovation.

There is some truth behind these economistic contentions. In the long sweep of human history, population growth does correlate with growing rather than declining resources, as well as improvements in human health, longevity, and well-being. Neo-Malthusian doomsayers rely upon an unrealistically static notion of the correlation of population and carrying capacity. Moreover, Malthusians underestimate technical inventiveness and the adaptability of market mechanisms.

Market mechanisms can be used to support sustainability and are surely a part of any solution for our environmental problems. Governments could cease subsidizing the depletion of resources by stopping

---

12. Pope John Paul II, "The Ecological Crisis: A Common Responsibility," January 1, 1990, no. 11.

oil depletion allowances and the cheap giveaways of water rights, grazing range, timber, and mineral rights on public lands. The oil industry
could internalize the real costs of maintaining the flow of crude oil from
the Middle East. The tobacco industry might internalize the health
costs that smoking produces. "Green taxes" could be levied to dis-
courage waste and stimulate eco-efficiency in the use of resources and
energy and packaging. And so on.

But in the last analysis, markets have limits. One, they reduce everything to its dollar value. So whether a product is produced by clean or
dirty technology or by well trained and well paid workers or by exploited ones does not matter on Wall Street. Second, as I have already
noted, goods valued for reasons that lie outside the market — for aesthetic reasons, say, or for ecological reasons — are discounted. A tree,
as we said, only counts as dead timber that can be sold. Its value for
other species, to the ecosystem, for watershed or habitat uses amounts
to zero in economic terms. Third, markets price things in terms of
present exchange values. To the question, Should we consume today
or save it for tomorrow? the answer is invariably short-term, to gratify
immediate needs or wants. Future value is speculative and discounted.
Finally, as Karl Marx observed, markets produce social inequality, with
long-term social costs that do not figure on the accounting sheets.

The New Colonialism

The ideology of economic growth continues to dominate our thinking because, in the aftermath of the collapse of the Soviet system, we
can imagine no clear alternative to neoliberal capitalist economics. It's
simply how the current global economy works. And the impact on the
environment can be discounted because for most of us in the affluent
West that impact is simply out of sight. We don't see the effect in the
third world. Nor, in terms of a declining resource-base even here in
the United States, do we see our own declining wealth. As I mentioned
in the last chapter, our GNP figure leaves out our losses, and hence
deceives us.

Because of the trading system, nations reach far beyond their own
borders to extract goods and services from distant ecosystems. And
the prices we pay here at home rarely reflect what is happening to
these distant ecosystems. What happens to the local ecosystem, then,
is no longer an adequate measure of the impact an affluent nation or
city is having on its environment. One needs to look at ecosystems
that are affected at great distances. Industrial nations act like giant
magnets, drawing everything into their maws. In doing so they expro-

priate the carrying capacity of other, usually poorer nations for their own use.

First off, even when we seem to do nothing, urban dwellers depend on the "goods and services" provided by tropical forests that form a broken band around the middle of the globe. Quite apart from the products these forests may supply to our pharmacies and other commercial outlets, they supply a sink for city-generated carbons, functioning to regulate global heat transfers and regulate the climate, as well as generating vital oxygen. Human high-rise dwellers are thus directly dependent on and sustained by these distant ecosystems, even when we are apparently keeping our power saws away from them.

When we buy our groceries, switch on the lights, the furnace, or the air conditioner, or take the kids for a drive, we are systematically blind to the impact our actions are having on ecosystems on the other side of the world. Green activists in Germany have focused attention on acid rain and the damage industry inflicts on native soil. Does that mean Germany is living within nature's carrying capacity? Not a bit. Germany, like every other affluent G-7 nation, appropriates carrying capacity far afield. Tropical forests in Brazil and other South and Central American nations have been cut down, in part to grow soybeans fed to German cows that produce surplus butter and cheese for foreign markets.

Or consider big cities, where half the world's population now lives. A city like New York, where I live, draws resources from everywhere and scatters consequences (waste) far and wide. (Think of that Long Island garbage scow that drifted around the world some years ago.) We expropriate carrying capacity all over the globe, and by virtue of urbanization and trade, I am screened both physically and psychologically from ever really seeing the impact on the ecosystems that sustain me. "Every city," say William E. Rees and Mathis Wackernagel in their study of this matter, "is an entropic black hole."[13]

This is what the global economy means. Theoretically, the role of trade in the standard economics text is to facilitate an exchange of goods that a particular culture could not produce itself. Each locale exploits its "comparative advantage" and offers what it can from its relative abundance, including human resources, and receives in return what it lacks. But what happens in reality, especially for poorer na-

---

13. William E. Rees and Mathis Wackernagel, "Ecological Footprints and Appropriate Carrying Capacity: Measuring the Natural Capital Requirements of the Human Economy," in *Investing in Natural Capital: The Ecological Economics Approach to Sustainability*, ed. A.-M. Jannson et al. (Washington, D.C.: Island Press, 1994), 370.

tions that lack high technology and the skills of the new information revolution? The system encourages poor nations to produce specialized commodities for export: Nikes and Adidas, cattle or crops for precious foreign currency. Land and resources are typically removed from their place in providing domestic staples for local markets in local communities, and peasants are driven off the good land to work marginal land, which means soil erosion and deforestation. Local land and resources are thus consolidated for consumption abroad, commonly in the form of high-energy, monocultural agriculture, or for the extraction of goods by mining and logging. Local sustainability for the long haul and for the many is thereby sacrificed for short-term gain by the few. Benefits largely accrue to international capital, transnational corporations, and the local elites who are tied to the export-oriented economy and international capital.

Other aspects of an expansionist economics worsen the environmental situation in the developing world. As we have observed, neoclassical economists and businesspeople operate with a "frontier paradigm" that assumes that there will always be plenty of the desired good available. For practical purposes, resources are presumed to be infinite. Scarcity is a nonproblem, because we can always find a substitute supplier of the desired good. What is substituted, however, is more of the same good — obtained elsewhere. If the Philippines runs out of timber, we turn to Chile or Malaysia or Indonesia. We never need take account of the replacement rate of such renewable resources or their local depletion, because we can always move on to some other supplier who is anxious for the business. Transnational corporations can continue stripping localities and their communities of their resources without looking back. The system pits one poor nation or region against another, in a constant competition to undercut its neighbor's price for labor, timber, cattle, minerals, or an export cash crop. In this way nations like Brazil, Indonesia, and Malaysia are being stripped of both their resources and the future of generations to come. (Market economics has no way of putting a price on the future — or on anything that is not currently for sale.) Meanwhile local production for local use by those with a life-investment in the land is sacrificed for cash in the hand, usually in the hands of local elites.

What we have here is an international trading system that promotes unsustainable development. Under this international regime, the ongoing growth and prosperity of the well-off in the first world are sustained by externalizing the costs to the third world, on the backs of already impoverished communities. Our prosperity is built on undermining local sustainability abroad. This is the new colonialism.

Sustainable Development vs. Sustainable Communities

According to current United Nations policy, economic growth is the magic bullet for everything that goes on under the title of sustainable development. Thus UN secretary general Boutros Boutros-Ghali's 1994 Agenda for Development heralds the "economy as the engine of progress." "Without economic growth," says this document,

> there can be no sustained increase in household or government consumption, in private or public capital formation, in health, welfare and security levels. . . . Accelerating the rate of economic growth is a condition for expanding the resource base and hence for economic, technological and social transformation. While economic growth does not ensure that benefits will be equitably distributed or that the physical environment will be protected, without economic growth the material resources for tackling environmental degradation will not exist, nor will it be possible to pursue social programmes effectively in the long term.[14]

With this policy, one avoids the more challenging path of trying to attack the inequitable distribution of power and resources. Instead, one makes economic development a priority, adding the secondary qualifiers of environmental protection and poverty reduction (which are frequently put into toothless "side agreements"). The Brundtland Commission, for instance, set up the target of 3 percent annual growth in income. But as we have just seen above, most market-oriented economic development does not benefit those most in need. It goes to the already well fed. Inequality between and within societies typically accompanies high growth rates.

The Worldwatch Institute's 1990 State of the World report punctures the illusions here. The average increase in global economic output in each of the last four decades has been colossal, equal to the total economic growth from the beginning of civilization until 1950! Average incomes soared. But at the same time environmental damage and the ranks of the destitute also rose. The World Bank puts the number of the "absolute poor," those who scrape by on a dollar or less a day per capita, at 1.2 billion people. Another 3.5 billion, the "managing poor," do more than subsist, but do not live well or without fear. Even with a 3 percent annual growth rate, the numbers of the destitute and the managing poor are almost sure to expand in coming decades. Economic

---

14. *An Agenda for Development: Report of the Secretary General to the Forty-Eighth Session of the General Assembly.*

growth neither eliminates poverty nor reduces environmental destruc-tion. World Bank and UN officials who think that economic growth correlates with either environmental protection or poverty eradication are dreamers — in the pejorative sense.

A very different approach begins not with economics but with ecol-ogy, and not at the global level but at the local and regional level. The World Council of Churches follows this latter path, emphasiz-ing not "sustainable development," a term it finds troublesome if not self-contradictory, but "sustainable communities."

The Zapatista rebellion in the southern Mexican state of Chiapas began in January of 1994, just hours after the North American Free Trade Agreement had gone into effect. The timing was no accident, and it symbolizes the difference between the standard, top-down de-velopment approach and an ecological approach that emphasizes the local community. The Chiapas revolt did not try to seize state power. Instead, it aimed to retrieve the power of the people (mainly Indians) to govern themselves within their own communities. The appeal was "for an end to 500 years of oppression and 40 years of 'development' "[15] — development that had benefits only for large landowners, not Indians. Behind the repudiation of "development" was President Salinas de Go-tari's repeal of the arrangement whereby the communal landholdings of indigenous peoples were constitutionally protected. The choice of NAFTA's inaugural date as the starting day of the rebellion was meant to contrast the Mexican government's growth-oriented strategies of de-velopment, which favor the wealthy, and the Indians' understanding of sustainable development. Larry Rasmussen sums up the difference:

> While conventional development revolves around economies and their growth in the form of free markets and economic glob-alization, the Indian notion of sustainability focuses on local land and the health of communities and societies tied more closely to self-reliance, indigenous social movements, culture, low-impact agriculture, sustainable energy use, environmental balance with locality and region, and community economic, social, and political accountability.[16]

Where conventional development qualifies its focus on economic growth with environmental sustainability, the alternative favored by the Indians (and WCC) works at increasing economic self-reliance

---

15. See Rasmussen, *Earth Community, Earth Ethics*, 130.
16. Ibid., 131.

within a framework of community responsibility and ecological balance.

For the Indians, the issue was not how to alter environments so as to serve the economy, but how to alter economies so as to serve environments ordered around healthy communities. "The difference," says Rasmussen, "is not subtle."

> Against the background of two centuries of industrial economies, it is the difference between an economic approach that begins with the notion of an "open," even "empty" and basically unlimited world, and an ecological approach that begins with a notion of a "full" and limited world that can only operate on a principle of borrowing. It is the difference between a mobile world (including mobile homes!) and a world of place and roots. It is the difference between viewing the whole world as sets of industrial and information systems that need to be managed globally as human and natural capital, and local and regional communities attending to home environments in a comprehensive way around basic needs and quality of life.[17]

The questions raised by the notion of sustainable community, then, are very different from the ones raised by sustainable development. What kind of planet do you want? the latter asks. The former: What kind of neighborhood? Sustainable development favors globalization from above, led by the institutional leaders of the developed world. Sustainable community means globalization from below, led by so-called "underdeveloped" people. I do not think these two approaches should be regarded as stark alternatives. There may be room for both.[18]

Civilizing the Global Marketplace

There is a season for everything — for planting and building and for uprooting and tearing down. The protesters who swarmed through the streets of Washington, D.C., over the weekend of April 14–16, 2000, during the annual meeting of the International Monetary Fund and the World Bank, seemed more interested in tearing down. They represented an unlikely coalition — of church people, consumer groups,

---

17. Ibid., 137.
18. It is currently fashionable in the academy to bash the World Bank for favoring big infrastructure projects — roads, hydroelectric dams, massive water projects — and to prefer local cultures and communitarian solutions. There is no hard and fast rule here. As the practice of clitoridectomy (genital mutilation) illustrates, local cultures can license all sorts of cruelty, oppression, and misery — especially for women, whose identity is typically construed in traditional cultures in relation to fathers, brothers, and husbands.

labor unions, protectionists, environmentalists, human rights activists, anarchists, economic nationalists, and isolationists — that had first assembled in Seattle in December of 1999 to shut down a meeting of the World Trade Organization. At their best, the protesters in Seattle and Washington were part of a necessary movement to civilize the global economy. At their worst they were playing into the hands of people like Texas Senator Phil Gramm, chairman of the powerful Senate Banking Committee, who is all too eager to eviscerate the I.M.F. and the World Bank by imposing restrictive new rules on their discretionary authority and lending. If he could, Senator Gramm would derail the whole campaign to relieve poor nations of crushing foreign debt.

The real problem is that for two decades now, under both Republican and Democratic leadership, the I.M.F., the World Bank, and the W.T.O. have lined up behind the so-called "Washington consensus" — the neoliberal belief that privatization, deregulation, and open capital markets do just about everything we want and need: create jobs, make companies more competitive, lower consumer prices, supply foreign capital and technology to poor countries, and by spreading prosperity establish the conditions in which democracy and respect for human rights may flourish. This is the new global economy, and according to enthusiasts like Thomas L. Friedman of the *New York Times,* it is as unstoppable as the spread of the new information technology that feeds its growth.[19]

Critics of this laissez-faire doctrine do not dispute all of its claims. Nor, if they are well informed, do they dispute that between 1965 and 1985, in part because of World Bank efforts and the private investment its seal of approval often unleashed, the lot of the poor in many developing nations improved dramatically. By whatever measure — whether it be increased income and consumption (the latter jumped by 70 percent per capita) or indices of social well-being like extended life-expectancy and improved levels of education — the world's have-nots were doing better. Overall, despite setbacks in sub-Saharan Africa and Latin America during the 1980s, that upward trend continues to this day. And again, part of the reason for such progress can be attributed to World Bank president Robert S. McNamara, under whose tenure (1968–81) a preference for huge hydroelectric and transport projects was balanced by a "basic human needs" approach that funneled money into agriculture, education, housing, nutrition, family planning, and health care.

---

19. Thomas L. Friedman, *The Lexus and the Olive Tree: Understanding Globalization* (New York: Farrar, Straus & Giroux, 1999).

But critics of the new global economy tell another side of the story — of World Bank projects like the Polonoroeste road building and agricultural project in the Brazilian state of Rondonia, which led to massive deforestation and social dislocation, or the bank's coal mining and power plant projects in Singrauli, India, which dislocated two hundred thousand people without compensation and created the greatest single source of carbon emissions on the planet. The World Bank conceded in a 1994 self-criticism that its decision-making procedures did not allow for input from those most affected by the Bank's decisions, even while conceding that local consent and involvement were crucial to the success of their projects. Nor were anthropologists and ecologists involved in Bank decisions, people who might offer another perspective to that of engineers and economists. Critics of the new globalism also speak of weak economies (witness Thailand, Indonesia, Russia, and Brazil) overwhelmed by easy money and vulnerable to volatile shifts in deregulated capital flows, of jobs less secure than the livelihoods abolished by globalization, of sweatshops, slave labor, and child labor, of wealth not enlarged but distributed upward to local elites and multinational corporations, and of intensified social and political conflict. The new global marketplace, say critics like William Greider, is a little like a Wild West show where institutions like the I.M.F. and the W.T.O. play sheriff and hanging judge, declaring the law and punishment on behalf of their wealthy patrons — the private first world bankers and brokerages that demand "transparency" and "due diligence" from the governments and banks of developing countries while exempting themselves from the same requirements.

The W.T.O. was created in 1995 as an extension of the previous General Agreement on Tariffs and Trade (GATT). Headquartered in Geneva, Switzerland, it makes and enforces the rules of international commerce, mainly by knocking down trade barriers (which are often another nation's health, safety, or environmental laws). Its blind spot lies in an exclusive faith in supposedly self-adjusting markets. After an occasional speculative overshoot like Thailand's 1998 real estate "bubble," things are supposed to return to normal with no help from governments. But prudent governments would be well advised to impose controls in order to stop frantic capital surges in and out, or to encourage long-term capital investment in what the nation decides are its own priorities. In practice, it often appears, the doctrinaire deregulation of international trade means that the biggest corporations are free to enter any market and to extract any resource without worrying much about labor, safety, or environmental constraints. As for the International Monetary Fund, it makes loans to troubled nations to prevent panics and in return demands sound management and transparent bookkeeping (all very sensible). But its bailouts also enable big Western banks like Chase and Citigroup — and offshore banking centers in places like the Cayman Islands, which specialize in laundering "dirty money" and avoiding national taxes — to walk away unscathed from reckless investments. Meanwhile the I.M.F.'s one-size-fits-all austerity programs undercut government programs that aim to protect people from the harshness of the market. The recent I.M.F. structural adjustment program in Indonesia, for instance, did not revive the economy but plunged it into depression, sinking half its businesses into bankruptcy, provoking massive social and political disorder, and making it harder than ever to restore the confidence of customers of Merrill Lynch and Goldman Sachs, whose flight caused the meltdown to begin with.

Whose interests do I.M.F. austerity programs serve? The 1998 Asian crisis, it turns out, offered a golden opportunity to push the American agenda. The U.S. had long viewed the Asian system of protectionism, industrial policy, and activist state intervention in the economy as a setup that handicapped our economic interests. United States trade representative Charlene Barshevsky explained to Congress that in the case of the I.M.F. program for Thailand, the "commitments to restructure public enterprises and accelerate privatization of certain key sectors — including energy, transportation, utilities and communications — which will enhance market driven competition and deregulation [are expected] to create new business opportunities for U.S. firms."[20]

It is time, therefore, for some rebuilding of international financial institutions. The great fiction of neoliberal dogma, that national governments must refrain from asserting themselves in the new global economy, is both unrealistic and counterproductive. For some time now, Chile has saved itself from economic, social, and political havoc by imposing controls on short-term capital flows, and a recent study for the prestigious Council on Foreign Relations under the direction of former Treasury chief Pete Peterson and former U.S. trade representative Carla Hill recommends this strategy. We probably also need some entirely new international institutions — a new system to prevent sharp swings in currency values from feeding speculative frenzies and the unproductive games of daily foreign exchange transactions amounting (presently) to $1.5 trillion; a new international bankruptcy court to set

20. Cited in William Greider, "Time to Rein in Global Finance," *The Nation* (April 24, 2000): 13–20.

rules for equitable settlements between creditors and defaulting nations so that the fallen country is not scavenged of its remaining assets while foreign investors walk away scot free, with no responsibility to answer for their mistakes. And perhaps we also require an international central bank that would, like our own Federal Reserve Bank, serve as lender of last resort in emergencies, provide temporary liquidity, and keep currency exchange values within agreed-upon ratios.

There is little question, too, that we need a mechanism to enforce international environmental and labor regulations to limit the unbridled exploitation of developing countries that are all too often at the mercy of a bidding war that amounts to a "race to the bottom." And finally we need generous funding for aid programs, especially for educational and social services, so that the disruptive impact of the I.M.F.'s stabilization programs does not fall disproportionately on workers and the poor, who should not be held responsible for the mismanagement and corruption of their political and business elites.

PART IV

THE ⊓EW COSⲘOLOGY

Science, I want to acknowledge, has contributed mightily to our sense of wonder at earth's bounty, beauty, and fragility. It has been profligate with its attention, introducing a new form of love into the world, a love of nature virtually unknown in the ancient world. I mean what Whitehead called that "vehement and passionate interest in the relation of general principles to irreducible and stubborn facts." In practice it has meant a massive dedication to the task of understanding the patterns of the natural world, from subatomic particles to galactic formation, from the mating habits of beetles to the migration paths of whooping cranes, from the reproductive behavior of fruit flies and mountain gorillas to the chemical properties of nitrogen and lithium. Literally anything and everything has been fair game. Nothing has been too small or too big to escape scrutiny and understanding — for its own sake, for the sheer wonder of it, without (at first) thinking of the practical applications of such knowledge or its monetary rewards. Simply (as with climbing mountains) because it, whatever the "it" is, is there. This kind of research is surely one of the glories of our species, and glorifies God.

Yet modern science, I have argued, has its dark side. It is in part responsible for our ecocrisis. It has played the role of sorcerer's apprentice to the world's conquistadors and industrial power grabbers. And in the form of the potent cultural idea of scientific materialism, it has tacitly denigrated matter and led to an adversarial relationship with the whole material world. But if science, or what more properly should be called scientism, is part of the problem, in the following section I want to argue that postmodern science is also part of the so-

127

lution. As in the seventeenth century, science is once again changing how we think of ourselves and our relationship to nature. It is reshaping our culture. We no longer live in a Newtonian world. And though people may have only a vague sense of what a post-Einsteinian physics is about, there is a widespread feeling in popular culture that the big story of the universe we are beginning to tell ourselves invites a new, positive relationship with the cosmos and a new understanding of our place in nature and history.

The question of our relationship to nature and of where we fit in the big scheme of things has to do with what has traditionally been known as cosmology. Cosmology in the modern, technical sense is not to be confused with the premodern concept of cosmology, and the distinction ought to be borne in mind. The highly dramatic cosmologies of the Babylonians, Israelites, and Aztecs spanned what we think of as philosophy, science, and religion and thus had room in them for creation stories, battles with dragons, and the release of an oppressed people from captivity. In the ancient and medieval worlds, then, cosmology located the human drama within the big story of the universe as a whole. It offered a theory of everything of overriding importance and concern to a society — what Joseph Campbell referred to as a "myth to live by," a way of articulating our ultimate meaning and destiny. This is the kind of cosmology I will be looking for in these final chapters.

In contrast, cosmology in the modern, technical sense is a science, and that means it prescinds from all questions of purpose or finality. More narrowly, modern cosmology refers to a subfield of physics having to do with theories about the origin, evolution, and present physical structure of the universe (e.g., "steady state" or big bang theories, accounts of the formation of galaxies, etc.). In turn, grand unified theories (GUTs) in physics, which sound as though they ought to approach a premodern concept of cosmology, thereby unifying everything in the whole universe, do nothing of the sort. In fact they leave out almost everything above the level of an electron.[1]

---

1. When Stephen Hawking tells us that he is searching for a "unification of physics" or what scientists sometimes call a "theory of everything," he is not to be taken literally (see *A Brief History of Time* [New York: Bantam Books, 1988], 156–75). First of all, there is the cautionary tale involved in Kurt Gödel's "incompleteness theorem." Our philosophies and science must remain inherently open-ended and exploratory — precisely because of the logical impossibility of any theory that proclaims its own completeness. Gödel's theorem, formulated in 1930, established that the full validity of any system, especially a scientific one, cannot be demonstrated within the system itself. A "theory of everything" that claimed to offer the definitive, last word about the physical structure of the universe would be a contradiction in terms, a sheer logical impossibility. It would have to reach outside its own postulates to "prove" itself, and by that very operation it would disclose its own incompleteness.

"In other words," as Timothy Ferris puts it, "the comprehensibility of a theory cannot be

In the following three chapters, I will try to lay out the new image of the biophysical world that is emerging from the new post-Einsteinian science — in effect, a new cosmology. The scientific part of the new cosmology is a story of how time and relationship return to our perception of nature and of how life and humanity cease to seem alien. Implicitly it will be an account of how the old dualism has been overcome and how the natural world regains its former sense of generativity. Science and religion, each from its own angle, can now join forces in appealing on behalf of the earth.

We are about to embark, then, upon an extended meditation upon the extraordinarily dynamic nature of matter and energy, one that differs markedly from the mechanical picture we got from Newtonian mechanics. "Thou art dust, and to dust thou wilt return," says the Ash Wednesday liturgy. What is the nature of this dust? Contemporary physics has an amazing story to tell of this dust. It is a new, post-Einsteinian cosmology. This places us in a universe that would have been familiar to the Hebrew prophets — one on the move, rich in possibility, rich in promise. The subjunctive mood has a secure place again in the nature of things. And paradoxically enough, it is all that turbulence and fluctuation in the cosmos that do this, that give all of nature's maybe's and might be's a chance to become true. Danger and risk there are. But in its own tacit, latent way, it as if the universe

---

established unless there is something outside the frame against which to test it — something beyond the boundary defined by a thermodynamic equation, or by the collapse of the quantum wave function, or by any other theory or law. And if there is such a wider reference frame, then the theory by definition does not explain everything. In short, there is not and never will be a complete and comprehensive scientific account of the universe that can be proved valid. The Creator must have been fond of uncertainty, for He (or She) has given it to us for keeps" (Timothy Ferris, *Coming of Age in the Milky Way* [New York: Doubleday Anchor Books, 1988], 384).

Secondly, the theory Hawking has in mind covers a limited sphere. It will explain "everything" only to the extent that everything in the cosmos is composed of subatomic particle-waves. Currently, Einstein's general theory of relativity, which describes the force of gravity and the large-scale structure of the universe, does not fit with quantum mechanics, which deals with subatomic phenomena. Hawking aspires to reconcile these two antithetical accounts by devising a quantum theory of gravity, which in effect would unify all of physics. But such a theory would be limited to explaining, at the most simple level of "bottom up" interaction, why subatomic particles have the mass, charge, and other characteristics that they do. But please note: Causality works from two directions, from the subatomic, bottom-up level of quarks and protons (which high energy physics attends to) and at higher levels of complexity from the "top down" (which physical chemists and biologists study). Hawking's great synthesis, if it happens, would do nothing to predict the "top down" behavior of things at more complex levels of organization — such as those of macromolecules, weather patterns, rain forests, jaguars, or human beings playing the stock market.

In short, what Hawking is about represents an abstraction from the whole of human experience, and to claim that this abstracted part is the whole (i.e., the "mind of God" or some such thing) is to commit what Alfred North Whitehead once called the "fallacy of misplaced concreteness." Hawking mistakes an abstraction for the concrete real.

dreams big, promises big, and is congruent with the human habit of hoping against the odds.

At this point, in order to see where I am going in the next chapters, it might be useful to lay out the differences between the classical Newtonian view of nature and the twenty-first century view. We are in the process of passing through a paradigm shift, engineered by science itself, that displaces one very manipulative idea of nature with an idea that is far more hospitable to an ecological ethic. Where the Newtonian understanding had viewed nature as a machine, understanding it as deterministic, atomistic, mechanistic, and dualistic, the new cosmology is evolutionary, unpredictable, relational, holistic, and interdependent. Gifford lecturer Ian G. Barbour gives the distinctive features of twentieth-century cosmology as follows:

- In place of immutable order, or change as rearrangement of the same, unchanging components, nature is now understood to be evolutionary, dynamic, and emergent. Its basic forms have changed radically and new types of phenomena have appeared at successive levels in matter, life, mind, and culture. Historicity is a basic characteristic of nature, and science itself is historically conditioned.

- In place of determinism, there is a complex combination of law and chance, in fields as diverse as quantum physics, thermodynamics, cosmology, and biological evolution. Nature is characterized by both structure and openness. The future cannot be predicted in detail from the past, either in principle or in practice.

- Nature is understood to be relational, ecological, and interdependent. Reality is constituted by events and relationships rather than by separate substances or separate particles. In epistemology, classical realism — the idea that the object can be known as it is in itself apart from the observer — now appears untenable.

- Reduction continues to be fruitful in analysis of the separate components of systems, but attention is also given to systems and wholes themselves. Distinctive holistic concepts are used to explain the higher level activities of systems, from organisms to ecosystems.

- There is a hierarchy of levels within every organism. (But not an extreme hierarchy of value among beings, as in the medieval view, which could be used to justify the exploitation of one group of beings by another.) Mind/body dualism finds little support in science today. The contemporary outlook is less anthropocentric; human beings have capacities not found elsewhere in nature, but they are the products of evolution and parts of an interdependent natural order. Other creatures are valuable in themselves. Humanity is an integral part of nature. The human being is a psychosomatic unity — a biological organism but also a responsible self.

- Nature is a community — a historical community of interdependent beings.[2]

This new understanding of things carries profound implications for both theology and ecology, which I will try to spell out in the next section. Western science and religion, after a period of temporary hostilities lasting a mere few centuries, I will claim, ought now to be seen as congruent with each other. This is not to say that science asserts exactly what the Judeo-Christian tradition preaches; science and religion have different things to tell us, each distinctive and irreplaceable. It is only to say that science and biblical faith are back on the same historical trajectory, neither one contradicting the other, each consonant with what the other is claiming. The biblical vision, I want to argue, provides a framework for the new science of an evolving cosmos.

2. Adapted from Ian G. Barbour, *Religion in an Age of Science* (San Francisco: HarperSan-Francisco, 1990), 1:220.

EIGHT

Evolution and
Theological Repair

A serious human life, no matter what religion is invoked, can
hardly begin until we see an element of illusion in what is really
there, and something real in fantasies about what might be there
instead.   — NORTHROP FRYE, *The Great Code*

> Now I am revealing new things to you,
> things hidden and unknown to you,
> created just now, this very moment.
>   —Isaiah 48:6–7

It is the fixed that horrifies us, the fixed that assails us with
the tremendous force of its mindlessness. The fixed is a Mason
jar, and we can't beat it open....The fixed is the world without
fire — dead flint, dead timber, and nowhere a spark. It is motion
without direction, force without power, the aimless procession
of caterpillars round the rim of a vase, and I hate it because at
any moment I myself might step to that charmed and glistening
thread.   — ANNIE DILLARD, *Pilgrim at Tinker Creek*

In a recent address to the head of the Vatican Observatory before a
major scientific conference, Pope John Paul II spoke of the urgent need
for a "vital exchange" between theology and the sciences. "Theology,"
he wrote,

> will have to call on the findings of science to one degree or an-
> other as it pursues its primary concern for the human person, the
> reaches of freedom, the possibilities of Christian community, the
> nature of belief and the intelligibility of nature and history. The vi-
> tality and significance of theology for humanity will in a profound
> way be reflected in its ability to incorporate these findings.

For its part, the pope went on, science should benefit from the exchange — insofar as "science develops best when its concepts and conclusions are integrated into the broader human culture and its concerns for ultimate meaning and value." Science, the pope concluded, "can purify religion from error and superstition; religion can purify science from idolatry and false absolutes. Each can draw the other into a wider world, a world in which both can flourish."[1]

What follows, then, will be an experiment in the kind of exchange between science and theology that the pope calls for. This will be an effort to locate the human drama within the big picture, the destiny of the cosmos as a whole. And for starters, I want to turn to the contrast between the scientific and the biblical vision of the whole. My thesis is basically this: So long as science viewed the cosmos as static, there could be no fundamental reconciliation between science and Western, biblical religion. But once science began to view the physical cosmos as a story of becoming, that is, in evolutionary terms, then a reconciliation between science and religion became possible. What connects science and religion is the accent on temporality and the motif of promise. The Bible is about nothing else than promise, and evolution discloses a universe that reinforces this theme.

Theology in a Static Cosmos

Biblical faith gives rise to both sharp criticism of the world, as we observe in the Jewish prophets, and a flight from the world, as in Platonism and Gnosticism. Christianity, we pointed out, is heir to both these impulses: the positive Jewish attitude toward time and the physical world that we saw in chapters 1 and 2, and the tendency to idealize the desire to escape the mortal bonds of body and earth. St. Augustine of Hippo (354–430 C.E.), the Western church's most influential theologian, conceives of God, in Platonic terms, as superabundant and overflowing goodness that must, of necessity, diffuse itself, give itself away, so that this inexhaustible, "never spent" goodness is ingredient in all creation. As we pointed out earlier, this theology provides the basis for world-affirmation, for a profound love of the created world. But it's also true that Augustine tilted Christianity in the direction of otherworldly pessimism by writing his monumental work on world history,

---

1. "Message of His Holiness Pope John Paul II to the Director of the Vatican Observatory," June 1, 1988. Reprinted in *Physics, Philosophy and Theology: A Common Quest for Understanding,* ed. Robert John Russell, William R. Stoeger, S.J., and George V. Coyne, S.J. (Rome: Vatican Observatory, 1997), M10, 13.

The City of God, in response to the sack of Rome by the Vandals in the early fifth century. And as Augustine lay dying in 430 C.E., his own North African city of Hippo lay under siege by these "barbarians." For the next thousand years, western Europe lived in the shadow of Augustine and the fall of the Roman Empire and understood the temporal world as a "vale of tears," a realm of decay, decline, and death. Long before Rudolph Clausius came up with the law of entropy in the nineteenth century, then, medieval Westerners had imagined that the world's energy was running downhill. The earth was thus understood as a point of departure or launching pad for another, supernal world. Life on earth was a kind of testing ground or "school for the soul"; the purpose of life was to prepare for the end of the world and life after death. Only in a very secondary sense did life's purpose involve responsibility for the state of the earth.

The classic medieval concept of God's transcendence reinforced this pessimistic otherworldliness. In order to protect divine freedom, the God of Aquinas and Bonaventure was conceived as having no internal relation to material creatures or to temporality. God's primordial perfection of being existed forever in a fixed realm "up above" creation, untouched by time. Hence the temporal realm of becoming could only be envisioned as a deficient reflection of, or deviation from, a "supernatural" world of timeless completion and fullness. The perfection of "Being" is already fully realized, a fait accompli existing from all eternity, and therefore the earthy arena of temporal becoming can bring about nothing truly novel or significant. Inevitably, the story of temporal becoming will turn out to be a tale of decline or straying from the already existing ideal.

It is no wonder, then, that the classic Christian spirituality of ascent is ambivalent toward the physical world and promotes a pervasive nostalgia for a lost perfection. At its worst it abhors the world of nature as the "Devil's realm," and it promotes an asceticism that is hostile to women, sexuality, the body, and the biophysical world. In ecological terms this strain of the tradition tends to reinforce a pattern of neglect of and flight from the earth. Because God is conceived as detached from the world and unaffected by time, the human ideal of perfection is conceived in terms of withdrawal from temporality, negation of the material world, and a shedding of the mortal body. This kind of spirituality justifies either neglect of or indifference to the material world; it hardly provides the basis for an ecological ethic.

Time and the Chancy Universe of the Prophets

At a deeper level, though, so long as the Judeo-Christian vision remains rooted in the Hebrew Bible, a spirituality of flight from the world and history can only represent an aberration. And so long as Christians remember their Jewish roots, they have to find a static Greek "block universe" foreign and alienating — somehow unbiblical. A Christianity that remembers its origins can only be at home with a metaphysics of the future. It will inevitably seek out an evolutionary, processive universe, a universe in the subjunctive mood, a world of contingency, possibility, and promise, of might be's and could be's.

As we have seen, scientists of the classical mode (and this would include Einstein) focus exclusively on the changeless redundancies of nature. Ironically enough, the Judeo-Christian objection to classical Western physics — at least when it offers to turn its implicit fatalism into an ultimate truth — is that it is unearthly, a kind of Platonism; it seeks an illusory transcendence of flux, change, and temporality. The cosmos of classical physics is inflexible, fixed, static; it is going nowhere. There is no give to it, no pliability or elasticity. It has no place in it for the kind of cosmos the Hebrew prophets assume to be the context of human life: the contingencies and ambiguities of earth and the cosmos, a setting whose beauty and wonder lie as much in its instability as in its stability. Above all, time counted in the world of the Hebrew prophets. It was a setting where the future is not determined by the past, where the future is open, so that there is much to be learned, to be discovered, to be invented.

If the Hebrew Bible is about anything it is about promise and possibility. A natural world, therefore, that would join forces with the prophets — with Moses, Isaiah, Jeremiah, Ezekiel, and Amos — must be eschatological, that is, on the move, full of promise and possibility. It must not only manifest stability and lawfulness, a sign of God's faithfulness, but must also provide space and time for the overturn of a given order. The great Hebrew prophets presuppose a world full of big chances, contingencies, and opportunities. They are on the lookout for breaks in symmetry and the direction of time. They are themselves harbingers of subversion and conflict. God knows the Bible chronicles enough episodes of oppressive business as usual. Stable order, however, is not the equivalent of the good or the better; it cannot hold the last word. The first and the last word of the Bible is the unprecedented, the new beginning. This note is sounded from the outset, with the story of Abraham leaving his father's dwelling in Haran. Abraham is called into *terra incognita,* the unknown, a complete departure from everything that has gone before in the long evolution of culture, which up until this time had known only cyclical time, the repetition of what had already been. As Abraham Heschel once put it,

> Judaism is a *religion of time* aiming at the *sanctification of time.* Unlike the space-minded man to whom time is unvaried, iterative, homogeneous, to whom all hours are alike, qualityless, empty shells, the Bible senses the diversified character of time. There are no two hours alike. Every hour is unique and the only one given at the moment, exclusive and endlessly precious.[2]

Heschel's "space-minded man" for whom time is "unvaried, iterative, homogeneous" applies perfectly to the mindset of the classical physicist (but not to Einstein's physics of relativity, as we shall see). In contrast to the classical mindset, the Bible is concerned with the "sanctification of time." It is not only space or the things of space that are sanctified but time, the day of the Sabbath, for instance, the days of the work-week, or the jubilee years during which debts were canceled and the land and its beasts of burden were given a well-earned rest.

Time, as Heschel puts it, "is perpetual innovation." Not repetition. In the biblical perspective, it is not time that is evanescent and per-ishing; it is the things of space that perish. Time itself never expires. Indeed, in attending to time, we attend to the transcendent. We find that which stands beyond our reach and power, something both near and far, intrinsic to all experience and yet transcending all experience. All the same, it is only within time that there is true fellowship and togetherness.

> Every one of us occupies a portion of space. He takes it up exclu-sively. The portion of space which my body occupies is taken up by myself in exclusion of anyone else. Yet, no one possesses time. There is no moment which I possess exclusively. This very mo-ment belongs to all living men as it belongs to me. We share time, we own space. Through my ownership of space, I am a rival of all other beings; through my living in time, I am a contemporary of all other beings. We pass through time, we occupy space. We easily succumb to the illusion that the world of space is for our sake, for man's sake. In regard to time, we are immune to such an illusion.[3]

---

2. Abraham Heschel, *The Sabbath: Its Meaning for Modern Man* (New York: Farrar, Straus & Giroux, 1951), 8.
3. Ibid., 99.

"Time, then," as Heschel has it, "is otherness, a mystery that hovers above all categories." He goes on,

> Time is the process of creation, and things of space are the results of creation. When looking at space we see products of creation; when intuiting time we hear the process of creation. Things of space exhibit a deceptive independence. They show off a veneer of limited permanence. Things created conceal the Creator. It is the dimension of time wherein man meets God, wherein man becomes aware that every instant is an act of creation, a Beginning, opening up new roads for ultimate realizations.... To witness the perpetual marvel of the world's coming into being is to sense the presence of the Giver in the given, to realize that the source of time is eternity, that the secret of becoming is the eternal within time.[4]

For the person of faith, then, time is essentially a medium of great promise, of God's fidelity to and love of the earth. This is what we meant earlier (chapter 2) by saying that the universe is sacramental. God's energy, glory, favor, and promise shine through the whole of things, not just at the beginning but throughout all time and history and at every instant, coming like the background radiation of the big bang from everywhere at once and with the same resonating intensity. It is to this rampant, quickening energy, the presence of the Holy Spirit immanent in the material world, that the Christian church and its saints testify. Today's Christians, like yesterday's, will want to sense in their bones God's promise, and that promise or blessing is not something apart from, but latent in, the very energies of the stars, the planets, and earth.

Hubble's Expanding Universe

To understand that God's blessing and promise are latent in the very energies of the stars, the planets, and earth, we need now to look at how time and possibility poured into the world once Darwin entered the debate. But first, let us take a brief look at how science has discovered not only that the earth has a history, but that this story extends to the whole cosmos. Once this storied cosmos is in place, I want to consider how this cosmic history should encourage us to do some serious theological repair work.

We hardly remember these days that even up to the first decades of the twentieth century most people, including the astronomers, believed

---

4. Ibid., 100–101.

that the universe was basically eternal and static. Things might change a lot, even evolve over millions of years, within our eccentric planet — so Charles Darwin had taught us — but otherwise, in the cosmos as a whole, nothing really essential changed. The cosmos did not have a history. So we wrongly thought.

All that has now changed. It is now understood that the cosmos does have a history.[5] It is common to say that the new picture of the cosmos was born in 1915, when Albert Einstein postulated in his general theory of relativity that everything from proton to star was a signal system warping space, and thus that time was inseparable from space. Stephen Hawking dates the shift in outlook even later, to 1924, when Edwin Hubble, working at the Mt. Wilson Observatory in California, tried to figure out whether the nebulae seen through the telescope were merely dust and gas sprinkled about the Milky Way galaxy, or whether they represented other "island universes," that is, other galaxies. Hubble showed that they were the latter, and that our Milky Way galaxy was thus not the only game in the cosmic town. At that point, most astronomers followed Fred Hoyle in thinking that our universe existed in a "steady state" and was virtually eternal. But then, in 1929, Hubble made the additional landmark observation that light reaching the earth from remote galaxies has a slightly different color from nearby ones. It is shifted, sometimes substantially, into the red region of the spectrum. The most sensible explanation for this shift, Hubble realized, is that the remote galaxies are moving away from us, in every direction, at a rapid rate. The greater the red shift, the faster the galaxy is moving, just like a speeding locomotive whose eerie whistle deepens in pitch as it moves away from an observer. To Hubble's initial surprise, the most distant galaxies were moving the fastest, as if everything in the universe were flying away from a great initial explosion at a single point in space and time.

One can hardly exaggerate the ramifications. Suddenly, cosmologists had a rational way of addressing the age-old questions of the structure and evolution of the universe as a whole. If the universe is expanding, does it have a center? Was there a beginning? Will it have an end? Are we to be the helpless victims of a cosmic cataclysm? Can we understand the "beginning," the putative big bang? The methods by which science pursues its answers to such questions could not be more different from the ways religion pursues its answers to such questions. But the questions are the same.

---

5. See Carl F. von Weizsacker, *The History of Nature* (Chicago: University of Chicago Press, 1949).

If the universe is truly expanding, argued Abbé Georges Lemaître, a Belgian priest-mathematician, space-time must be blooming out from a "primeval atom" of unimaginably compacted energy some 15 to 20 billion years ago. British astronomer Fred Hoyle would derisively name this initial event the "big bang" — and the name stuck. It seemed, after all, that maybe the universe had a beginning. In 1963 two Bell Laboratory scientists, Arno Penzias and Robert Wilson, confirmed this suspicion by accidentally picking up the primordial sound wave of the birth of our universe on their big radio antenna in Holmdel, New Jersey. Suddenly, the cosmos had a history, a narrative story, going from almost nothing to a very big something in very short order. Astrophysicist Robert Jastrow described the phenomenon this way:

> At this moment it seems as though science will never be able to raise the curtain on the mystery of creation. For the scientist who has lived by his faith in the power of reason, the story ends like a bad dream. He has scaled the mountains of ignorance; he is about to conquer the highest peak; as he pulls himself over the final rock, he is greeted by a band of theologians who have been sitting there for centuries.[6]

The Cosmic Clock

What are we to make of a universe that we now know consists of some 125 billion galaxies? That is estimated to be 15 to 20 billion years old? That has a diameter of 30 billion light years? The distance light travels in a year is about six trillion miles, so to reach a diameter of 30 billion light years, one multiplies 30 billion by six trillion to get some 180 sextillion miles. This is a very, very long trip. The spatial scale of the universe is mind-boggling. Yet, as physicist John Polkinghorne reminds us, we should resist being daunted by such immensity.

> Those trillions of stars have to be around if we are to be around also to think about them. In modern cosmology there is a direct correlation between how big a universe is and how long it has lasted. Only a universe as large as ours could have been around for the fifteen billion years it takes to evolve life — ten billion years for the first generation of stars to generate the elements that are the raw materials of life, and about a further five billion years to reap the benefit of that chemical harvest.[7]

6. Robert Jastrow, *God and the Astronomers* (New York: W. W. Norton, 1978), 116.
7. John Polkinghorne, *Beyond Science: The Wider Human Context* (Cambridge: Cambridge University Press, 1996), 84.

Thus forewarned, we can turn forthrightly to the temporal scale. We can now put Darwin together with Einstein and Hubble. When the Christian creed fails to connect with these scales of time, when it loses its link to the galaxies or its necessary ingredient of wildness, it begins to feel conventional, domesticated, tamed, and without power. Something essential has been lost. The juice has gone out of it. As the late literary critic Northrop Frye once observed, with the coming of the seventeenth-century scientific revolution our biblically based sense of "dominion" over creation began to be exposed as a paranoid delusion.

> From Copernicus onward, man seemed increasingly to have only an accidental relation to the spatial world of the stars, where conscious life has not so far been found, and to the temporal world of evolution, in which man is a late and perhaps an intrusive development. As the sheer size of scientific time and space expanded so hugely, the traditional view of creation began to look paranoid, a complacent and unwarranted illusion on man's part that everything had been created for him.[8]

Suppose, then, that we place ourselves within astrophysical time. What is the effect? Would it not humble our arrogance? And would it not admonish us to remember our cultural roots in the Yahwist's tradition of humble service of the land we inhabit?

And suppose, for another thought experiment, we folded astrophysical time into the framework of the biblical vision. What would that do for the process of evolution? Would that not suggest that the evolutionary struggle for existence, despite all the competition and blind alleys and waste, is finally meaningful — even when we cannot fathom that meaning?

Consider, in any case, the way in which Carl Sagan, in *The Dragons of Eden,* tries to get across to us the history of our universe and our relative place in it. He asks us to imagine a "cosmic clock," the 15-billion-year lifetime of the cosmos compressed into the span of a single year. Within this compass, every billion years of earth history would correspond to about twenty-four days of this cosmic year. That would mean that the big bang would occur on January 1 and the whole of recorded history would fit into the last ten seconds of New Year's Eve, December 31.[9] The moral lesson Sagan seeks to draw from all this is not dissimilar to the Yahwist's theology of humble service that we

---

8. Northrop Frye, *The Great Code: The Bible and Literature* (New York: Harcourt Brace Jovanovich, 1981), 74.
9. Carl Sagan, *The Dragons of Eden: Speculations on the Evolution of Human Intelligence* (New York: Random House, 1977), 14–16.

examined in the first chapter. Sagan wanted to remove us from our pedestal, to put us in our humble place in the big scheme of things. But the story also describes a process of complexification, diversification, and the emergence of novelty. Nature, as the ancients had it, constantly gives birth to the new. The story goes something like this:

January 1   Big Bang

May 1   Origin of the Milky Way Galaxy

September 9   Origin of the solar system

September 14   Formation of the earth

September 25   Origin of life on earth

October 2   Formation of the oldest rocks on earth

October 9   Date of oldest fossils (bacteria and blue-green algae)

November 1   Invention of sex (by microorganisms)

November 12   Oldest fossil photosynthetic plants

November 15   Eukaryotes (first nucleated cells) flourish

December 1   Oxygen atmosphere begins to develop on earth

December 5   Extensive vulcanism and channel formation on Mars

December 16   First worms

December 17   Precambrian ends. Paleozoic Era and Cambrian Period begin. Invertebrates flourish

December 18   First oceanic plankton. Trilobites flourish

December 19   Ordovician Period. First fish and vertebrates

December 20   Silurian Period. First vascular plants. Plants begin colonizing land

December 21   Devonian Period begins. First insects. Animals begin colonizing land

December 22   First amphibians. First winged insects

December 23   Carboniferous Period. First trees. First reptiles

December 24   Permian Period begins. First dinosaurs

December 25   Paleozoic Era ends. Mesozoic Era begins

December 26   Triassic Period. First mammals

December 27   Jurassic Period. First birds

December 28   Cretaceous Period. First flowers. Dinosaurs become extinct

December 29   Mesozoic Era ends. Cenozoic Era and Tertiary Period begin. First cetaceans. First primates

December 30   Early evolution of frontal lobes in brains of primates; First hominids. Giant mammals flourish

December 31   End of the Pliocene Period. Pleistocene and Holocene Period. First humans

Human beings, then, would not emerge until late in the last day of the year, and all recorded history would fit into the last ten seconds. As evolution proceeds, one of its most striking features is that at each stage of biotic development, the tempo accelerates. It took about 3.9 billion years, some eight-tenths of earth's history, to generate photosynthesizing bacteria. The entire development of plants and animals has occurred in the last one-ninth of the planet's history. And within that history of land animals, human beings occupy a mere fraction of the time, some 400,000 years, or less than one-tenth of 1 percent of earth's history. Our putative "control" or "dominion" over the creatures of earth began only with the development of agriculture some 12,000 years ago, and it was probably pioneered not by men but by women, since their plant-gathering activities would most likely have led them to observe the growth of plants from seeds, and hence to the idea of planting and tending plants themselves. Twelve thousand years is roughly 2 percent of human history. For some 4,599,600,000 years, then, the earth got along quite well without us. Thus put in our place, let us resume with the count-down on December 31.

1:30 P.M.   Origin of Proconsul and Ramapithecus, probable ancestors of apes and men

10:30 P.M.   First humans

11:00 P.M.   Widespread use of stone tools

11:46 P.M.   Domestication of fire by Peking man

11:56 P.M.   Beginning of most recent glacial period

11:58 P.M.   Seafarers settle Australia

11:59 P.M.   Extensive cave painting in Europe

11:59:20 P.M.   Invention of agriculture

11:59:35 P.M.   Neolithic civilization; first cities

11:59:50 P.M.   First dynasties in Sumer, Ebla, and Egypt; development
of astronomy

11:59:51 P.M.   Invention of the alphabet; Akkadian Empire

11:59:52 P.M.   Hammurabic legal codes in Babylon; Middle Kingdom
in Egypt

11:59:53 P.M.   Bronze metallurgy; Mycenean culture; Trojan War;
Olmec culture; invention of compass

11:59:54 P.M.   Iron metallurgy; First Assyrian Empire; Kingdom of
Israel; founding of Carthage

11:59:55 P.M.   Asokan India; Chin Dynasty China; Periclean Athens;
birth of Buddha

11:59:56 P.M.   Euclidian geometry; Archimedean physics; Ptolemaic
astronomy; Roman Empire; birth of Christ

11:59:57 P.M.   Zero and decimals invented in Indian arithmetic; Rome
falls; Moslem conquests

11:59:58 P.M.   Mayan civilization; Sung Dynasty China; Byzantine
empire; Mongol invasion; Crusades

11:59:59 P.M.   Renaissance in Europe; voyages of discovery; Ming
Dynasty China; experimental method in science

Now   Widespread development of science and technology;
emergence of global culture; acquisition of the means
of self-destruction of the human species; first steps in
search for extraterrestrial intelligence.

An astrophysical angel, you might say, would scarcely have time
to notice us, much less figure out what such mites were doing in the
cosmos. Once again, by the cosmic clock scale the birth of Christ would
have occurred only seconds ago — at precisely 11:59 and 56 seconds
P.M. And the Renaissance only two seconds later. Can we say we realize
what such events mean when (from this perspective) they are barely
past us?

People will someday wonder, the philologist Owen Barfield wrote
in 1957, how we could have missed the congruence between evolution
and a religion that was so attuned to history. How could we be so
blind that

a religion which differed from all others in its acceptance of time, and of a particular point in time, as the cardinal element in its faith; that it had, on the other hand, a picture in its mind of the history of the Earth and man as an evolutionary process; and that it neither saw nor supposed any connection whatever between the two.[10]

One would have expected, Barfield continues, that those who considered Jesus of Nazareth to be the culminating point of the history of the earth, indeed its savior, would "feel that we are still very near to that turning point, indeed hardly past it; that we hardly know as yet what the Incarnation means." For against the 4.6 billion-year history of the earth, not to mention the age of the cosmos, what is a mere two thousand years? Do we comprehend any event that we are "hardly past," that in astrophysical terms happened but seconds ago? And how can we begin to apprehend such an epiphany if we do not have our ears to the ground — to hear the primordial Sound, the subtle vibration that John's Gospel calls the "Word made flesh," that was in the beginning, that resonates still through all created things?

No God of the Gaps or Big Explainer

One thing ought to be eliminated at the beginning: the habit of plugging God into the gaps in our scientific knowledge. Stephen W. Hawking, the current occupant of Isaac Newton's Lucasian Chair of Mathematics at Cambridge University, makes this mistake when he pits belief in a Creator against scientific interpretations of the big bang (like his own). At one point in *A Brief History of Time,* he assures his readers that "so long as the universe had a beginning, we could suppose it had a creator." But in his model of a "completely self-contained universe, having no boundary or edge," the universe would have neither beginning nor end; it would simply be. "What place, then," he asks, "for a creator?"[11]

Hawking misunderstands what believers are getting at when they say the universe is created. Creation, first of all, is not to be viewed as an act that has happened once upon a time back in the immemorial past. The issue is not how things happened (which science covers) but why there is anything at all. Strictly speaking, creation is not concerned

10. Owen Barfield, *Saving the Appearances: A Study in Idolatry* (Middletown, Conn.: Wesleyan University Press, [1958] 1988), 167.

11. Stephen W. Hawking, *A Brief History of Time: From the Big Bang to Black Holes* (New York: Bantam Books, 1988), 140–41.

with an absolute beginning at all. The act of bringing the world into existence and replenishing it is a continuous process; every instant is an act of creation, a flash of a great beginning. That is why the issue of an absolute beginning of time doesn't really matter for Jews and Christians. When we confess our faith in God, creator of heaven and earth, we are making no claims about, offering no explanation for, the initial conditions of the universe. The effect of saying that God makes everything effortlessly, *ex nihilo,* out of nothing, is precisely to make this point. As British theologian Nicholas Lasch puts it,

> The effect of this quite crucial clarification is to rule out the possibility that the concept of God may properly serve as a principle of explanation. Explanations are stories of causes and effects. There is no causal story which could start with "Nothing." From "nothing," there is no move the mind could make (what would the next sentence be?). To confess that God creates the world *ex nihilo* is thereby to acknowledge that there is an end to explanation, that it makes no more sense to seek for "ultimate" explanations of the world than it would to ask what the "solution" was to the "plot" of the world's history.[12]

Stephen Hawking doesn't understand this. The universe might well be self-contained, without boundary or edge, as Hawking claims. And it may be eternal, without beginning or end, as the Russian astrophysicist Andrei Linde believes. In no case are either of these hypotheses a threat to faith — unless you are a biblical literalist. The issue for believers is why there is something rather than nothing.

Christians sometimes make the same mistake atheists do in this regard: imagining that God is a principle of explanation, that God answers all our questions. Not so. Again, as Nicholas Lasch has it,

> To confess the world to be created out of nothing is to acknowledge its contingency. But, from contingency, nothing follows. Here we are. This is how things are. That's it. No safety belts, no metacosmic maps or guidebooks, no mental cradles for our "ultimate" security. The recognition of contingency, what Schleiermacher called the sense of absolute dependence, may (like vertigo) be intermittently exhilarating, but its more lasting moods lie somewhere between sheer mind-stopping awe and stark terror.[13]

12. Nicholas Lasch, *Believing Three Ways in God: A Reading of the Apostles' Creed* (Notre Dame, Ind.: University of Notre Dame Press, 1993), 39.

13. Ibid.

God provides no escape from this sense of contingency. Nor does God offer escape from unyielding laws and forces, which God also creates — of gravity and economics, entropy and institutional inertia, genetic mix-ups and the unforeseen consequences of trivial and distant human acts. Trusting in God can give one courage, but it does not stop the world from being chancy and dangerous. If anything, by not blinking at chance accidents, suffering, or death, the biblical worldview not only offers no safety net; it exposes us, like Job, to the harshly unpredictable catastrophes of time and history.

Christian Spirituality in an Evolving Universe

For what, then, can we hope? For most Christians, that is a question, as it was for Immanuel Kant, about the reality of life-after-death. But today, we must also turn it in the direction of earth and the temporal order. Is there hope for the earth? As Georgetown University's theologian John Haught has argued, as long as nature is viewed as static or eternal, it has no real future of its own to offer. In the classical scheme of things, either ancient or Newtonian, the order of nature appears to be nothing but repetition of the same; either it is going nowhere or, according to the law of entropy, it is going downhill, and hence there can be no hope at this level of things. With these presuppositions in place, human hope for what is truly new and fulfilling had to turn elsewhere, to another dimension, to an entirely different, supernatural world. In other words, we were led to withdraw from the natural world in order to experience a mystical breakthrough from another dimension. Or we detach ourselves from nature in order to arrive, after death, at a purely spiritual world situated, as it were, "up above." "The gist of such a view of truth and being — no matter how much its devotees seek to polish it up," says Haught, "is that nothing really new is ever going to happen."[14]

But after Darwin, after the idea of an evolving world was introduced into our horizon, the cosmos acquired a history and a future. And hence the horizon of human expectation could shift toward a future that includes the universe and the entire breadth of evolutionary time. In this way, argues Haught, evolutionary science not only opens up space for the insertion of hope within the temporal sphere; it also provides theology with the chance to get over its fascination with God as control freak and power-monger. The picture of nature

---

14. John F. Haught, *God after Darwin: A Theology of Evolution* (Boulder, Colo.: Westview Press, 2000), 187; see also 38–39.

that evolution offers — of random genetic mutation, natural selection, and immense stretches of time — is of a wild lottery riddled by chance, struggle to survive, waste, dead ends, and tragic outcomes as well as unaccountable good luck. For many a scientist, in fact, the picture is so grim as to render the notion of a benevolent "intelligent designer" God utterly incomprehensible, for the designer of so much misfortune and lucky accident, mass extinction and cruel competitive struggle would have to be a sadist. Indeed, even for those who persist in believing, adjustments will be required. For if the God of evolution is not to seem a sadistic control-freak, then God cannot be conceived as first of all a designer of all the dead ends, cruelty, and vast wastage of evolutionary eons. The God of evolution must take chances or "play dice." In other words, God must be conceived in more Taoist terms of noncoercive "nondoing" and "letting be."

Instead of constituting a loss or disadvantage, however, this will prove a positive gain. After all, the Unmoved Mover of Aristotle or the oriental despot who determines everything that happens down to the last twist and turn has never born any resemblance to the God of the Bible. Ridding ourselves of these notions of omnipotence, then, should bring us closer to the biblical image of God — to the God who lets creation develop in relative autonomy, who lets the world be, who renounces power and empties himself, who hears the cry of the poor and suffers with us. An evolutionary perspective, moreover, could also stimulate us to retrieve the ancient religious intuition that redemption involves more than the human family. It is, as the Epistle to the Romans says, the entire creation that "groans" for ultimate fulfillment (Rom. 8:22). After Darwin, that is to say, we can once again understand, as St. Paul did, that cosmic destiny and human destiny belong inseparably together.[15]

What we encounter in the detached God of classical theism is a profoundly anti-social and anti-ecological notion of transcendence. As we noted above, it offers us a model of God, an "eternal presence" located vertically up above, and as such, unrelated to earth, the body, and mortality. It is a concept of God that consequently promotes a spirituality of escape from the body and earth. For once, Hebrew and Greek notions of perfection coincide in embracing the same fallacy. In the classic Hebrew conception, procreational potency is denied to the female and earth, and entirely appropriated by a male divine power standing above and outside the earth. Earth and women remain completely passive, mere receptacles for the form-implanting male energy.

---

15. Ibid., 38–39, 105–20.

But this is also Aristotle's view. For him, the procreative seed and form derive from the active male principle, and matter and woman are purely passive and receptive. Aquinas follows this tradition in believing that women are deficient males, only partly ensouled. As we said above, the dominant Christian pedagogy of redemption has been an earth-fleeing spirituality, one that subtly discredits the natural and lends itself to ecological abuse. We have been taught to look away from the mutable world's cycles of birth, decay, and death, and to ascend to a disembodied state. Needless to say, this is not a spirituality that encourages care for the earth.

What is needed here is revision of the classic notion of God, beginning perhaps with a reflection on the religious inadequacy of a notion of perfection that would entail the absence of relation and receptivity. Does it make religious sense to speak of a God who is unrelated to the world, or a God who cannot be affected by anything occurring in the world — a God, in other words, whom we would have to call supremely autistic or narcissistic, totally wrapped up in himself? Would it not make more sense to conceive of perfection, as process philosophers do, as being unsurpassably related to all events, as well as unsurpassably receptive to all events? This would certainly appear to be the kind of God revealed in the pages of the Bible.

We can get some conceptual corrective from the process cosmology of Alfred North Whitehead and Charles Hartshorne, and the first advantage of this reworking of traditional theism is that it is hospitable to evolution.[16] God is understood as the primordial source and stimulus for cosmic evolution. God is the creative eros, the inspiration and attractive "lure" at the bottom of things, that arouses the world to the evolutionary movement toward life, consciousness, and civilization. God is the "force" behind the world's order, but also the creativity behind the emergent novelty and contrast that makes for beauty and the intrinsic value of all things. In this conception, it is the divine bounty and dynamism that perpetually intensify beauty, and the human role in this ongoing process is to contribute to the adventure of enhancing the beauty of the universe.

The second important aspect of process cosmology is the conviction that what happens in the material world happens also to God. God is unsurpassably related to all events in the cosmos and affected by them. In contrast to the Greek notion of a perfection untouched by time, tragedy, and suffering, this notion of an unsurpassably related

---

16. See Charles Hartshorne, *A Natural Theology for Our Time* (LaSalle, Ill.: Open Court, 1967); also *The Divine Relativity: A Social Conception of God* (New Haven: Yale University Press, [1948] 1964).

God approaches the biblical idea of a God who fully participates in the life and sufferings of the world. As John Haught puts it,

> Unlike some traditional theologies that locate God "up there" totally apart from the world, process theology maintains that God's being, without in any way jeopardizing the divine transcendence, actually includes the world. God is not a reality that we reach only by leaving this world behind. Rather, God is the reality into which all events in the universe are finally synthesized and preserved as they aim toward a continually more expansive beauty. Thus we may say that the conservation and prolongation of nature's beauty actually contribute intensity and beauty to God's life. God is internally affected, indeed changed, by what happens in the cosmic process. When nature suffers, God suffers.[17]

Technically, this is called panentheism (God-in-all, all-in-God). God is eternal, but it is an eternity that is inclusive of, rather than separate from, temporality. God takes in all the events of the world's temporality, including its suffering, weaving them into the fabric of his own everlasting life and thereby preserving their value forever. In Whitehead's own words, God is the "tender care that nothing be lost."[18]

Correlatively, the reality of God can also be relocated — from the One who dwells vertically "up above" to One who comes into the world from out of the realm of the future, from "up ahead." This is a common theme among Catholic and Protestant theologians in recent decades. Jesuit paleontologist and theologian Pierre Teilhard de Chardin was famous for claiming that evolution requires us to imagine God not as driving or determining events from behind or from the past, but as drawing the world from up ahead toward the future. Only a God who functions out of the future, he insisted, can satisfy us in an evolutionary world.[19] Karl Rahner, arguably the most influential Catholic theologian of the twentieth century, spoke of God as the "Absolute Future."[20] Protestant theologian Jürgen Moltmann consistently reminds us that in the biblical view the word "God" means, first of

---

17. John F. Haught, *The Promise of Nature: Ecology and Cosmic Purpose* (Mahwah, N.J.: Paulist Press, 1993), 35. For an overview of process theology, see John B. Cobb Jr. and David Griffin, *Process Theology: An Introductory Exposition* (Philadelphia: Westminster Press, 1976). For the implications of process cosmology for ecology, see Charles Birch and John B. Cobb Jr., *The Liberation of Life* (Cambridge: Cambridge University Press, 1981).

18. Alfred North Whitehead, *Process and Reality: An Essay on Cosmology* (New York: Harper Torchbooks, 1960), 525.

19. Pierre Teilhard de Chardin, *Christianity and Evolution*, trans. René Hague (New York: Harcourt Brace, 1969), 240.

20. Karl Rahner, *Theological Investigations*, vol. 6, trans. Karl and Boniface Kruger (Bal-

all, "Future," and his colleagues Wolfhart Pannenberg and Ted Peters refer to God as the "Power of the Future."[21]

Once again, an evolutionary perspective provides theology with a reason to reconceptualize our understanding of transcendence in a way that actually corresponds to the God of biblical revelation. For the God of the exodus from Egypt is a God of the future who "goes before" the people and leads them out of bondage to liberty. Accordingly, the same promise that brought Israel into being must now be conceived as encompassing the whole of creation. As Second Isaiah and the Book of Revelation have it, God is the one who "makes all things new" (Isa. 43:19; Rev. 21:5).

Causality vs. Vision

The Bible relates fundamentally to faith, hope, and vision, whereas science, being preoccupied with established fact, is locked into the past. As Moltmann puts it, eschatology (theory about the final direction or end of all things) is not a merely ancillary part of Christian faith. It is at the center and heart of that faith.

> From first to last, and not merely in the epilogue, Christianity is eschatology, is hope, forward looking and forward moving, and therefore also revolutionizing and transforming the present. The eschatological is not one element of Christianity, but it is the medium of Christian faith as such, the key in which everything in it is set, the glow that suffuses everything here in the dawn of an expected new day.... Hence eschatology cannot really be only a part of Christian doctrine. Rather, the eschatological outlook is characteristic of all Christian proclamation, of every Christian existence and of the whole Church. There is therefore only one real problem in Christian theology...the problem of the future.[22]

---

timore: Helicon, 1969), 59–68. See also Rahner, *Foundations of Christian Faith,* trans. William V. Dych (New York: Seabury Press, 1978), 178–95.

21. See Jürgen Moltmann, *The Coming of God: A Christian Eschatology* (Minneapolis: Augsburg Fortress, 1996). Also Wolfhart Pannenberg, *Faith and Reality,* trans. John Maxwell (Philadelphia: Westminster Press, 1977), 58–59; Ted Peters, *God — The World's Future: Systematic Theology for a New Era,* 2d ed. (Minneapolis: Fortress Press, 2000).

22. Jürgen Moltmann, *Theology of Hope,* trans. James Leitch (New York: Harper & Row, 1967), 16. Does this future orientation make for ecological problems? A number of pro-environment theorists certainly think so. For instance, the Catholic "geologian" Thomas Berry argues that the biblical motif of promise is not helpful in grounding an ecological ethic (see Berry, *Dream of the Earth* [San Francisco: Sierra Club, 1988], 114–15). Following the historian Arnold Toynbee, Berry claims on the contrary that Western culture derives its obsessive dream of progress from the biblical vision of the eschaton, and it is this vision that has made our culture so impatient with the present, so manipulative of nature, so eager to sacrifice what we see before us on the altar of our destructive futurism.

Let me elaborate on this statement by contrasting, as the literary critic Northrop Frye did, science's search for causality with the Bible's concern with faith and vision.

The most important single fact about the Hebrew Bible, argues Frye, is that "the people who produced it were never lucky at the game of empire." The biblical vision is typically looking at the social structure from the bottom up, from the vantage point of the "have-nots." Except at rare intervals under David and Solomon, temporal power lay in heathen hands; consequently "history became reshaped into a future-directed history, in which the overthrow of the heathen empires and the eventual recognition of Israel's unique historical importance are the main events, though events still to come."[23]

For the Christian the great events of the Old Testament — Exodus, Sinai, Exile, and Restoration — find their full meaning in the story of Jesus of Nazareth. For Jews, the full meaning is still to manifest itself, when the Messianic age dawns. Underlying this future-directed mode of thought, says Frye, is a theory of history or of historical process. The Bible assumes that history is one-directional and irreversible. It assumes that history has a point, that there is some meaning to it, and sooner or later some event or series of events will occur which will disclose what that meaning is. In biblical terms, the event which suddenly reveals the meaning of the past — like the climax of a dramatic play — becomes the fulfillment of what has happened previously. The roots of Western culture's distinctive confidence that history is going somewhere, says Frye, lie in the Bible.

> Our modern confidence in historical process, our belief that despite apparent confusion, even chaos, in human events, nevertheless those events are going somewhere and indicating something, is probably a legacy of Biblical typology: at least I can think of no other source for this tradition.[24]

The contrast with causal thinking could not be more striking. Causal thinking insists on staying within the same dimension of time. The causes must lie in the same temporal plane as their effects, or they will be rejected out of hand. If one ascribes an illness, for example, to the will of God or the action of a magic spell, this is not considered causal thinking. In contrast, biblical stories often point to future events that transcend time, so that, as Frye has it, "they contain a vertical lift as well as a horizontal move forward."

---

23. Frye, *The Great Code,* 83.
24. Ibid., 81.

The metaphorical kernel of this is the experience of waking up from a dream, as when Joyce's Stephen Dedalus speaks of history as a nightmare from which he is trying to awake. When we wake up from sleep, one world is simply abolished and replaced by another. This suggests a clue to the origin of [biblical] typology: it is essentially a revolutionary form of thought and rhetoric. We have revolutionary thought whenever the feeling "life is a dream" becomes geared to an impulse to awaken from it.[25]

But the difference between visionary and causal thinking has an even more remarkable feature. Causal thinkers confront a mass of data that they suppose they can understand only by taking them as effects, after which they search for their prior causes. The crucial point to note here is that the movement of causal thinking is essentially backward — to the past. As in Plato's view of knowledge as anamnesis or recollection, the new is recognized as something to be assimilated to the old, to what we have observed as having already happened. For the sake of clarity in exposition, this movement backward can be reversed, proceeding forward from cause to effect, but it is clear that in the order of discovery one moves from effect (in the present) back to cause (in the past). Thus, in the case of some evolutionary novelty, classical science always tries to eliminate the novelty by reducing it to the impersonal unfolding of a mathematical simplicity that occurred in the dim past.

Scientific predictability only appears to violate the rule of thinking backward, not forward. But it doesn't. Future phenomena are predictable precisely because they are mechanical or behave mechanically. That is, they perform in a redundant or repetitive manner. The pattern is cyclical and set in stone, as it were, a repeat of what has happened before. And hence one can assimilate the new to the old, as with astronomical predictions of an eclipse or the reappearance of a comet. What classical science is constantly reinforcing is the idea that there is nothing new under the sun. For scientific materialists, as we just said, all the diversity of life that we now see on the planet is reducible to some simple relationships in the remote past. The complex hierarchies and wholes of the present world are dissolved into their constituent parts: quarks, atoms, chemicals, genes. The complex systems are said to represent nothing but the reshuffling of the same lifeless elements that have virtually always been there. According to this reading of Darwinism, argues John Haught, the entire cosmic process, including the story of life-forms and mind, "rather than being evidence of nature's

---

25. Ibid., 82–83.

openness to the arrival of genuine novelty, is only the explication of what was fully latent already in lifeless matter from the time of cosmic beginnings." He continues:

> Evolutionary materialism locates the source and substance of life's diversity in the purely physical determinism that, allegedly, has led, step by fateful step, out of the dead causal past to the present state of living nature in all its profusion of complexity. Such a metaphysics no more allows for the emergence of real novelty in evolution than does a religious metaphysics fixated on the eternal present.[26]

Where classic theism implicitly denies novelty by saying that everything has been determined "from above" or is merely a weak reflection of a lost eternal and perfect world, scientific materialism suppresses novelty by saying that all present and future states of the universe were virtually given in full in the remote cosmic past, say in the first three seconds after the big bang. In neither standpoint is there room for the emergence of real novelty, and "so both standpoints imply that the future will be inherently barren."[27]

But evolution, if it is to be granted any significance, is decidedly not the recycling of the past or some second-rate imitation of Platonic ideas in another realm of perfection. It is something definitively new, something unheard of before, in its own right. When Darwin said that variation occurs by chance, he was in effect saying that real novelty remains an utter conundrum, something unexplained and irreducible to the past. "Ironically," says Haught,

> the hierarchical cultivation of an eternal present [as in mystical breakthrough from a supernatural realm of perfection] locks hands under the table with modern scientific materialism in neutralizing the dimension of futurity to which the promise of evolution awakens us once again. Far removed as they may be from each other, materialism and supernatural theism both share a remoteness from the implicit metaphysics of the ancient Hebrews and the early Christians, which gave primacy to what is yet to come. If they were true to the spirit of their father Abraham, followers of biblical faiths would once again seek to live out of the future. From this future, they would anticipate the arrival of God and the new creation of the cosmos.[28]

---

26. Haught, *God after Darwin*, 86.
27. Ibid., 95.
28. Ibid., 187.

The restoration of a harmonic relationship to nature, please note, lies very much at the center of biblical futurology. "What does the Bible look like," asked Frye, "when we try to see it statically, as a single and simultaneous metaphor cluster?" His answer:

> We are perhaps not too surprised to discover that there is a factor in it that will not fit a static vision. Ordinarily, if we "freeze" an entire mythology, it turns into a cosmology.... But what the Bible gives us is not so much a cosmology as a vision of upward metamorphosis, of the alienated relation of men to nature transformed into a spontaneous and effortless life — not effortless in the sense of lazy or passive, but in the sense of being energy without alienation.[29]

But what is "upward metamorphosis" but a fancy term for evolution? And what does Frye have in mind by the phrase "energy without alienation"? It is the dream of Eden, wherein human beings and animals dwell together in complete peace. But his arcadian dream is projected into the future. It becomes the end time, the "fullness of time," the Day of Judgment when humans will have stopped their destructive behavior and it becomes clear what kind of world we are really in. The real world lies beyond time, but can be attained only by a process that goes on in time. As T. S. Eliot put it, only through time is time conquered. The prophet Isaiah gives an intimation of what this fulfillment will look like:

> The wolf also shall dwell with the lamb, and the leopard shall lie down with the kid; and the calf and the young lion and the fatling together; and a little child shall lead them....
>
> They shall not hurt nor destroy in all my holy mountain: for the earth shall be full of the knowledge of the Lord as the waters cover the sea. (Isa. 11:6, 9)

To be sure, God is rock-like, and reflected as such in nature's stability. But to the prophets, the Holy One is primarily the source of the new and barely imagined. Empirical events such as the exodus or the return from exile only foreshadow what is to come. The Holy One of Israel is the God of unguessed novelty, who holds out the promise of turning a barren wasteland into a land running with rivers. God's promise, it is clear, extends to all of the created universe.

> Behold, I am doing a new thing; now it springs forth, do you not perceive it? I will make a way in the wilderness and rivers

---

29. Frye, *The Great Code*, 76.

in the desert. The wild beasts will honor me, the jackals and the ostriches; for I give water in the wilderness, rivers in the desert, to give drink to my chosen people, the people whom I formed for myself that they might declare my praise. (Isa. 43:19–21)

As this text attests, God's promises are not exclusively for his "chosen people"; they are for the "jackals and ostriches" as well. The promise here echoes the great primordial covenant with Noah, wherein God remembers not simply the stalwart Noah and his family, but "every living thing, and all the cattle that were with him in the ark" (Gen. 8:1; also 9:16).

This means that, through faith, the whole of nature can be interpreted as a great promise. Again, as John Haught says, the implication is that we can treasure nature,

not simply for its sacramental transparency to God but also because it carries in its present perishable glory the seeds of a final eschatological flowering. Hence, by allowing the embryonic future to perish now at the hands of our own ecological carelessness and selfishness we not only violate nature's sacramental bearing but also turn away from the promise that lies embedded in all of creation.[30]

---

30. Haught, *God after Darwin*, 151.

NINE

A Physics of Promise

Certainly nature seems to exult in abounding radicality, extremism, anarchy. If we were to judge nature by its common sense or likelihood, we wouldn't believe the world existed. In nature, improbabilities are the one stock in trade. The whole creation is one lunatic fringe....No claims of any and all revelation could be so far-fetched as a single giraffe.

— ANNIE DILLARD, *Pilgrim at Tinker's Creek*

The unpredictable and the predetermined unfold together to make everything the way it is. It's how nature creates itself, on every scale, the snowflake and the snowstorm. It makes me so happy. To be at the beginning again, knowing almost nothing...the ordinary-sized stuff which is our lives, the things people write poetry about — clouds-daffodils-waterfalls-and what happens in a cup of coffee when the cream goes in — these things are full of mystery, as mysterious as the heavens were to the Greeks. We're better at predicting events at the edge of the galaxy or inside the nucleus of an atom than whether it'll rain on auntie's garden party three Sundays from now. Because the problem turns out to be different. We can't even predict the next drip from a dripping tap when it gets irregular. Each drip sets up the conditions for the next, the smallest variation blows predictions apart, and the weather is unpredictable the same way, will always be unpredictable. When you push the numbers through the computer you can see it on the screen. The future is disorder. A door like this cracked open five or six times since we got up on our hind legs. It's the best possible time to be alive, when almost everything you thought you knew is wrong. — TOM STOPPARD, *Arcadia*

In the classical view — and here we include quantum mechanics and relativity — laws of nature express certitudes. When appropriate initial conditions are given, we can predict with certainty the future, or "retrodict" the past. Once instability is included, this is no longer the case, and the meaning of the laws of nature changes radically, for they now express possibilities or probabilities. — ILYA PRIGOGINE, *The End of Certainty*

What are we to make of our relationship to the cosmos? What is our role and function within the big scheme of things? That is the larger question and theme of these chapters. Obviously, the answer that we give to such a question hinges on what science has to tell us about this greater scheme of things. For in our culture science holds a virtual monopoly over the interpretation of what sort of sign nature provides — whether one of hope, of despair, or of something in between like stoic resignation.

Is the universe for us or against us — or merely indifferent? What sign does it give? Do we have reason to hope? Or reason to despair? Without exception, all the great religions of the world announce, in one way or another, that the universe (or the Creator of the universe) is for us and with us. There is therefore hope, and as we saw above, in the Jewish and Christian traditions, that hope is embedded in the promissory character of the material world itself. A long and respectable scientific tradition, on the other hand, reads things differently — as if the universe were against us. As Alfred North Whitehead once remarked,

> The pilgrim fathers of the scientific imagination as it exists today, are the great tragedians of ancient Athens, Aeschylus, Sophocles, Euripides. Their vision of fate, remorseless and indifferent, urging a tragic incident to its inevitable issue, is the vision possessed by science. Fate in Greek Tragedy becomes the order of nature in modern thought.[1]

Is science, then, on a collision course with a religious vision of the cosmos? Depending on whom you listen to, it can seem that way. Reports from the scientific front, one can agree, are at least conflicting or ambiguous — as conflicting and ambiguous as nature itself. Our present cosmos of complex galaxies and at least one habitable solar system, we are told, has evolved from the hot plasma of a big bang some 15 billion years ago. Things have constantly metamorphosized, going from simple to complex, from utter flux to increased states of organization, from quarks to conscious minds. One can cite amazing examples of altruism and self-organization that suggest that the uni-

---

1. Alfred North Whitehead, *Science and the Modern World* (New York: Macmillan, 1926), 15.

verse is oriented to maintaining life. Take the earth itself, which lives off a constant flux of energy and matter radiated from the sun. Since the beginnings of life on the planet it is estimated that the sun's output of energy has increased by 30 percent, which should have been enough to fry every living thing into a cinder. But no, it hasn't happened. The earth seems to have maintained a relatively constant temperature, in effect compensating in some magical way for the upsurge in the sun's heat. How has this been accomplished? Atmospheric chemist James Lovelock hypothesizes that starting with the primitive blue-green algae, living systems cooperate on a massive scale to keep things hospitable to life. Lovelock argues that through a complicated set of internal feedback loops linking plants and rocks, animals and atmospheric gases, micro-organisms and the oceans, the earth operates like a single cell, regulating its own climate, the chemical composition of the atmosphere, and the salinity of its oceans. The planet acts holistically, that is to say, it acts as a self-organizing, autopoietic system not reducible to its component parts.[2]

On the other hand, the second law of thermodynamics suggests that the universe is dead set against the experiment of life. It tells us that the cosmos's quality of organized energy is degrading, running inexorably downhill toward a final state of random disorganization. The all too familiar and unsatisfactory way of dealing with this ambiguity, and others like it, has been to take a dualistic stance. We read our favorite novels, listen to Bach or Brubeck, and reassure our children when they awake with nightmare dreams, but meanwhile this world of human interest has no connection with the world that the natural sciences reveal to us. We split ourselves down the middle, confining human values and concerns to intrapsychic space, thus subjectivizing them and leaving the realm of cold "fact" to the scientists. We keep two separate accounts, one for the dynamics of the physicist's energies and another for the dynamics of the human life-world. In short, we accept the rule of Cartesian dualism, keeping the affairs of science in one compartment and the doings of the human spirit in another compartment — and there is no connection between them. Historically, those who follow Immanuel Kant have tended to accede to such double accounting. Some of us, however, reject this solution; we want our spirituality grounded in the great outdoors, in the same universe of hard fact that modern science investigates.

---

2. See James Lovelock, *Gaia: A New Look at Life on Earth* (New York: Oxford University Press, 1984).

Cosmic Pessimism

Many scientists advocate a kind of cosmic pessimism. The universe, they keep declaring, is utterly "alien" or openly "hostile" to the human species. So far as anyone can reliably say, it is "sound and fury signifying nothing." Classical physics, as we saw in chapters 3 and 4, offers a clue, a sign, that the universe is purely redundant, going nowhere; material nature sounds like a stuck, monotone telephone signal. The sign, one might say, is of death — of no message at all.

Face it, the late French biologist Jacques Monod once insisted, the great cosmos is deaf to our music, as indifferent to our hopes as it is to our sufferings and crimes. Human beings, he sternly exhorted, are aliens in the universe and ought to cast off their infantile dreams, their impetuous hopes.

> Man must at last finally awake from his millenary dream; and in doing so, awake to his total solitude, his fundamental isolation. Now does he at last realize that, like a gypsy, he lives on the boundary of an alien world.[3]

Nobel laureate Steven Weinberg essentially agrees. He is all for the dialogue between science and religion, but sees no possibility of its being a "constructive" dialogue. "One of the great achievements of science," he writes, "has been, if not to make it impossible for intelligent people to be religious, then at least to make it possible for them not to be religious."[4] Citing pogroms, crusades, jihads, and the harm done by religious enthusiasms over the ages, he finds the moral influence of religion, on balance, to have been "awful." And the more he studies the cosmos, the more he finds it "pointless." While jetting over the great plains at an altitude of thirty thousand feet, Weinberg summed up his understanding of things by saying:

> Below, the earth looks very soft and comfortable — fluffy clouds here and there, snow turning pink as the sun sets, roads stretching straight across the country from one town to another. It is hard to realize that this all is just a tiny part of an overwhelmingly hostile universe. It is even harder to realize that this present universe has evolved from an unspeakably unfamiliar early condition, and faces a future extinction of endless cold or intolerable heat. The

---

3. Jacques Monod, *Chance and Necessity* (New York: Vintage Books, 1972), 172–73.
4. Steven Weinberg, "A Designer Universe?" in the *New York Review of Books*, October 21, 1999, 48.

more the universe seems comprehensible, the more it also seems pointless.[5]

Many distinguished scientists still see it this way. On the basis of his reading of evolutionary biology, British zoologist Richard Dawkins assures us that from behind the scenes, our "selfish genes" govern all our strategic decisions in life, as they govern the lottery of evolution itself. "We are survival machines — robot vehicles blindly programmed to preserve the selfish molecules known as genes."[6] The world disclosed by evolution, Dawkins insists, is an amoral, if not immoral, story of eat-or-be-eaten. It is not at all the kind of world one would expect were it designed by the benevolent God worshipped by Jews and Christians. Think of the cannibalism of blackheaded gulls, which congregate in large colonies with nests only a few feet apart. When the chicks hatch they are small, defenseless, and easy to swallow. When one gull leaves the nest, it is common for a another to save itself the trouble of having to go out and catch a fish by gobbling up its neighbor's chicks, swallowing them whole. Female praying mantises exhibit a similar appetite for their mates. They are carnivorous and normally eat smaller insects such as flies, but they will attack almost anything that moves. During mating, the male creeps up on the female, mounts her, and copulates. But if the female gets half a chance, she will devour the male, beginning by biting off his head, either as he approaches, after he mounts her, or after they part.

The world ruled by the materialist suppositions of chance mutation and natural selection, Dawkins says,

> would be neither evil nor good in intention. It would manifest no intentions of any kind. In a universe of physical forces and genetic replication, some people are going to get hurt, other people are going to get lucky, and you won't find any rhyme or reason in it, nor any justice. The universe that we observe has precisely the properties we should expect if there is, at bottom, no design, no purpose, no evil, and no good, nothing but blind, pitiless indifference.[7]

As Dawkins describes the process of evolution, life occurs by means of a cruel and wasteful crapshoot in a chillingly heartless cosmos. For him,

---

5. See Steven Weinberg, *The First Three Minutes*, updated edition (New York: Basic Books, 1993), 154.

6. Richard Dawkins, preface to 1976 edition of *The Selfish Gene* (New York: Oxford University Press, 1989), v. Cf. also Dawkins, *The Blind Watchmaker* (London: Heinemann, 1986), 126.

7. Richard Dawkins, *River Out of Eden* (New York: HarperCollins, 1995), 132–33.

Darwinism not only provides a superior explanation for evolution, which renders the intervention of God otiose; natural selection also constitutes something of a scandal incompatible with biblical theism. No benevolent God, he believes, would have concocted (or "designed") such a harsh, wasteful, and might-makes-right system for growing a simple world into a complex one. (Biologists estimate that since the origins of life, some 99 percent of living species have become extinct.)

But if Darwinism doesn't rule out God, many a scientist thinks the second law of thermodynamics ought to do the job. Thermodynamics gives no grounds for hope in a good outcome; rather, it portrays great nature as running out of steam, as the carrier of death that will inevitably devour all creatures, including us and all our little victories. Nature is thus our invincible adversary, the biggest competitor of all. In the end this enemy is bound to win out over our paltry efforts and wishful thinking by killing us. The second law of thermodynamics may be kept at bay for a while, but it will have the last word in the cosmos.

The central insight of the second law of thermodynamics is this: With the elapse of time, the organized, kinetic energy available for mechanical work — whether electrical, chemical, or thermal — inevitably has to be paid for in waste, irretrievable structural dissipation, decay, and aging. In 1850 Rudolph Clausius labeled this erosion of usable energy "entropy," which he then formulated as the second law of thermodynamics: "The entropy of the world endeavors to increase." That is, over time organized energy wears down, loses its oomph. Whether artificial, inorganic, or organic, machines and bodies that contain energy wear down, age, and decay. Mountains erode, metals rust, wood rots, hot coffee cools, snowmen melt — things die. And these processes are not reversible: Broken crockery does not mend itself, Niagara Falls does not suddenly run backwards, death is not retractable. What such facts translate into is an irreversible process, a one-way trend and transition from organization to disorder — or what physicists call thermal "equilibrium," a chill state of undifferentiated uniformity or maximum disorganization. The universe as a whole, it is said, is headed in this direction, to a so-called "heat death." Thus it is no exaggeration, claim scientists like Monod and Weinberg, to say that the universe as a whole seems hostile to the experiment of life.

Not only are we humans mortal, but so is our solar system. The minor yellow star about which our planet gravitates, which has been shining for some 5 billion years, will — in about another 5 billion years — eventually burn up all its hydrogen fuel. Thereupon it will enter the next stage of stellar evolution, turning into a grossly swollen "red giant," extending beyond the earth's orbit in the solar system and burning up any life remaining here before finally collapsing into what is known as a "white dwarf." That will be the end of us — unless, before that time, we have immigrated to a different solar system with a longer lasting star at its center.

As for the cosmos as a whole, it's a tug-of-war between the expansive forces released by the big bang, propelling matter apart, and the contractive force of gravity, pulling matter together. Are the two forces evenly balanced? Or does one have an edge? Recent evidence suggests that the universe may expand forever, in which case the galaxies will continue to fly apart. Within each of the galaxies, gravity may score a local victory, causing them to condense into gigantic black holes. Over immense periods of time these will ultimately decay into low-grade radiation — meaning that some solar systems, perhaps whole galaxies, will end in a long, drawn out whimper.

If, on the other hand, our current belief in expansion proves wrong, gravity will cause the universe to halt and reverse its flight outward. Galaxies will come flying back together and what began as a big bang will end in the cosmic melting pot of a "big crunch." Either way, carbon-based life appears to be a transient episode in the history of the cosmos. Does this condemn the universe to purposelessness, as Monod and Weinberg conclude? The error these thinkers make is to confuse a final physical state with the question of whether the universe has a purpose or not. These are distinct issues. Knowing that I am subject to the second law of thermodynamics and will die in no way prevents me from having worthwhile purposes.[8] And so for the universe as a whole: It may perish with a pop or a whimper, but along the way it may realize many worthwhile purposes.

Ironically, scientists of the cosmic pessimist school find the field of their investigations, great nature itself, an unwelcoming, alien, and hostile terrain, if not precisely evil, then at least something profoundly foreign and estranging. In this regard, Monod, Weinberg, and Dawkins, it seems to me, are virtually indistinguishable from Cartesian dualists. For Dawkins, nature confronts us with "pitiless indifference." Nature, Monod asserts, is "alien." Weinberg goes further: Nature is

---

8. As British philosopher Keith Ward puts it, "There is no reason to think that this final physical state of the universe is the purpose for its existence, any more than my final physical state, my corpse, is the purpose of my life. If I have purposes, they will be achieved, not at the very end of my life, but at some point during my life. When I die, I can, if I am lucky, die knowing that I have achieved my purposes. If the universe has a purpose, it will lie not at its physical end, but in the creation and contemplation of worthwhile states during the course of its existence. If such states come to exist, then even if they pass away and cease to be — as they will — the purpose of the universe will have been achieved." See Keith Ward, *God, Chance and Necessity* (Oxford, England: Oneworld Publications, 1996), 50–51.

positively "hostile," the enemy of the human experiment. Question: Why, given these alienating characterizations, should we care about serving or preserving the physical world? (In Part II, chapters 3 and 4, I have already given my reply to this question.)

In this context, the human mind appears as a freak event, a stranger in a strange, mechanical desert — precisely as Descartes held nature to be. Humans come across, then, as cosmically homeless; we do not really belong here. We are nothing but atomized individuals. Running through the cosmic pessimism of Monod, Weinberg, and Dawkins is the tacit fallacy of reducing wholes to their component parts. They implicitly assert that a human being is nothing but a collection of cells, which themselves are nothing but bits of DNA, which in turn are nothing but strings of atoms — and therefore they conclude that life has no significance. This is muddle-headed reasoning, as if to say that the equations of subatomic physics could possibly replace or substitute for what the biochemist, at a more complex level, has to tell us about the function of cellular ribosomes in the production of the animal body's proteins and enzymes. It ignores the distinction between different conceptual levels that correspond to different levels of organization. Paul Davies points out the error:

> In the case of living systems, nobody would deny that an organism is a collection of atoms. The mistake is to suppose that it is nothing but a collection of atoms. Such a claim is as ridiculous as asserting that a Beethoven symphony is nothing but a collection of notes or that a Dickens novel is nothing but a collection of words. The property of life, the theme of a tune or the plot of a novel are what have been called "emergent" qualities. They emerge only at the collective level of structure, and are simply meaningless at the component level. The component description does not contradict the holistic description; the two points of view are complementary, each valid at its own level.[9]

The failure to distinguish these different and complementary levels of description has the ironic effect of disconnecting human beings from earth. Loosed from tradition and communal bonds, shut out indeed from nature or any kinship with nature, cosmic pessimists are forced to the conclusion that human beings do not share any community of interest with other creatures of the earth, either animate or inanimate. On this account we are on our own, left to pursue the selfish

---

9. Paul Davies, *God and the New Physics* (New York: Simon and Schuster Touchstone Books, 1983), 62.

self-interest of our genes by battling solo against brute necessity and blind chance in a perversely unfair and heartless universe. Cut off from nature (and nature's God), our ethics finds no root or grounding in the nature of things.

Does the modern Western ethos tend to degenerate into hypertrophic introspection and narcissistic navel-gazing? If it does, I believe that part of the reason is that the so-called "hard sciences" mislead us, as Monod, Weinberg, and Dawkins would mislead us, into thinking that great nature demands that we seal ourselves up within the prison-solitude of our own hearts. And what is so disturbing about this self-portrait is that it disconnects human destiny from the fate of the earth and the cosmos. As such it is a prescription for political impotence and carelessness about our natural environment.

In order to ground an ecological ethic, we need to get potency, time, and the subjunctive mood back into nature and the physics that tells its story. How do irreversible time, possibility, and promise reenter physics? Or, to put the matter more directly, how is it that the laws of physics become open to the unpredictable future and hospitable to the experiment of life? The future-orientation and promissory character of nature reenters physics, I will try to show, through randomness, chance, and irregularity. The key is not the dominance of the past or the redundant order of classical physics; the key is nature's indeterminacy, its openness to the incalculable future.

Arrows of Time: Darwinian vs. Thermodynamics

Classical physics, as we have observed, had understood matter as essentially inert and uncreative. In defiance of the very etymology of the word "physics," the physical world no longer gave birth. Physics focused exclusively on redundant patterns and effectively denied the reality of irreversible time. Throughout the nineteenth century, physics remained the solitary holdout in this regard. For starting with geology and running up through biology and the life sciences, the big intellectual event of the late eighteenth and early nineteenth century was the discovery of time and history. This was the period, after all, when archeologists were digging up the ruins and artifacts of ancient cultures and, more to the point, when geologists were finding "deep time" in the form of primitive fossil remains — all of which was leading to the conclusion that the earth was much older than the four thousand years presupposed in the biblical accounts of creation.

In the last chapter we saw how time and possibility entered into biology and astrophysics. How, we may now ask, did time, generativity, and self-organization reenter into physics and chemistry? Physics began to seriously entertain the idea of the irreversibility of time with the nineteenth-century invention of the steam engine. It was the century of energy and the dynamo. Scientifically, that translated into the study of heat and its transformations — what is known as thermodynamics. Thermodynamics marked the shift from the laminar flows and geometrical trajectories of Newton's machines to the fiery physics of Fulton's steam engines and Bessemer's smelters. Fire freed matter from imprisonment in Newton's geometrical diagrams of fixed form. It melted all the straight edges, made matter vibrate, oscillate, and explode into clouds. Contingency, chance events, and chaos thus began to insinuate themselves into the fatalistic laws of classical physics. And this change in perspective would eventually open the door to the discovery of atomic and nuclear dissemination at the beginning of the twentieth century.

For physics, then, thermodynamics represented the transition to process thinking or historicity. It brought irreversible time into the equations. In a larger, cultural sense, thermodynamics also represented a study in paradox and contrast. On the one hand, it grounds our understanding of death and the fragility of life and the perishability of everything we human beings build in time. On the other hand, while tracking how things run down and die, thermodynamics also specifies the conditions whereby the tendency to disorder and death can be overcome. It is at once the science of both disorganization and organization, of dying and self-renewal.[10]

By measuring the qualitative state of the energy in a system — the movement from differentiated order to a less differentiated state — thermodynamics made it possible for physics to clearly distinguish the past from the future. The time symmetry assumed by classical physics was thus broken, and thermodynamics came up with an arrow of time. But it was not the promising time of the Hebrew prophets or of Darwinian evolution. Rather, it was the time of Hindu myth, of time running down. Time had a direction, but it was downhill, from order to disorder. In contrast, biological evolution is counter-entropic (or negentropic), manifesting a growth in structural organization running from atoms to molecules to simple cells to multicellular organisms. It discloses life as becoming more, not less, organized through time, as simple creatures evolved into more complex ones. In other words,

---

10. On the new science of chaos and complexity, see the essays in Robert John Russell, Nancey Murphy, and Arthur R. Peacocke, eds., *Chaos and Complexity: Scientific Perspectives on Divine Action* (Berkeley, Calif., and Vatican City: Center for Theology and the Natural Sciences and the Vatican Observatory, 1995).

the vast experiment in life that Darwin described appears, in thermo-dynamic terms, as a highly improbable freak of nature, something wholly unexpected.

Lying smack in the middle of nineteenth-century science, then, lay this huge conflict between two polarized arrows of time: (1) a cosmic time that seemingly runs universally downhill and (2) Darwinian bio-logical evolution that runs uphill, against the tide of entropy. We are left with two arrows of irreversible time running in opposite directions. How reconcile the two theories?

How does evolution happen? How does Darwinian evolution beat the odds of entropy and introduce novelty into the scheme of things? Does it violate the second law of thermodynamics? Somehow evade the logic of entropy? The answer is no; the second law is not abro-gated. The equation for the second law clearly indicates that entropy can be successfully opposed for periods of time by an input of en-ergy. If the system is closed in on itself, it will gradually and invariably degenerate; entropy always has the upper hand. But if the system is open to inputs of energy from outside, this free energy — the differ-ence between the energy input and the loss of energy to the system — works against the tide of entropy. In this way, counter-entropic organi-zation can temporarily gain the upper hand within a particular system, while the entropy outside the system increases. And thus Darwinian evolution and an upwardly directed arrow of time become possible in principle.

For all that, classical nineteenth-century thermodynamics provoked the feeling that, in the big picture, the universe was somehow set against the experiment of life, which would ultimately be swept away into the dark night of randomness. For a different view, we would have to await contemporary nonequilibrium thermodynamics and chaos theory, to which we now turn.

Open, Nonequilibrium Systems

Classical thermodynamics is very successful in dealing with closed dy-namical systems at or near thermal equilibrium (that is, very near utter stasis). In common usage, "equilibrium" denotes stable order. In a thermodynamic context, however, equilibrium represents just the opposite, a limit case of disorder or random activity without rhyme, reason, or pattern. In biological terms, maximum entropy or equi-librium translates into biological death. In cybernetic or information theory, this is called "noise" — again a limit case of total randomness or disorganization that bears little resemblance to the complex order of most chemical and biological systems. Similarly, at the opposite end of things, one must bear in mind that the "limit case" measure of order in thermodynamics is the perfect, static order of a crystal lattice, the repetitive pattern of wallpaper, or a stuck, monotone telephone signal — again, another sign of death, only this time from rigidity.

Classical thermodynamics is incapable of handling open dynamical systems far from equilibrium. Amazingly, it turns out that classical physics fails at what it boasted of being best at: its analysis of dynamic systems. The mistake was to have focused its attention too narrowly upon closed, integral systems. When attention turns to nonlinear, open, and chaotic systems, as it has in recent decades, the universe begins to appear quite different. The "tame" systems investigated by classical physics emerge as the exception to the rule; their dynamical behavior is untypical. Information theory reminds us that the idealized limit cases of classical thermodynamics — complete randomness (called thermal equilibrium) or rigid, crystalline order — leave out most of the actual complex systems of nature, which exist somewhere in between and involve both some random behavior (so-called "noise") and a degree of regularity or redundancy. In other words, they involve both chance and necessity.

The vast majority of natural systems, from the Andromeda constellation to an amoeba, are signal systems that exist far from equilibrium and far from the frozen structure of a crystal or of the repeated patterns of wallpaper. What we find are systems that exchange energy and matter with their environment; they are open to turbulence, fluctuation, and a degree of random chance. And yet by employing a standard code or set of rules that generate a wide variety of programs and messages, they maintain their identity against the flood of entropy.

An exclusively deterministic description of a physical system, which admittedly works for a pendulum or the structure of a crystal, no longer works for the vast majority of systems operating far from thermal equilibrium. For the most part, the utterly predictable behavior of static systems is to be found only in a laboratory or other very artificial environments. The typical dynamical system — physical, chemical, biological, or neurological — is almost never truly isolated or self-contained; it is, first, an "open" system exchanging energy and matter with its environment. Most natural systems are radically interconnected with their environments in a host of different ways. Moreover, such systems are rarely linear, moving only in straight trajectories. On the contrary, they are likely to be marked by nonlinear feedback loops, moving in all directions at once. This means that their behavior can be described only by considering the interaction of the components within the whole system involved and not simply, as reductionists would maintain, by the addition of the component elements. In other words, the sum of a nonlinear system is qualitatively different from its parts because its parts act on each other to produce complex and unpredictable behavior. Systems of this sort exhibit both complex order and turbulent instability. That is, they are marked not only by stability but by randomness and a chancy character that can only be specified in terms of probabilities. From this point of view the universe ceases to be an exclusively deterministic order; what we have instead is a stochastic order, that is, a set of probabilities or a vast array of gambles on the future.

Consider a supposedly well-determined system, the successive collisions of a collection of many billiard ball–like objects. The differential equations for such a simple system should have one single, clear solution. But they don't — for the simple reason that the outcome becomes progressively more complicated as each ball is deflected in a slightly different angle by each successive collision. Small differences in the angle of impact rapidly accumulate to produce exponentially diverging consequences. Or, to put it another way, small causes have giant and quite unpredictable effects. Molecules in a gas behave in similar ways. After only 10^{-10} seconds, fifty or more impacts have taken place for each molecule. Even after so few collisions, the outcome is so sensitive that it would be affected by the variation in the gravitational field due to an extra electron on the other side of the universe. Predictability and control are impossible. Instead of determinism we have open possibility. In short, the system becomes unstable, and what distinguishes its behavior is known as "sensitive dependence on initial conditions."

Sensitivity to initial conditions means that small fluctuations at the beginning of a process can amplify through positive feedback and lead to large-scale, unforeseeable consequences. This came to be known as the "butterfly effect" — the half-joking assertion that the air stirred by the flap of a butterfly's wing in Bali could lead in the next month to a hurricane over New York City.

Dissipative Structures and Emergent Complexity

Molecular biologists of the cosmic pessimist bent can match Steven Weinberg's cosmic pointlessness by moving in the opposite direction from numbing necessity. Their mantra is "pure chance." They end up so stressing the role of randomness in evolution that it becomes equivalent to irrationality. "Pure chance," says Jacques Monod, absolutely free but blind, at the very root of the stupendous edifice of evolution: this central concept of modern biology is no longer one among other possible or even conceivable hypotheses. It is today the sole conceivable hypothesis, the only one compatible with observation and tested fact.[11]

This is perfectly correct so far as it goes.

Where Monod oversteps the evidence, however, is when he goes on to raise chance to the level of a metaphysical principle, arguing that all the works of nature are the products of a perfect crapshoot, and therefore pointless, lacking any cosmic significance. It has been one of the great discoveries of modern physics that chance events at the microscopic, quantum level can translate at the large-scale macroscopic level into "lawful" behavior. So the occurrence of chance mutations at the molecular level does not preclude these events turning into law-like effects at the level of populations of organisms or whole ecosystems. In this sense chance events can feed into well-ordered, replicative, and interlocking mechanisms which constitute the continuity of a complex, living form. Once again, we have the difference between description at the elemental level of component parts (say subatomic structure) and description at higher, holistic levels of organization.

Molecular biologist Arthur R. Peacocke notes how chance and necessity are connected in the normal course of natural selection:

Instead of being daunted by the role of chance in genetic mutations as being the manifestation of irrationality in the universe, it would be more consistent with the observations to assert that the full gamut of the potentialities of living matter could be explored only through the agency of the rapid and frequent randomization which is possible at the molecular level of the DNA. In other words, the designation "chance" in this context refers to the multiple effects whereby the (very large) number of mutations is elicited that constitute the "noise," which, via an independent causal chain, the environment then selects for viability. This role of chance is what one would expect if the universe were so constituted as to be able to explore all the potential forms of organization of matter (both living and non-living) which it contains.[12]

---

11. Monod, *Chance and Necessity*, 110.
12. Arthur R. Peacocke, "Chance and Law in Irreversible Thermodynamics, Theoretical Biology, and Theology," in *Chaos and Complexity: Scientific Perspectives on Divine Action*, ed. Robert John Russell, Nancey Murphy, and Arthur R. Peacocke (Berkeley, Calif., and Vatican City: Center for Theology and the Natural Sciences and the Vatican Observatory, 1995), 127.

Over billions of years, that is to say, evolution wanders through the archive of every conceivable replicative structure and sequence of DNA, trying out countless possibilities until it chances upon what is adapted to various environments and thus able to survive and reproduce. In this sense the combination of chance mutation and natural selection is nature's way of exploring its own prodigious creativity.[13]

The classical attitude of someone like Weinberg or Dawkins, says Peacocke, puts us "in the position, as it were, of the audience before the pianist begins his extemporizations — there is the instrument, there is the range of available notes." But what the classical scientists have nothing to tell us about is "what tune is to be played and on what principle and in what forms is it to be developed."[14] Or, to use a computer analogy, the classical laws of physics give us the fixed hardware, but they do not tell us what software program nature will use.

Ilya Prigogine was awarded the Nobel Prize in 1977 for developing the nonequilibrium thermodynamics to fit unstable flow-through systems.[15] The phenomenon can be found across the board, in both nonliving and living systems. The earth itself is one such open network; plants and cells and stars are others. Prigogine calls such systems "dissipative structures" because they dissipate high levels of heat in the process of maintaining an equally high level of organization. Organization and random behavior coexist in them. They maintain themselves far from equilibrium, "at the edge of chaos," producing a high level of entropy in the form of waste transferred to the environment. Literally created by the continual flux of matter and energy that flows through them, they constitute eddies in the stream of energy in which they occur. Some systems like the carbon dioxide or hydrological cycles will be structurally stable, damping down any turbulence in their organization, and can be described in deterministic terms. Others will undergo phases of instability which turn out to be moments of unpredictable creativity. It is the very instability — in effect, the "noise" or chaos in the system — that provides the new principle of order, and thus a key to evolutionary change.

Think of all of the matter in the universe as so many islands of order in a vast sea of turbulence or entropic energy. Under the right

---

13. See Arthur Peacocke, "Biological Evolution — a Positive Theological Appraisal," in *Evolution and Molecular Biology: Scientific Perspectives on Divine Action*, ed. Robert John Russell, William R. Stoeger, S.J., and Francisco J. Ayala (Vatican City and Berkeley, Calif.: Vatican Observatory and Center for Theology and the Natural Sciences, 1998), 357–76.

14. Peacocke, "Chance and Law," 123.

15. Ilya Prigogine and Isabelle Stengers, *Order Out of Chaos: Man's New Dialogue with Nature* (New York: Bantam Books, 1984). See also James Gleick, *Chaos: Making a New Science* (New York: Viking, 1987).

conditions, the tides of the vast sea overtake these islands or pockets of order, causing fluctuations, disturbances in the field. The new science of chaos suggests that we have to think of these fluctuations as being the seeds of a deeper level of pattern. If the turbulence or chaos is not damped down by the reigning order, but rather amplified by feedback loops, the deeper pattern concealed in the turbulent "noise" will typically take over the whole system. The system then changes its whole structure to a new ordered state. This shift is called a "bifurcation point," a juncture of sudden turbulence out of which new forms often emerge. At a bifurcation point the system branches unpredictably, guided by what mathematicians call the "strange attractor." In ordinary dynamic systems — dynamics being the study of the way in which systems change — an attractor will either be a fixed point where a trajectory ends, as life ends in death, or it is a "limit cycle," the point at which the trajectory becomes periodic, as in the to-and-fro movement of a pendulum. But insofar as the components of a nonlinear system act on each other, their trajectories develop differently, the system's equilibrium is unstable, and the attractor works in indeterminant ways. A strange attractor is strange precisely because it leads to the phenomenon we have already referred to: a "sensitivity to initial conditions" that leads to widely variant and unpredictable consequences. In layman's terms the attractor is strange because it works mysteriously and is itself strangely complex.

One of the most common consequences will be a more complex new order that repeats itself at successive scales of magnitude, from the microscopic to the macroscopic. (What is known as "fractal geometry" has been developed to describe these jagged geometrical shapes.) At a bifurcation point, the path the system will take is wholly undecipherable — a mystery. But once the new organization is in place, the system normally settles down to a law-like steady state that is again describable in deterministic terms. The whole process exhibits the interplay of both necessity and chance, both determinism and unpredictable chaos. But the term "chaos" is misleading, for the instability conceals a new level of organization (as in the neo-Darwinian notion of genetic mutation).

What is an organism in this perspective? Michel Serres sums it up:

> First, [an organism] is an information and thermodynamic system. Indeed, it receives, stores, exchanges, and gives off both energy and information — in all forms, from the light of the sun to the flow of matter which passes through it (food, oxygen, heat, signals). This system is not at equilibrium, since thermodynamic

stability spells death for it, purely and simply. It is in a temporary
state of imbalance, and it tends as much as possible to maintain
this imbalance. It is hence subject to the irreversible time of the
second law, since it is dying. But it struggles against this time.... In
and by its imbalance, it is relatively stable. But here invariance
is unique: neither static nor homeostatic, it is homeorrhetic [the
same flowing]. It is a river that flows and yet remains stable in the
continual collapse of its banks.[16]

In classical thermodynamics, it looked as if the small enclave of
biotic organization on our planet was fighting a losing battle against the
whole trend of the universe toward heat death. The picture of life that is
emerging from the more recent thermodynamic analysis of dissipative
structures has a far different tenor. The stream as a whole continues to
move in the direction of increased entropy and disorder. But the eddies
that form within this flux of entropic energy use it to create new forms
of order. That is, the flux not only casts the shadow of decay and death
over every pocket of order in the universe; flux is simultaneously the
secret source of creativity and renewal. As Arthur Peacocke puts it,

> the movement of the stream itself inevitably generates, as it were,
> very large eddies within itself in which, far from there being a
> decrease in order, there is an increase first in complexity and then
> in something more subtle — functional organization. Now there
> could be no eddies without the stream in which they are located
> and so may it not be legitimate to regard this inbuilt potentiality
> for living organization that the entropic stream manifests as being
> its actual point — namely, why it is at all? There could be no self-
> consciousness and human creativity without living organization,
> and there could be no such living dissipative systems unless the
> entropic stream followed its general, irreversible course in time.
> Thus does the apparently decaying, randomizing tendency of the
> universe provide the necessary and essential matrix (*mot juste!*)
> for the birth of new forms — new life through death and decay of
> the old.[17]

We are no longer trapped in a repetitive order of cyclical time or a
cosmos running exclusively downhill. As Annie Dillard puts it,

---

16. Michel Serres, *Hermes: Literature, Science, and Philosophy*, ed. Josué V. Harari and
David F. Bell (Baltimore: Johns Hopkins University Press, 1982), 74.
17. Peacocke, "Chance and Law in Irreversible Thermodynamics, Theoretical Biology, and
Theology," in *Chaos and Complexity*, 143.

Certainly nature seems to exult in abounding radicality, extremism, anarchy. If we were to judge nature by its common sense or likelihood, we wouldn't believe the world existed. In nature, improbabilities are the one stock in trade. The whole creation is one lunatic fringe.[18]

The whole cosmos, it now turns out, is a tissue of improbabilities, of new possibilities spun paradoxically out of chaotic entropy. The past no longer decides everything that comes; the future is once again back at the forefront of physics. Nature, it begins to appear, is a great river of wild, generative energy within which are strewn islands of fragile order that form out of its chaos. As St. Paul intuited in Romans 8, this flood of energy strains toward the future and is seeded with promise. Why do we care about nature? Because it is "pregnant with the mysterious future."[19]

In this context life is not some anomalous, misbegotten freak or alien intruder. Life is to be expected, the outcome of a cosmos that is riddled with chance, with risky, self-organizing systems.

The Big Bang and the Anthropic Principle

But can we go farther in seeing the universe as promising and standing behind the experiment of life? This brings us to the so-called "anthropic principle."

The big bang is called a "singularity" because at an estimated 100 billion degrees Centigrade no stable particles could take shape, and thus none of the current laws of physics apply at that point. You also cannot imagine it as a TNT blast, starting from a definite center and then engulfing the preexisting container-space around it. No, it is more useful to imagine it as analogous to the first fortissimo chord of Beethoven's Fifth Symphony, occurring simultaneously everywhere — except that here you have to imagine that vibratory chord expanding, and as it does so, creating the "everywhere" of space-time itself, like a huge ballooning sound wave. Only as this initial plasmic wave cooled did the microscopic stuff of stars, planets, and DNA molecules begin to weave themselves out of the initial chaos. It was the beginning of an epic story.

---

18. Annie Dillard, *Pilgrim at Tinker Creek* (New York: Quality Paperback Book Club, 1990), 144.
19. John Haught, *The Promise of Nature* (Mahwah, N.J.: Paulist Press, 1993), 110; see also 88–125.

Big bang theories — and there are several — do not necessarily imply a Creator. Sadly, says Timothy Ferris, science as such can tell us nothing about God:

Cosmology presents us neither the faces of God nor the handwriting of God nor such thoughts as may occupy the mind of God. This does not mean that God does not exist, or that he did not create the universe, or universes. It means that cosmology offers no resolution to such questions.[20]

Nor will science reassure us about an absolute beginning of time. If physicist Hugh Everett is right, our universe may just be one of many existing simultaneously (the others being unknown to us). Or, if Andrei Linde of Stanford is right, our universe may have ballooned out of a prior universe; it could be just one of many in a sequence, like the branches of a tree spreading in different directions. And needless to say, the whole works of our present universe could be destined to collapse into a dense black hole, from which — who knows? — another universe might spring. (A few years ago two teams of astronomers concluded that the current evidence points to an ever-expanding universe.) Or, if Hawking's theory is correct and finite space-time has no boundary or edge, the universe may be completely self-contained.

But if big bang theories do not logically demand a Creator, they definitely do have implications for how mind or consciousness fits in to the general picture of nature. Up until very recently it has been almost standard scientific dogma that nature is mindlessly indifferent to the presence of beings who think, reason, plan, and comprehend. Consequently mindful creatures are viewed as cosmic anomalies — alien and absurd intruders into the big scheme of things.

But what if this is untrue? Suppose we really belong here, are in fact a part of nature's thrust, as nearly everyone before the seventeenth century claimed. What if the evolution of mind is what this universe has been about since the first three seconds? Curiously, physicists now toy with the notion that mind, after all, may be a fundamental aspect of nature, and not just an incongruous accident. It all began with a lecture given by the physicist Brandon Carter of Cambridge University at the 1973 meeting of the International Astronomical Union in Krakow, Poland. Using insights from relativity and particle physics, plus observations from astronomy, Carter pointed out that the seemingly arbitrary and unrelated constants in physics have one very odd

---

20. Timothy Ferris, *The Whole Shebang* (New York: Simon and Schuster, 1997), 303–4. For a different view, see Gerald Schroeder, *The Science of God: The Convergence of Scientific and Biblical Wisdom* (New York: The Free Press, 1997), esp, 176–90.

thing in common: they are precisely the values you need if you want to have a universe capable of producing carbon-based life. Life is no random accident. From the first nanosecond — against all probability — the cosmos has been so arranged as to make the emergence of life a high probability. Carter called this strange coincidence the "anthropic principle" (from the Greek word for "human being").[21]

The question of the significance of the anthropic principle is a scientific metaquestion; it arises from scientific insights but goes beyond what science itself is competent to answer. The issue is not a matter of physics but of metaphysics — the purpose or nonpurpose of the universe.

What amazes Stephen Hawking and many other physicists about the earliest seconds of our universe is the observed constants: the exact rate of expansion (the Hubble constant), the precise numerical values of the force fields that hold things together (nuclear forces, electromagnetism, gravity), and the particle-antiparticle ratio. No one now understands exactly why these constants have the precise values that they do. But what is clear and startling is that the initial conditions of the universe are so very fine-tuned for the development of life — in some region of the galaxies at some time, and perhaps in more locales than planet earth.

Consider the particle-antiparticle ratio: If in the very early universe every proton had been matched by an antiproton, they would have annihilated each other — and the story would have been over almost before it started. Or consider the force of gravity and the expansion rate: If either had been only fractionally different than it is, either smaller or larger, the universe would either have collapsed very quickly or it would have ballooned out too rapidly for stars and planets to form, and since nuclear star factories produce the heavier chemical elements needed for life, without stars the universe would be lifeless.

The case is the same with the nuclear bonding properties: If the "strong force" that holds atomic nuclei together had deviated from its actual strength by as much as 1 percent, no carbon atoms, the basic building blocks for DNA, would have been able to form inside stars. In turn, if the nuclear "weak force" responsible for radioactive decay had been a mite stronger, all hydrogen would have immediately dissolved into helium, and without hydrogen there could be no carbon, oxygen, or nitrogen. Again, if the binding force of electromagnetism responsible for light and all electrically charged particles had been even marginally

21. See John D. Barrow and Frank J. Tipler, *The Anthropic Cosmological Principle* (New York: Oxford University Press, 1986).

stronger than it was, stars would have remained too chill to explode as supernovas — and since exploding supernovas seed the planets with the heavier, life-giving elements, our planet (and any other one) would have remained a dead wasteland.

But our planet is not a wasteland. Somehow, from the very outset, the universe was exactly calibrated so as to favor life. Is this mere coincidence? Or is something more — and something very akin to teleology — afoot here?

The anthropic principle limits acceptable cosmological theories to those that take human existence, or at least life, into account. Others would put it more strongly, saying that the range of possibilities is restricted by the conditions necessary for the presence of observers like ourselves. There are actually two versions of the anthropic principle. The so-called "weak" version, which, emphasizing the vast number of galaxies besides our own, limits itself to saying that the conditions necessary for intelligent life are met in certain limited regions of time-space and, accordingly, since we (and our physicists) are here, we find the conditions that produced us. As Hawking wryly quips, this "is a bit like a rich person living in a wealthy neighborhood not seeing any poverty."[22]

In the "strong" version, however, teleology reenters cosmology (much to the horror of many scientists). As John Barrow and Frank Tipler express it, "The Universe must have those properties which allow life to develop within it at some stage of its history." Or, to put it another way, the universe is the way it is for our sake — because of mind. To suggest, however, that the evolution of 125 billion galaxies exists simply for our sake seems a bit much: anthropocentrism gone wild, and an invitation to self-inflation. (The believer has a different way of putting it: The universe is the way it is for the glory of God.)

A softer version of the principle would merely note the extraordinary fruitfulness of the universe and acknowledge that this calls for an explanation, which might well lead to the notion of a purposive cosmic mind. The universe has not been indifferent to life. Physicist Freeman J. Dyson looks at the anthropic principle and arrives at a conclusion just the opposite of Steven Weinberg's:

I do not feel like an alien in this universe. The more I examine the universe and study the details of its architecture, the more

---

22. Stephen W. Hawking, *A Brief History of Time: From the Big Bang to Black Holes* (New York: Bantam Books, 1988), 124.

evidence I find that the universe in some sense must have known we were coming.[23]

From the very beginning, we might say, the cosmos has been silently working toward us, distilling a sounding board and a voice that might speak for it. We are no longer strangers in a hostile or indifferent cosmos. We belong here, are a vital part of the universe's immense journey. As Thomas Berry expresses it, "In this perception the human is seen as a mode of being of the universe as well as a distinctive being in the universe. Stated somewhat differently, the human is that being in whom the universe comes to itself in a special mode of conscious reflection."[24]

What one can safely say is that the universe favors the experiment of life. That is the implication of the anthropic principle. It is also the implication of the new dynamics of complex systems. Whether modern star-gazers reflect on the startling initial conditions of the universe or the behavior of complex, dissipative structures, they contemplate an amazing grace. In a very real sense the cosmos stands behind us, is with us. Quite literally, we are the fallout of the stars and the lucky outcome of a succession of contingent transformations that have emerged out of chaos. British novelist Sara Maitland catches the implications exactly:

> It is terrifying. God plays preposterous games. God allows complexity, encourages complexity. God obliges us to play the game of becoming. . . . We have to struggle to replace the functionalist, bureaucratic God with an artist God—that is to say a God who loves both beauty and risk. . . . God's willingness to run risks for the sake of a risky delight should boggle our minds.[25]

And our role in this mind-boggling creation? Unless there are extraterrestrials, we are the only ones in the cosmos who will be able to tell its story and say what it shall mean.

---

23. Freeman J. Dyson, *Disturbing the Universe* (New York: Harper & Row, 1979), 250.
24. Thomas Berry, *The Dream of the Earth* (San Francisco: Sierra Club, 1988), 16.
25. Sara Maitland, *A Big Enough God: A Feminist's Search for a Joyful Theology* (New York: Henry Holt, 1995), 43.

TEN

The Voice
of the Hurricane

Now, even though the realms of religion and science in themselves
are clearly marked off from each other, nevertheless there exist between the two strong reciprocal relationships and dependencies.
Though religion may be that which determines the goal, it has,
nevertheless, learned from science, in the broadest sense, what
means will contribute to the attainment of the goals it has set up.
But science can only be created by those who are thoroughly im-
bued with the aspiration towards truth and understanding. This
source of feeling, however, springs from the sphere of religion.
To this there also belongs the faith in the possibility that the
regulations valid for the world of existence are rational, that is,
comprehensible to reason. I cannot conceive of a genuine scientist without that profound faith. The situation may be expressed
by an image: Science without religion is lame, religion without
science is blind. — ALBERT EINSTEIN, *Science and Religion*

We are submerged to our neck, to our eyes, to our hair, in a
furiously raging ocean. We are the voice of this hurricane, this
thermal howl, and we do not even know it.

— MICHEL SERRES, *Hermes*

If the military file conception of nature proposed by classical Newtonian physics shattered the sort of communion with the cosmos that
Francis of Assisi could take for granted, post-Einsteinian cosmology
begins to restore that communion. Due to a number of developments
over the last century, including the strange unpredictability of subatomic phenomena and complex systems, the great distance between
models of life and the mechanical models preferred by classical physics
is measurably reduced. The gap is closing, and as it closes, two trends
emerge: The cosmos begins to appear to be a lot more irregular, even
chaotic, than we had supposed, and the Cartesian gap between nature

and human beings closes. We appear to belong here, and, conversely, impersonal nature regains its creativity, and hence its resemblance to human nature. The poetry is back in nature.

The late Erich Jantsch, systems theorist at the University of California at Berkeley, articulated the general laws of nature's dynamics, as envisioned by the new scientific outlook, as follows:

> The basic themes are always the same. They may be summarized by notions of self-determination, self-organization and self-renewal; by the recognition of a systemic interconnectedness over space and time of all natural dynamics; by the logical supremacy of processes over spatial structures; by the role of fluctuations which render the law of large numbers invalid and give a chance to the individual and its creative imagination; by the openness and creativity of an evolution which is neither in its emerging and decaying structures nor in the end result, predetermined.[1]

Clearly, self-organization, interconnection, process, fluctuation, and openness mark the dynamics of human culture. But if the dynamics of nature are also characterized by these same features, then, as Jantsch observes, "the dualistic split into nature and culture may now be overcome." We no longer need that double-accounting procedure of putting the physicist's energy systems in one box and the energy systems of our life-world in another. Distinctions may still have to be drawn to avoid reducing the human to an electron or a "selfish gene," but what we have here is continuity — or something like the ancient notion of an analogy of being. All beings in the great sea of energy released by the big bang are interrelated, just as all living organisms are descended from common ancestors and thus effectively kin to each other. Moreover, as we survey the principal features of this post-Einsteinian world in what follows, step by step we will be moving into the Hebrew prophets' eschatological world. A universe bound fast to grim, timeless necessity gives way to a stochastic or chancy universe in which contingency and irreversible time begin to count again. For Western culture, which has always been essentially time-oriented, this is of enormous importance. It means that our physics and astrophysics can be contextualized within the biblical perspective. Let me now summarize what we have been developing.

---

1. Erich Jantsch, *The Self-Organizing Universe: Scientific and Human Implications of the Emerging Paradigm of Evolution* (New York: Pergamon Press, 1980), 8.

The Unpredictability and Interconnectedness of Matter-Energy

What we think of as matter — whether it be a subatomic quark, a yellow star like our sun, or a bee hive — must be thought of as bound and condensed energy, captured in an eddy out of the torrential, buzzing flow set loose by the first chord of our cosmic symphony. We, the plants and the stars, are warps or disturbances in the field of this ballooning, random energy. The ancient Greek atomists and Hindu mythologists were on target: All object-like entities in the universe are vortices or whirlpools in a vast cosmic river of free energy that flows through them and simultaneously creates them. And, as we discovered with the atom bomb, the potency of this bound energy is almost unimaginable; to measure it, one must multiply mass by an enormous constant, the velocity of light squared ($E=mc^2$).

Moreover, when not contained, this random flood of energy is impossible to pin down; it simply dances and is fundamentally indeterminate. Should you try to locate a subatomic particle's position in a nuclear cloud chamber, its velocity will elude you; and conversely, if you try to determine its speed, its position will remain unknown (Werner Heisenberg's "uncertainty principle"). As Stephen Hawking puts it, quantum mechanics, which formulates the laws of this subatomic domain, "introduces an unavoidable element of unpredictability and randomness into science."[2]

The problem for a classical, deterministic physicist is that this elemental stuff acts like both wave and particle. On the one hand, Max Planck demonstrated that subatomic phenomena exhibit particle-like behavior; they come, like monetary denominations, only in certain sized packets or quanta. On the other hand, these same particles also behave like sound or light waves; they are not localizable but diffused, which does not permit scientists to predict a single definite outcome of an observation. Instead all one can do is predict a number of possible outcomes and tell how probable each one is.

Gone is the Newtonian world of inert, disconnected matter. The constituents of everything in the cosmos — molecules, atoms, and subatomic particles — are signal systems in a state of constant motion, linking up with each other and with everything in the cosmos.

The issues involved in special and general relativity, it turns out, are finally very similar to those raised by quantum physics. Physicist Lee Smolin puts it well:

---

2. Stephen Hawking, *A Brief History of Time: From the Big Bang to Black Holes* (New York: Bantam Books, 1988), 55.

What is at stake in the conflict between the absolute and the relational views of space and time is then much more than the academic question of how space is to be represented in physics. This question goes to the roots of the whole of the scientific conception of the universe. Does the world consist of a large number of independently autonomous atoms, the properties of each owing nothing to the others? Or, instead, is the world a vast, interconnected system of relations, in which even the properties of a single elementary particle or the identity of a point in space requires and reflects the whole rest of the universe? The two views of space and time underlie and imply two very different views of what it means to speak of a property, of identity, or of individuality. Consequently the transition from a cosmology based on an absolute notion of space and time to one based on a relational notion — a transition that we are now in the midst of — must have profound implications for our understanding of the place of complexity and life in the universe.[3]

Hard science has thus been forced to recognize two major consequences: First, Newton's laws of motion and the orderly grid of the periodic table of chemical elements have to be understood as exercises in statistics. Lawfulness at the macroscopic level, it now appears, rides in fact on a wildly chancy underworld of vibrating, oscillating, aleatory clouds. Hence the great nineteenth-century dream of scientific determinism — Laplace's boast to Napoleon that if he knew the complete state of the universe at any one time he could then predict whatever would follow — is a delusion. The subatomic underworld does not resemble a geometric diagram; it looks more like a painting by J. M. W. Turner or Jackson Pollock.

Second, since elemental matter exhibits the characteristics of a field or wave, this means that the universe is radically interconnected. Through their fields, the atoms of one thing entangle themselves with the fields of another — and thus everything is internally related to everything else. The mutual impact may be negligible, but the Andromeda constellation doesn't make a move without affecting you or me, nor do we make a move without affecting it. In this understanding, the word "atom" should connote just the opposite of what Newton supposed. At the most basic physical level, at least, everything is implicated in everything else — the one in the many, the many in the one. The truth is that matter-energy is profoundly social; communion, not isolation, is the rule.

---

3. Lee Smolin, *The Life of the Cosmos* (New York: Oxford University Press, 1997), 221.

A Semiotic Universe

In a Newtonian universe of big-scale phenomena, matter is inert and dumb: the mere repetition of the same prosaic routine by a "closed system." In such a world, perfect equilibrium is the norm. The redundant swing of a pendulum or the reiterated pattern of wallpaper, therefore, would serve as paradigmatic examples of lawfulness in the timeless Newtonian scheme of things. In a post-Einsteinian universe, however, most systems are "open," active, and wildly or moderately exchanging energy with their environment. In this context, matter-energy is an information system that gives signs; it is semiotic. Anything, from a quasar to a DNA molecule, constitutes itself as a time series, a sequence of signals that govern its behavior and vary according to some sort of statistical regularity.[4] The understanding of such processes falls under the sway of information physics, the theory that underlies the functioning of the transistors and integrated circuits of our television sets and computers. As we saw in the last chapter, information, which is equivalent to organization, is a form of counter-entropy — a warp in time-space that works against the odds, against the trend toward incoherence or sheer "noise."

Molecules and stars — and everything in between like ourselves — do not operate like wallpaper. We are all thermodynamic systems (heat users), and that means we are precarious balancing acts, moment by moment converting random energy into information/organization and, in the enterprise, loosing structured energy in the form of waste or noise (i.e., producing entropy). If there is too much randomness, the result is mere chaotic buzz — the system simply dissipates into unbound energy that does no work. On the other hand, if, as in Newton's ideal, there is too much redundancy, the result will be ironbound rigidity — the wallpaper effect or something like the monotone of a stuck telephone signal that communicates nothing. Complex signal systems balance between these two extremes and are thus neither completely regular nor completely irregular. They exist far from equilibrium. Necessity and chance, or order and disorder, intermingle in them. They are essentially ambiguous, and the more complex a system is, the more unstable and innovative.

In effect, everything that we spoke of as weaving itself out of the random energy of the big bang is self-organizing, or "autopoietic." And how does such self-organization proceed? Things maintain themselves in being, that is, order the disorder they devour, by using a standard

---

4. For a lucid account of information physics, see Jeremy Campbell, *Grammatical Man: Information, Entropy, Language, and Life* (New York: Simon and Schuster, 1982).

code or protoalphabet that regulates their signals. The protoalphabet is analogous to a set of grammatical rules which generate, within limits, a wide variety of programs or messages. The code of the spiral DNA macromolecule discovered by Crick and Watson in 1955 is a good example: An "alphabet" consisting of four nucleotides forming three-letter "words" for twenty amino acids is arranged into "sentences" that will specify one of thousands of proteins necessary for organic life.

The implications? Information physics has returned us by a detour to a semiotic universe, a nature that — like the medieval sacramental universe — carries messages. The universe is a gigantic communications network, a complex circuitry of instructions, most of which we can barely decipher. Consequently, the gap between nature and human culture has narrowed considerably. We no longer need to carry the physicist's energy and the humanist's signs and symbols in separate accounts. One balance sheet will do. The natural sciences, we may now say, do archeological digs into the primitive signs and protolanguages of atoms and DNA molecules; the humanities deal with the more developed sign systems and meanings of the animated stardust we call human cultures. An analogy of being is back in place — and will be more firmly in place with what follows. As Michel Serres articulates it,

> It is no longer necessary to maintain the distinction between introspective knowledge, or "deep" knowledge, and objective knowledge. There is only one type of knowledge and it is always linked to an observer, an observer submerged in a system or in its proximity. And this observer is structured exactly like what he observes.... There is no more separation between the subject on the one hand, and the object, on the other.... Instead, each term of the traditional subject-object dichotomy is itself split by something like a geographical divide: noise, disorder, and chaos on one side; complexity, arrangement, and distribution on the other. Nothing distinguishes me ontologically from a crystal, a plant, an animal, or the order of the world; we are drifting together toward noise and the black depths of the universe.... Knowledge is at most the reversal of drifting.[5]

If I get it right, then, information physics authorizes us to return to the idea, so keenly felt by the ancient Greeks, that the dramas of Aeschylus and Sophocles confront the forces of nature within us: the hurricane, the raging ocean, the wail of the wind, thunder and light-

---

5. Michel Serres, *Hermes: Literature, Science, Philosophy,* ed. Josué V. Harari and David F. Bell (Baltimore: Johns Hopkins University Press, 1982), 83.

ning. Indeed, these plays resonate with the vibrations of subatomic particle-waves and the thermodynamic turbulence of stars. Given all the unpredictable chanciness we have discovered in post-Einsteinian nature, it is no wonder that Freudian psychoanalysis is interminable.

Order Out of Chaos

The etymology of the word "nature" suggests birth and engendering the new, and as we saw at the outset, this sense of nature's promise was vital to a biblical (and especially a prophetic) cosmology. A classical deterministic physics seemingly put an end to this biologistic way of thinking. Newton focused on what physicists call "integral systems," stable, closed systems whose final state would not differ from their initial conditions. Psychological time, in which present and past differ from each other, was therefore viewed as a mirage. He thus gave us a science of dead things that recopy the same writing in the same atomic letters — and hence a frozen, unpromising world in which there could be nothing new under the sun.

As we saw in the last chapter, however, the new post-Einsteinian physics has begun to pay more attention to the nonlinear, erratic side of things, and with such phenomena we tacitly reenter the eschatological universe of the Hebrew prophets. Along with molecular chemists and climatologists, physicists are now looking at systems of middle-range size and of some complexity which exist "far from equilibrium," for instance, the galactic clustering of stars, the microscopic intertwining of blood vessels, or the shapes of clouds and lightning. This new focus has not only forced them to recognize how changes in larger wholes — say of a solar system, an atmosphere, an ecosystem, or a brain — can reorganize molecular and atomic structures (top-down causality); it has also given them new insight into how disorder functions in nature to give birth to more complex levels of organization. In this manner, physics at last has a way of understanding how some complex systems move uphill against the tide of entropy — to a future that is richer than their pasts. It has a handle, that is, on the evolutionary arrow of time.

Unlike the closed, linear systems examined by classical physics, which for the most part are found only in a laboratory, the new physics pays attention to nonlinear thermodynamic systems whose dynamics are marked by relative instability. Here the rule is that the outcome of the dynamic process is so sensitive to initial conditions that a minimal change in the situation at the beginning of the process results in a large difference at the end. Time counts, is intrinsic to the process. And so do small numbers count. A small imbalance in the particle-antiparticle ratio of the early universe, for example, leads to a cosmos of 125 billion galaxies and a habitable planet earth. A small change in cholesterol content can produce disproportionately large changes in cell functioning. The flapping of a butterfly's wing in South Asia may alter the ensuing weather over San Francisco.

Physicists call it complexity theory or, somewhat misleadingly, chaos theory. What they really have in mind is the germ of a new order that is present in near random activity — and which acts as "strange attractor" for the whole system. Complexity/chaos theory focuses on open systems that exchange lots of energy with their environment. Some of these systems, for instance dying stars, are wholly dissipative; entropy is dominant and they are wearing out. Others like the recently discovered nascent star near the constellation Aquilla or the blue-green algae which first created a breathable atmosphere on planet earth are equally unstable, but exhibit an extraordinary feature: They break symmetry by flirting with the disorder or noise they constantly take in, and it is apparently this chaos in the system, a minor fluctuation at first, that triggers the emergence of an often beautiful and thoroughly unpredictable novelty that reorganizes the whole system and keeps it moving uphill, against the odds of dissipation and death.

That is, in some but not all instances, the minor fluctuation overcomes the weight of large numbers, and thus the redundancy, of the prior system and reorders it. The signal changes. And when this happens, the direction of the time arrow changes — from negative (degrading, aging, entropic) to positive (upgrading, complexifying, negentropic). Nature's story, then, is only partly grasped as one of determinism. Redundancy there is, but it is only part of the picture. The other, complementary part is the story of turbulence or fluctuation that begets continual metamorphosis. Irreversible time — a present and future that differs from the past — is thereby written into the fundamental script of nature.

Examples of the eating habits of nonlinear, open systems abound in nature. The interstellar gas left over from the big bang in the course of time manufactured carbon and various organic compounds, and when supernovas exploded, their meteorites very likely bore these vital "waste products" to earth, where they proceeded to convert the energy of the sun to new uses. To the sun, of course, the photons it casts off are waste, sheer noise; but to emerging blue-green algae, busy with the alchemy of photosynthesis, such waste is nutriment to be converted into information/organization. In turn the algae break down carbon dioxide and give off excess oxygen, again so far as the algae are concerned sheer waste, but the staff of life for emerging animal organisms.

In sum, complex nature devours noise and transforms its random non-sense into information or structure. In the case of the star this process directs thermonuclear operations, in the case of plant life it controls photosynthesis, and in animals it turns up as DNA code and enzyme production. Open systems are converters of random energy into order, the original self-organizing, alchemical agents. From neutrinos to stars, nature has from the beginning been a technologist, making the new out of the old, pouring new wine into the old skins.

The basic rules for open energy systems seem to be that (1) they never give back energy in precisely the same form in which it has been taken in; (2) big numbers don't always win out; small numbers and minority reports matter; (3) it is precisely the ingestion of chaos or noise — an irregularity — that catalyzes a potentially new level of or-ganization (a chance variation); (4) the more complex the system is, the more unstable and innovative it is. Are we describing nature's process of surprise, or that of human beings? It is difficult to tell. From the very beginning, nature, too, has been metamorphic, a technological trans-former of raw energies into more diverse and complex organization. In short, there is plenty of prefigurative precedent in nature for changing water into wine, or bread and wine into one's body and blood. From the very beginning of the universe, transubstantiation has been nature's commandment.

So where does this put us cosmologically? It puts us, I think, in a universe that would have been familiar to the Hebrew prophets — one on the move, rich in possibility, rich in promise. The subjunctive mood has a secure place again in the nature of things. And paradoxically enough, it is all that turbulence and fluctuation in the cosmos that does this, that gives all of nature's maybe's and might be's a chance to become true. Danger and risk there is. But in its own tacit, latent way, it is as if the universe dreams big, promises big, and stands fully behind human hope.

The Anthropological Fallout

How do organisms — living systems — appear within the above per-spective? First, an organism is an information and thermodynamic system, receiving, storing, and giving off both energy and information in all its forms, from the light of the sun to the flow of food, oxygen, and heat passing through it. It is not at equilibrium, neither static nor homeostatic; it is a vortex ferrying both order and disorder in a state of imbalance, and it tends to maintain this imbalance, struggling upriver against the entropic drift of decay. As Michel Serres puts it

The organism is a barrier of braided links that leaks like a wicker basket but can still function as a dam. Better yet, it is a quasi-stable turbulence that a flow produces, the eddy closed in on itself for an instant which finds its balance in the middle of the current and appears to move upstream.[6]

Second, an organism can be defined only in a global perspective; for the circulation of energy from the sun and the black depths of space is integral to its precarious balancing act. Indeed, without the great river of flux let loose by the big bang, there could be no eddy, no knot of bound and structured energy to push upstream. Indeed, this temporary knot of energy is woven out of all times. Embedded here is the whole vast evolution of its chemical elements, its genes and their erratic variations. The nuclei of its carbon atoms were assembled inside a star that exploded long before the sun was born; and deeper still lie the quarks making up each proton and neutron of every atomic nucleus, quarks that were bound together when the universe was but a few seconds old. Says Serres,

> Now, and here is the crux of the matter, all times converge in this temporary knot: the drift of entropy or the irresistible thermal flow, wear and aging,... the conservative invariance of genetic nuclei, the permanence of form, the erratic blinking of aleatory mutations, the implacable filtering out of non-viable elements.... The living organism is of all times. This does not mean it is eternal, but rather that it is an original complex, woven out of all the different times.... All the temporal vectors possessing a directional arrow are here, in this place, arranged in the shape of a star. What is an organism? A sheaf of times. What is a living organism? A bouquet of times.[7]

And what are we — we human "bouquets of times"? Look at the palm of your hand. Imagine you could examine it through an electron microscope. What would you see?[8] First of all cells. And within them those meandering mitochondria and starburst centrioles devoted to respiration, sanitation, and energy production that keep you and your cells going. Though the cells you would see may be only a few years old, their architecture dates back more than a billion years, to the time when nucleated cells first evolved on earth.

---

6. Ibid., 75.
7. Ibid.
8. I borrow this example from Timothy Ferris, *Coming of Age in the Milky Way* (New York: Doubleday Anchor Books, 1988), 338–40.

To see where these cells obtained the blueprint that told them how to form, turn up the magnification on a cell nucleus. And behold the spiral DNA macromolecules secreted within your genes. Each holds a wealth of information about the size of the *Encyclopaedia Britannica,* accumulated over 4 billion years, specifying how to make a human being, from skin to bones to brain cells.

The DNA molecule is itself composed of many atoms whose outer electron shells joined up with their atomic nuclei more than 5 billion years ago, in the starry nebula from which planet earth was formed. Increase the magnification a hundred thousand times and the nucleus of a single carbon atom may swirl into view. It was assembled inside a star that exploded before the sun was born — anywhere from 5 to 15 billion years ago.

Finally, peering down even farther, you can make out the trios of quarks that make up each proton and neutron in the nucleus. When the big bang occurred, these quarks were the first minute eddies to weave themselves out of the great river of random energy in the first nanoseconds. They are the most fundamental constituents of everything, making up atomic nuclei, which in turn make up stars, solar systems, bacteria, and you and me. (Caltech's Murray Gell-Mann won the Nobel Prize in 1969 for discovering and naming them from a whimsical text in James Joyce's *Finnegans Wake.*)

What are we — we human beings? Like the stars or the weather patterns of our atmosphere, we too are open thermodynamic "wicker baskets," quasi-stable turbulences in the field and flow of energy and information stretching back to the big bang. Indeed, as the most complex creatures that we know of in our region of space-time, we are the most unstable — and that means the most recycled. Though we cannot regrow major organs, we do regrow nearly everything else about our physical being constantly. The DNA structure of our genes, of course, remains constant, but nothing in our genes was present a year ago. The tissue in our stomach renews itself weekly, the skin is shed monthly, and the liver regenerates every six weeks. Every moment, a portion of the body's trillions of atoms is dissipating to the world outside, and 98 percent of them are replaced annually. Each time we breathe, we take in a quadrillion atoms breathed by the rest of humanity within the last two weeks, and more than a million breathed personally sometime by each and any person on earth.[9] So much for the strictly bounded, separate individual!

---

9. See Larry Dossey, *Space, Time, and Medicine* (Boulder, Colo.: Shambhala, 1982), 72–81.

Like other organisms, we cannot be defined except globally, indeed cosmically. We are, first of all, creatures of the soil and utterly dependent on the teeming life underneath our feet. Paul and Anne Ehrlich remind us that a gram of forest soil (less than a twenty-fifth of an ounce) has been found to contain over a million bacteria of one type, almost 100,000 yeast cells, and some 50,000 bits of fungus. Similarly, a gram of agricultural soil may contain over 2.5 billion bacteria, 400,000 fungi, 50,000 algae, and 30,000 protozoa. It isn't the sheer numbers that are important; it's the role these microorganisms play in converting nutrients like nitrogen, phosphorus, and sulfur into forms that are usable by the higher plants upon which our life depends. Most green plants flourish only because of intimate relationships with special kinds of soil fungi. The plants nourish the fungi, which in exchange transfer essential nutrients into the roots of the plant. In many forests, the trees are utterly dependent upon the activity of such fungi. And on farms, other microorganisms serve parallel critical functions in transferring nutrients to crops like wheat and corn.[10]

As Lewis Thomas was fond of pointing out, without the huge swarm of plant chloroplasts and mitochondria swimming in our cells, we could neither breathe, move a muscle, nor think a thought.[11] Quite literally, of course, we are descendants of the stars, for without star factories to convert helium out of hydrogen, there would be no oxygen, carbon, or iron; and without these there would be no amino acids or proteins for life. Fifteen billion years of evolution, a proliferation of forms out of chaos, are inscribed in our bone marrow, in our nerves and tissue. Each of us is a distillation, a condensed centrifuge of cosmic energy. We may leak like a sieve, but we dam up the whole sidereal river.

Order, complexity, and arrangement on one side, chaos, noise, and disorder on the other, there is nothing that separates us structurally from a crystal, a plant, an animal, or the whole order of nature. Together we struggle upward and drift toward death. And like the rest of nature both determined and riddled by chance, we too give signs, leave our mark or scrawl here.

The poet can be at home in such a universe, for it is riddled with correspondences and parallels between the human and the nonhuman — a veritable goldmine of metaphors. Said Rainer Maria Rilke,

---

10. See Paul R. Ehrlich and Anne H. Ehrlich, *Healing the Planet: Strategies for Resolving the Environmental Crisis* (Reading, Mass.: Addison-Wesley, 1991), 23–24.

11. Lewis Thomas, *The Lives of a Cell: Notes of a Biology Watcher* (New York: Bantam Books, 1975), 2ff.

> Ah, not to be shut off
> not through the slightest partition
> shut out from the law of the stars.
> The inner — what is it?
> If not intensified sky, hurled through with birds
> and deep with winds of homecoming.[12]

There once was a time, entranced by Newton's "one-eyed sleep," when we were sure Rilke's identification of inwardness with sky was nothing but a flight of fancy, the ravings of a romantic. The poet's habit of saying that I am rock, river, animal, and sky was taken at best as tolerable exaggeration, at worst as shoddy thinking. In neither case was it taken seriously. No more. In light of quantum physics and nonequilibrium thermodynamics, we have to say that such poetry captures the literal truth. The taboo against identifying psyche with nature has been lifted. Star time and earth time speak through us; we are their sound, their tongue.

We must recenter, reorient ourselves, to serve the earth and all sentient beings. The argument for ecocentrism and the intrinsic value of the biophysical world makes eminent sense if it widens the horizons of our moral concern and is taken as a sharp rebuke to utilitarian shortsightedness and egocentrism. But if it forces us to an either/or choice between care for Monarch butterflies, say, and care for the people who share their habitat, there is probably something wrongheaded going on. If, in order to qualify as an environmentalist, one has to check one's humanistic credentials at the door, we must be rapping at the wrong door. I refuse to believe that in order to love old-growth redwoods I have to be a misanthrope.

We are both a part of nature and exceptional, akin to all other things, plants, and animal species and, at the same time, a distinctive, even unique, species. On the one hand we are defined by our relationships, unmistakably embedded in the web of life and in the matrix of atoms, stars, and galaxies. As such we are one species among many, both in terms of our biological makeup and our dependence for food and energy on the resources of the earth and other species. But this does not mean we don't have a unique role in the history of the cosmos. The human brain is the most complex system that has been found in the natural world, containing some 100 billion neurons, each connected with hundreds or thousands of other neurons through synaptic junctions, perhaps some 100 trillion of them. We require at least two

---

12. Rilke in Stephen Mitchell, ed., *The Enlightened Heart: An Anthology of Sacred Poetry* (New York: Harper & Row, 1989), 144.

languages to make sense of ourselves: the language of biochemistry to explain neurophysiological phenomena, and the language of selfhood or moral agency to account for the causal efficacy of our free choices. We dwell both within and outside the natural world, being the unique makers of technologies and sociocultural living spaces that have the singular power to change, manipulate, destroy, and transcend natural environmental limits. Biologists and ecologists emphasize one part of this double truth — our belonging to the natural world. Social scientists and humanists emphasize the other.

Coming at the end of a vast chain of conversions of chancy energy, we are simply the final alchemists, the last transformers and interpreters, the ultimate black box of nature. We do not hear its thermal din, all the raucous noise random energy makes, because it is filtered out by the enormous chain of energy-converters that came before us. As Michel Serres says, "We are submerged to our neck, to our eyes, to our hair, in a furiously raging ocean. We are the voice of this hurricane, this thermal howl, and we do not even know it."[13]

---

13. Serres, *Hermes*, 77.

PART V

EARTH ETHICS:
DOING JUSTICE TO CREATION

How does one pray and act in a post-Einsteinian cosmos? There are no dragons here, but it is awesome enough, unimaginably vast and ancient, blessed with steadfast stability but still more remarkably graced with process, self-organization, interconnection, communication, fluctuation, and openness. It is a universe in the subjunctive mood, one that is congruent with the biblical sense of promise. "We are the voice of this hurricane, this thermal howl." What do we make of it?

Is there a purpose at the heart of that noise, that howl? Does the universe care about us, stand with us? Or against us? We asked these questions before; we now raise them again. Where do we fit? How shall we understand ourselves within this new story of how nature works? What are we to make of ourselves in this new context? How are we to understand our role, our responsibilities, our destiny?

This is a universe whose fullness, diversity, promise, and risk simply dazzle. We have no further reason to feel estranged or alien. We can be at home and treat nature as our home. The old Cartesian dualism between the domain of matter and the domain of mind has given way, replaced by a new sense of continuity, interrelation, kinship. Life and mind are no longer to be considered alien anomalies in nature. There are grounds for discerning a subtle teleology running through all creation. Suddenly, after the hiatus of the Cartesian-Newtonian world, we have a material world that unfolds, as human life does, in the form of a great experiment, an adventure story. From the outset the universe has been fine-tuned for the emergence of carbon-based life. It is once

193

again a nexus of connections, a place we can truly and rightly love —
without suspecting ourselves of sentimentality or the pathetic fallacy.
On every scale the universe is irreversibly temporal and historical, as
we are. From its first moment and from the bottom up it is loaded with
promise, and possibility — and high risk. The risks and uncertainties
are in direct proportion to the possibilities and chances.

The new cosmology has to make a difference to our conception
of God, our prayer life, our work and action. Let me spell this out,
speaking out of my own experience of faith. News from the Hubble
space telescope or from a nuclear accelerator will not give you the interpretation that follows. Here, while building on the preceding analysis, I
follow the news I get from the New Testament and from the depth probe
of my soul's experience, which in the final analysis reaches farther than
scientific apparatus into the secret design of things. The points I want
to make pertain to one basic question: What is all this cosmic circuitry
for? What, if anything, is the message of the Ultimate Dispatcher?

And what, if we sense what that message means, is the implication
for what we do or how we act in this world? Does it mean something
for the way we regard the earth? Does being here — just once, no more,
and never again — carry obligations to the earth? We are involved, it
would appear, in a big gamble. God seems to have taken a huge chance,
uncertain of the outcome. We must do the earth justice. There may be
other minds distributed around the galaxies (from whom we have yet
to hear), but so far as we know, we are the only conscious, intelligent
beings in our part of the Milky Way. It is our responsibility to keep
planet earth running in good condition. The quarks, the mitochondria
in our cells are speechless. It is our responsibility, if I am not mistaken,
to say what the purpose of earth shall be.

This is a daunting responsibility, and I see no way of avoiding it in the
ill-founded hope that things would improve if we left nature alone. We
cannot pretend that we don't have duties in a way we never did before.
Our technology forces these obligations upon us. The task seems likely
to tax us to the limit, and it induces in me a biblical "fear of the Lord." I
pray for a proper humility and the Yahwist's sense of service in us all —
in the face both of what we should like to know and what we do not.
I have already commented above about the new mood of uncertainty
that currently prevails among ecologists: they no longer feel so confident
that they can tell policy-makers where and when nations and industries
may be overharvesting nature's reserves. My worry is their new "permissiveness," that failing scientific certainty they may be disposed to
let the ideologically driven managers and free marketeers imagine they
have the expertise to go at the earth without restraint or mercy.

ELEVEN

The Fallout for Spirituality

Even if there is only one possible unified theory, it is just a set of rules and equations. What is it that breathes fire into the equations and makes a universe for them to describe? . . . Why does the universe go to the bother of existing?
— STEPHEN W. HAWKING, *A Brief History of Time*

Before you the whole universe is as a grain from a balance,
or a drop of morning dew come down upon the earth.
But you have mercy on all. . . .
For you love all things that are
and loathe nothing that you have made;
for what you hated, you would not have fashioned.
And how could a thing remain, unless you will it;
or be preserved, had it not been called forth by you?
But you spare all things. . . .
For your imperishable spirit is in all things.
—Wisdom 11:22–12:1

God does not offer himself for observation.
— G. W. F. HEGEL

A mistake about nature, I have been assuming, will rebound as an error about God. Conversely, getting the truth about the nature of matter should bring us closer to the truth about nature's Creator. Christianity, as we have noted, has been ambivalent about the natural world. The tradition has divided between two basic paths: those that follow a spirituality of escape from time, and those that trust in the ultimate meaning of temporality. Christianity, we said, inherits both traditions. And we can see that in the very different notions of God we use.

On the one hand we have what we might call the "Hellenic" heritage, the so-called philosopher's God, who is identified by uncovering the properties of perfect being, where perfection is largely defined as

195

the opposite of anything finite, earthly, and changing. This interpretation of God posits a timeless ground of Being above the temporal flux: the Unmoved Mover and supreme substance existing in itself, eternally the same, independent of all others. This is the immutable God of classical Western theism, unaffected by anything created, an utterly detached God who has no intrinsic stake in the well-being and unfolding of nature in time. In a remarkable way, classic Newtonian physics imitates this atemporal theology. It too posits timeless laws above the temporal flux and treats its ultimate entities (atoms) as if they were immutable, eternally the same, independent of and unrelated to anything else.

Biblical

Then there is the God of the Bible, whose identity consists in self-constancy rather than sameness. This God identifies himself in relation to the temporal order, in relation to the unfolding of cosmic and planetary history. The primordial covenant, as we saw, is with all living creatures. God reveals himself to Israel as Yahweh and ties his name to a promise: he is the one who hears the cry of the poor, who delivers the Israelites from slavery in Egypt. In short, God's identity does not consist in otherworldly properties of sameness, as with the Greeks, but is linked to the power to do what God says he will do. In the Hebrew understanding, the principle of permanence lies in keeping one's word. In this sense the conception of deity is "personal," established by words and commitments, by the faithfulness of later acts to the promises made in earlier acts. As theologian Kevin J. Vanhoozer puts it, "The Hebrew interpretation of God sees God not as standing apart from time but standing faithful through it. God is not true because God lies unperturbed outside time but because God can be relied upon in time, and until the end of time."[1]

The Hebrew God is a God who freely defines himself by his relationships to the created other. As Eternal Wisdom she is a God who involves herself in her creation, who loves what she has created. And dwells in all things that are created. As the Book of Wisdom has it, the world and everything in it is holy because "the imperishable spirit" of God lives in all things.

> For you love all things that are
> and loathe nothing that you have made;
> for what you hated, you would not have fashioned.
> And how could a thing remain, unless you will it;

---

1. Kevin J. Vanhoozer, "Does the Trinity Belong in a Theology of Religion?" in *The Trinity in a Pluralistic Age: Theological Essays on Culture and Religion*, ed. Kevin J. Vanhoozer (Grand Rapids, Mich.: William B. Eerdmans, 1997), 49.

> or be preserved, had it not been called forth by you?
> But you spare all things. . . .
> For your imperishable spirit is in all things!
>   (Wis. 11:22–12:1)

Those that serve the Holy One, the God of Israel, will — so far as they can — embrace, cherish, and care for what God mothers and cares for. We will, of course, fall short, because the Creator's embrace is all-encompassing whereas ours is not.

In classic Greek thought, there were two separate worlds, one the immutable, intelligible order of the super-celestial spheres accessible to scientific understanding, the other the mutable, sensible sublunar world of which no scientific understanding was possible. Christianity denied this division; for it there was but one world of experience — founded on faith in the invisible Creator of heaven and earth. At the Council of Nicea in 325 C.E., the church broke decisively with classic antiquity's disjunction between time and eternity, or being and becoming, and explicitly qualified the notion of a transcendental deity exclusive of becoming or movement.[2] Godhead, the council asserted, presented itself in trinitarian form, and therefore our language about God had to be threefold. There was something deficient, these early Christians thought, in speaking of God as exhaustively, formlessly transcendent (as the mystical traditions of East and West do). At the same time it is false to speak of God as wholly immanent in or identical with the world (pantheism). Similarly, God cannot be spoken of as identical with some creature (idolatry). Not this, not that. . . . As Aquinas would later maintain, our knowledge of God is finally negative. We know best what God is not.

Christians believe in God in three ways, ways that are narrated in the three articles of the Creed: Father, Son, and Holy Spirit. To be more accurate, there are three ways in which God is — creator, redeemer, sanctifier — for each of which we conventionally use the term "person." The term "person," however, is misleading. For us, a person is an individual agent, a conscious center of memory and choice, of action, reflection, and decision. But when we speak of God as "three persons," we do not mean that God has three minds, three memories, three wills.[3]

---

2. See Charles Norris Cochrane, *Christianity and Classical Culture* (New York: Oxford University Press, [1940] 1968), 236–37.
3. See Nicholas Lasch, *Believing Three Ways in God* (Notre Dame, Ind.: University of Notre Dame, 1992), 31–32.

The three ways in which God is God correct each other. If transcendence and utter qualitative difference were the only truth about God, we would be impelled to rise above the earth, and abandoning earth for beatific vision would constitute the higher and only wisdom. But this is not the only truth about God. Unlike the abstract being of Greek philosophy, the great I AM of Sinai encompasses both being and becoming, order and movement. According to the trinitarian protocol, God's overflowing goodness must be sensed as both "beyond" the world and simultaneously poured out and manifest in the world. God, the Holy Spirit, is thus immanent "within" all created being (hence the truth of sacramentality and even of pantheism), and is the source of both life and perfectibility in the universe. For Christians, moreover, God is poured out and emptied in time and human flesh, notably in the lineage of the Hebrew prophets, from Moses to Jesus the Christ, even to the point of embracing death.

If the only truth were transcendence, all we could say would be *neti, neti* — God is neither this nor that — and atheists and agnostics would have the last word. Spirit being immanent and incarnate, however, we have access to the unspeakable. Gerard Manley Hopkins has it right.

> Glory be to God for dappled things....
> All things counter, original, spare, strange;
> Whatever is fickle, freckled (who knows how?)
> With swift, slow; sweet, sour; adazzle, dim;
> He fathers-forth, whose beauty is past change;
> Praise him.[4]

Christianity, as we said many chapters ago, walks a fine line regarding its attitude toward the earth. It not only supports a spirituality of ascent that promotes detachment and criticism of the temporal world; it also evokes a spirituality of immanence that is only a hair's breath away from pantheism. In the doctrine of the Incarnation, moreover, we have a spirituality of descent and embodiment (as in the "heaven-on-earth" architecture and art of the European Baroque) that leads us, or ought to lead us, to cherish earth and the changeable things of earth. The ecological situation of our time demands that we hold on to all these motifs.

---

4. From "Pied Beauty," in *A Hopkins Reader*, ed. John Pick (New York: Doubleday Image Books, 1966), 50–51.

A Big Enough God and the Spirituality of Ascent

The universe we have surveyed in the last several chapters is far different from the one Francis of Assisi dwelt within, but even more than his, it declares the glory of God. The grounds it gives for seeing "how God works ... in all created things, ... in the heavens, elements, plants, fruits, flocks" are staggering. For in a static, Ptolemaic "block universe," the Creator may very well seem like a boring old emperor. A post-Einsteinian universe, on the other hand, offers signs of grace and gives birth to diversity on a scale never dreamed of by our medieval ancestors. More than Ptolemy's tightly concentric cosmos, this is the world-in-movement of the Hebrew prophets, a world full of possibility and promise. The sheer scale and immense generativity of the cosmos can serve the believer as an allusion to the greatness, creativity, and generosity of the Holy One who breaks our boundaries, with whom we must stretch, whose "thoughts are not your thoughts" and whose ways are "as high as the heavens above the earth" (Isa. 55:9).

My first conclusion is that the kind of God we imagine ourselves in communion with cannot be a small tribal or household god, much less one confined to feeding hyperthyroid consumer desire. As we saw earlier, if you were to condense the whole 15-billion-year evolution of the cosmos into one year, all of recorded human history would fit into no more than that year's last ten seconds! Humans are latecomers, still trying to hire on for a bit part in a very big cosmic drama. But what is the play about? Only God knows — and there's the rub. For given the huge time scale and 125 billion galaxies, the Author of the script stands beyond reckoning, has to be big and unfathomable. Thus the Ur-Mystery we worship must be the Unnameable One/Ancient of Days of the mystics, of whom one can only speak negatively (not this, not that), a "wholly other," hidden God of Glory, the *mysterium tremendum et fascinans,* of unsurpassable centripetal and centrifugal radiance. To use other than metaphorical language of such a God (i.e., literalistic, descriptive terms) is to lose our way. The nuclear generators we call stars provide signs, halting metaphors of the God of glory.

As Hegel observed, "God does not offer himself for observation." We would do well to recall that the Bible calls upon a whole range of metaphors for the Holy One, both human and nonhuman.[5] But con-

---

5. Some of the biblical images: God is faithful husband, boxer, warrior, potter, judge, physician, thief, farmer, redeemer, executioner, slaveowner, destroyer, hero, archer, savior, consoler, strong arm, teacher, bridegroom, midwife, mother, jealous lover, stranger, seducer, enemy, butcher, guard, and mason. God is also lion, dew, light, tree, stream, bear, stumbling stone, trap, shelter, shade, drought, restaurateur, rock, crown, bird, the sun, fortress, eagle, a mace, shield, stronghold, thunderstorm, lamp, song, wind, cloud, and fire.

temporary physics supplies other appropriate metaphors, metaphors that correct the impression (created in part by classical Newtonian physics) that the Holy One is a static "thing," a kind of remote, super-spy satellite "way up there" orbiting earth, that might be defined by a noun. No, transcendent Spirit — essentially verb, not noun — is better imagined as the Great Initial Conditioner and Ultimate Strange Attractor of this or any other universe, and hence as limitlessly charged energy field, force, a process accomplishing itself and yes, unsurpassably related to everything that is. Like the wave-particles of high energy physics, the Strange Attractor cannot be pinned down or defined. Our Hebrew and early church ancestors knew this: that God is no idler but the great Energy Field in whom all creation lives and moves and has its being.

Our ancestors also knew that this is the God of the rainbow covenant — and we must remember that. The God of our Scripture is primarily concerned with renewing, or re-membering, the whole of creation and is not simply preoccupied with the human race. Redeeming the Israelites as a "light to the nations" ultimately serves a larger design, involving the whole cosmos. The Noah story is paradigmatic. In that mythical time out of time, after having almost repented of creation when, because of us, it went so haywire, God made the primordial rainbow covenant with earth, equivalently with all creation. "Never again will I curse the earth because of man," God said (Gen. 8:21). The covenant was not just with humankind but "also with every living creature to be found with [Noah], birds, cattle and every wild beast...everything that lives on the earth" (Gen. 9:10). Human redemption thus appears as a subordinate clause within the larger matrix of creation theology.

From the very beginning, the Unnameable wore many names — Brahman, Tao, Yahweh, No-Thingness, Unconquerable Sun, Grandfather Spirit, Ultimate Dispatcher, Absolute Future, and Strange Attractor. We keep dreaming them up. Though "All Circumstance are the Frame / In which His face is set," said the poet Emily Dickinson, she called God a "Force illegible." From the beginning — and continuously since — the Ultimate Strange Attractor overshadows random energy, breathes into what passes for established order and that peace which is no peace. The Strange Attractor stirs things up, is the Restless One, a God of the future.

> Now I am revealing new things to you,
> things hidden and unknown to you,
> created just now, this very moment.

Of these things you have heard nothing until now,
so that you cannot say, "Oh yes, I know all this."
You had never heard,
you did not know,
I had not opened your ear beforehand.

(Isa. 48:6–9)

God is Creator/Destroyer — a revolutionary. "Lift up your eyes to the heavens, look down upon the earth. The heavens will vanish like smoke, the earth wear out like a garment . . . but my salvation shall last forever and my justice have no end" (Isa. 51:6). The Just God exhibits few signs of a restorationist mentality, looking back to some Edenic bliss. The movement is ever forward thrusting, to the extent that, even in the Book of Revelation's vision of the end-time, God's last word is: "Now I am making the whole of creation new" (Rev. 21:5).

Yes, the Master of the Universe must be a God of order — and of beauty, subtlety, and compassion beyond telling — but to square with the chancy universe we have just surveyed, the Holy One cannot be the cuddly Super-Therapist proposed by New Agers. God has filled the universe with contingencies, with chances. The Creator of so much turbulence must be Job's God of the whirlwind, a God of "holy discontent" who is manifest as fire, devouring lion, and enemy, to disrupt and displace the reigning order of things. From the vantage of the putatively powerful, this can only look like Holy Terror, sheer chaos rather than planting the germ of a new order in the old. But so it is that the God of the whirlwind works to transform and make new, whether that be with self-organizing stars, planets, paramecia, and species of finches or with autopoietic emissaries like Moses, Lao Tzu, the Buddha, and on down to Gandhi, Rosa Parks, and Andrei Sakharov.

The Holy One is a gambler, plays the odds, takes chances. Don't count on a safety net. That we hope in God and the promising world we have been given does not mean that the world is not a dangerous, risky place. According to certain medieval Talmudic texts, twenty-six attempts at creation preceded our present world, all of which were destined to fail. The present creation, they say, has arisen from the debris of those twenty-six others, and it too is exposed to the risk of failure and a return to nothingness. As God created this universe, said the rabbis, He exclaimed, "Let's hope it works!"

In terms of spiritual practice, then, the many-named Ur-Mystery we have just evoked demands distance from our small personalities. That is, it suggests the way of detachment and ascent from the busyness and chatter of earth, a strategic withdrawal, as it were, for later reentry into

the world. Solo flights of the "alone to the Alone," at least for begin-
ners, are not recommended. A religious tradition, with creed, ethical
code, and communal ritual, comes to our aid here, mapping the terri-
tory of peak experience, providing guides and critics, setting our neural
pathways to the frequency of the Creator's music — slowly. For, as all
seasoned ascenders know but individualistic Americans tend to forget,
contact with the divine energy field can be "too much," can blow all
your circuits. The challenge is to learn, step by step, how to stand such
intensity, to be a conduit for that energy and the big dreams it begets —
without flying off into bliss-out, outer space, or without immediately
dissipating the energy by breaking down under the burden of dashed
hopes. A religious tradition, if it does its job, grounds us and thereby
enables Blessing to radiate earth.

The Source of the radiance is beyond all, far out, way up (metaphors
that have as reference point the human body); here is the Lawgiver
of Sinai's peak, Plato's Good, the Big Sky God of the ancient desert
monks and holy women (for whom you needed a ladder of ascent),
the supreme Beauty pursued up the chain of being in St. Bonaventure's
classic *Itinerarium mentis in Deum* (the journey of the mind to God).
Historically, this is the "wholly other" God of the mountaintop and
far horizon, who has been imagined, at least in the West, primarily in
masculine terms. "He" encourages a kind of top-down social order.
As the Hebrew tradition's Abraham and Moses stories have it, the
Holy One is the Aboriginal Dispatcher who calls people out from a
settled life to find or create a new world. Classically, therefore, the
spirituality of men is inward/upward that it may finally be outward-
bound and world-changing. Moses is paradigmatic: When he glowingly
descends the mountain, he brings a new code that will fashion together
a people and take them to a land they had never previously imagined.
He embodies God's imagination for the elements, for the world.

Pneumatology and a Spirituality of Descent

"The presentation of God under the aspect of power," remarked Alfred North Whitehead, "awakens every modern instinct of critical
reaction."[6] There is, however, a more down-to-earth approach to the
Author of the cosmic script. It might be called the way of descent or
immanence, and it is picked up and embraced by the male seers of the
Wisdom Books of the Hebrew Bible. Says the Book of Sirach when

---

6. Alfred North Whitehead, *Science and the Modern World* (New York: Macmillan, 1926),
274.

it personifies the hidden Wisdom of God as female and giver of new birth,

> Alone I have made the circuit of the vault of heaven
> and have walked in the depths of the abyss.
> In the waves of the sea, in the whole earth,
> and in every people and nation. (Sir. 24:5–6)

This is, of course, the wind-breath-sound that the Creator breathes forth into primordial, big bang chaos, the "gentle breeze" that walks with Adam and Eve in the garden, Elijah's "small, still voice," the Shekinah/Glory of the rabbis, the Advocate-Spirit that "blows where it will" through the Gospel of John, and of course, Gerard Manley Hopkins's Holy Ghost that "over the bent / World broods with warm breast and with ah! bright wings."

The Holy Ghost "with warm breast" sounds like the Great (Good) Mother of everyone's dreams, very different from the Roarer of Sinai who spits lightning and thunder. Serene and infinitely subtle, the metaphors are primarily feminine. She is first of all poet-muse, one who takes meaningless matter-energy and breathes meaning into it. She rejoices and dances — and so is to be found around hearth and full table, in laughter and, as the Song of Songs has it, in intense love matches. In contrast to the commanding mountain-peak God who is obsessed with ethics and more familiar to top-down men, the stress here falls on relationship and connection. What we have here is the conception we adverted to in chapter 8, the God who is "unsurpassably related" to everything, who, as the Sufi Muslims say, is nearer to us than the vein in our own throat. It turns out that, disguised as a thief in the night, the Aboriginal Dispatcher has entered the world secretly from below — and at that ever so quietly, anonymously, and erotically. (There is more to Id that met Sigmund Freud's eyes.) It's something to make the mountains clap their hands, for Wisdom identifies with groaning earth.

Women, I suspect, have always been especially sensitive to this path, a more bottom-up spirituality than the ascension approach preferred by men. The earth and all of nature, women know, is holy, made so by the fact that the First Poet "above and beyond" also moves in the atoms, in the "deep down freshness" of all dappled things. And hence it is this underground Current that women — and some men — try to tap into in their spiritual practice: in prayer, reading, and retreats, wilderness trips and jogging, listening to classic jazz, Mozart, or Gregorian chant. It sometimes feels quite impersonal, this Current does, but it's like a vast cleansing river, bringing unaccountable love and forgiveness, enabling a new beginning. Fire and water at once.

"Where you are not," says the poetic Sequence for the Pentecost liturgy, "man is naught, / Nothing good in deed or thought, / Nothing free from taint or ill." It goes on to pray,

> Heal our wounds, our strength renew;
> On our dryness pour your dew;
> Wash the stains of guilt away:
> Bend the stubborn heart and will;
> Melt the frozen, warm the chill;
> Guide the steps that go astray....

In this connection I think of Whitehead's sense of God as the "lure" behind all becoming and movement in the universe, or of Dante's "Love that moves the sun and the other stars." God works not by power but by a kind of magnetism in the mode of what Quakers call "gentle persuasion." Hence Whitehead's description of the spirit of hope (and not illusion) to be found in religion, in its root sense of reconnecting and rebonding to the heart of reality. "Religion," he said in *Science and the Modern World,*

> is the vision of something which stands beyond, behind, and within, the passing flux of immediate things; something which is real, and yet waiting to be realized; something which is a remote possibility, and yet the greatest of present facts; something that gives meaning to all that passes, and yet eludes apprehension; something whose possession is the final good, and yet is beyond all reach; something which is the ultimate ideal, and the hopeless quest.[7]

In this light, spirituality, whether ascending or descending, acquires a new context. Spiritual practices, we have to understand, are not undertaken out of curiosity or for our exclusive private benefit; they are undertaken for the sake of registering in our bones the primordial rainbow covenant: All is blessed; nothing is to be lost. As the Mahayana Buddhists have it, the point — God's point, we would interject — is to save all sentient beings. For it is through cherishing them that we redeem the meaning of the inanimate universe that sustains and buzzes within them. As a species, one human race, we hold in our hands the fate of the cosmos. Man or woman, the trick is to learn how to open to the Spirit, to say with the earth-born virgin mother, "Be it done unto

---

7. Ibid., 275.

me according to your will." In short, let Spirit-Energy flow through our sieve-like, leaky baskets!

Christology and the Dream of Earth

For Christians, of course, the decisive clue to all that I have been developing in this chapter is Jesus of Nazareth, for us God's Word, God's anointed. From the great silence, the ultimate Strange Attractor addresses us, speaking as Ignatius of Antioch described it, "from the very *bythos* or depth of nature." Is there a purpose at the bottom of things? Is the universe against us, indifferent to us — or by some wild stretch of the imagination, possibly for us? Put these questions to nature and the reply is silence or thoroughly ambiguous. Science occasionally stumbles on an intimation, a dim clue, like the anthropic principle, that suggests maybe the cosmos had observers like us in mind from the outset. Maybe. But one would hesitate to take it for certain or bet one's life on it. And strictly speaking, scientific method interdicts such speculation. In the final analysis, in response to the questions that move our souls, science remains mute.

Does the universe care whether we live or die? Are we loved? And what is the efficacy of love? What can it do? Will it overcome death? Again, if all we had to go on was the Holy Mystery, either transcendent or immanent, to which we have just alluded above, the questions would remain hanging. We have inklings, intimations, guesses — when, as it were, the clouds part, sky opens up, and one feels bathed in sunlight and blessing. Such moments evoke what a more innocent, less skeptical age than ours once called a sense of divine providence. Like Ludwig Wittgenstein's inexplicable "experience of feeling absolutely safe . . . whatever happens." As if the cosmos somehow held him in its embrace.[8]

But for the most part it is only when purpose or providence or love is embodied, when it takes on a face and a name — and speaks our name — that we can fully trust it. For Christians, Jesus Christ is that embodiment, God's Eternal Word-in-the-flesh, telling us that "God so loved the world that he sent his only Son. . . . It was not to judge the world that God sent his Son into the world, but that through him the world might be saved" (John 3:16, 17).

Jesus is the pattern for our lives, Christians are used to saying, and that is certainly part of it. But given our individualism, this saying

---

8. See Norman Malcolm, *Ludwig Wittgenstein: A Memoir* (New York: Oxford University Press, [1958] 1967), 70.

tends to have a narrowly anthropocentric focus. No, to address the big questions we have about the purpose of the universe, about a possible cosmic design or providence, about the meaning of our living and dying, Jesus has to be something more than a moral example; he has to be the Holy One's word of address to us. Has to be revelation of a "mystery hidden from eternity."

Who is Jesus of Nazareth? Christians insist that his life makes no sense unless we understand him, born of woman and the Hebrew gene pool, as primarily born and borne up by the Spirit's wind. He is earth-stuff doing the will of the Father of Mercies. The assertive (masculine) God of Sinai and the (feminine) Spirit of humble, earthen things intersect in him. He is both God's Word of address to us (as in "Let there be light"), and immanent Spirit/Wisdom sounding from star-carbon. In him taciturn earth awakens to infinite love and speaks through the throat of a man.

Like us "in everything but sin," as the tradition insists, Jesus can be understood only in global terms. He is the cosmos become conscious; he provides it with soul-space. But in him the cosmos finally finds adequate soul-space, a cavern of interiority big enough to contain the fullness of divine love and compassion. (Unlike us, he isn't a shallow container; he doesn't babble nonsense or go haywire under the strain of too much possibility.) We don't take his words as some freak, unprecedented event in the history of the world. Jesus was a Jew. He recapitulates a lineage, a crowd of witnesses, without which we, their descendants, would hardly be able to imagine that the dizzying process whereby dark matter, the galaxies, and black holes occur is "parented," fathered-forth by a boundless Love. Without these witnesses, without their boldness in pulling back the curtain of obscurity, we would not have the courage to call the creator of this vast cosmos "Father." Much less utter the more familiar term that Jesus himself uses for the "illegible Force" — namely, *Abba*.

Jesus, we believe, intensifies what God has particularly chosen the people of Israel to meditate and mediate: the meaning of everything from quarks to cities; nothing is too small or big or unclean as not to merit passionate interest and attentive understanding. Through this son of Israel Christians discover that the Ur-Mystery lives in human blood, would act through us, speak through us — to a world where today fully a fifth of the planet's 6 billion people is starving. The word we hear is a word of compassion. The voice belongs to the God of Moses, who hears the cry of the poor, which today is also the cry of the earth.

The Torah, the big dreams of the Hebrew prophets, and the poetry of the Wisdom literature speak out through him; Jesus is intelligible only within this lineage. He is heir of the prophets, itinerant preacher of good news to the poor, liberty to captives, sight to the blind, freedom to the downtrodden, the jubilee year of the Lord's favor (Isa. 61:1–2; Luke 4:18–19). The land will rest.

If the story of Jesus displays God's power, it is power emptied, rendered vulnerable. "I have not come to be served," Jesus says, "but to serve." The era of "dominion," of "lording it over" another, is declared at an end. Dostoyevsky's Grand Inquisitor parable had it right. If Jesus be a manifestation of God's way with earth, it is the way of weakness. No power plays. No material inducements. No miracles that would usurp our freedom. No bread and circuses, no easy ways out of our conflicts and confusions. "God has chosen what the world counts as folly," says St. Paul. "He has chosen things low and contemptible, mere nothings, to overthrow the existing order" (1 Cor. 1:27–28). Jesus dines with the wrong crowd. He stands with the pariah people, the scapegoats, the outcastes, castaways, and outsiders, all those who don't belong, won't fit, and upon whom a society projects its own evil and fear of death. He is a scandal, a stumbling block to the worldly-wise. So he must be sacrificed. As today the land — air, water, soil, and forest — is sacrificed, handed over to the exactions of short-term self-interest.

Weakness and vulnerability. Yet the message is not one of scarcity but of plenty, of abundant life for the impoverished and the broken, for those who mourn and those who thirst for justice. Forgiveness for the sinner — how many times? Seventy times seventy. (It's when people feel there's not enough to go around, when they feel up against the wall, that they start looking to exclude the foreigner, find a scapegoat to blame, etc.) The lowly of this earth are to be lifted up, brought into the action, into the unfolding story. "Blessed are the poor.... Blessed the gentle.... Blessed those who mourn.... Blessed those who hunger for justice.... Blessed are the merciful...the peacemakers...the persecuted" (Matt. 5:3–10). Let all come into the big drama and be fed with what the earth longs for and what the Father of Mercies desires to give: justice and abundant life.

There is no greater sin for Christians than anti-Semitism. For the cross exposes the horror show, the repetition compulsion, of a social order built on the habit of projecting evil onto others, on the device of making victims. As, historically, Christians have done with Jews, thus showing that we missed the whole point of Jesus' life and death. For the cross declares the era of scapegoating and bloody sacrifice to have come to an end — to be replaced by grace abounding, an unbloody sacrificial love and kinship, a communion that knows no ethnic, national, gender, or racial boundary. That knows no sharp boundary between the human and the material universe, for what we now behold is an earth community, kinship all around. We are the offspring of stars.

In hindsight, the church has understood Jesus in cosmic terms. As the New Testament testifies, Jesus has to be taken as prototype of our species and, better yet in cosmic-ecological terms, as the archetype of what the quarks and the molecules, from the beginning, were predestined to become — one resurrected body. Jesus is not simply a moral example. He is, as St. Paul would have it, the axis of cosmic time and the prototype and fullest embodiment of our species-role: the carrier and vessel, the fleshing out of the Creator's great dream for the universe. He embodies the rainbow covenant, reveals what from the outset the Poet-Creator imagined for the profusion of quarks that over the course of 15 billion years would take the form of human beings. Our leaky sieves are to dam up more than a sidereal river.

This is an ancient understanding that goes back to St. Paul and the Gospel of John. For them the doctrine of creation held a certain priority. "In the beginning was the Word, and the Word was with God...and through him all things came to be" (John 1:1). In this sense the doctrine of creation encompasses the doctrine of redemption as a corollary. Or to put it another way, creation and salvation are not split off from each other, but form a basic unity. For the original followers of Jesus, it sounded as if the desire of the everlasting hills had at last surfaced in the throat of a man; in hearing Jesus, they thought they heard the voice of the Creator — who would have the very atoms of their bodies leap in ecstasy. The primordial Word, they cheered, "was made flesh, he lived among us, and we saw his glory...full of grace and truth" (John 1:14). A minority of one, a miniscule disturber of the field of first-century Palestine, would alter the course of history.

This is clearly how Pauline tradition also thought of Jesus.

> He is the image of the unseen God
> and the first-born of all creation,
> for in him were created
> all things in heaven and on earth:...
> As he is the Beginning,
> he was first to be born from the dead,
> so that he should be first in every way;
> because God wanted all perfection

to be found in him
and all things to be reconciled through him and for him,
everything in heaven and everything on earth....
(Col. 1:15–20)

Within this vision of things, salvation or redemption encompasses far
more than humanity; it takes in the destiny of the whole natural order.
In other words, it embodies the primordial covenant made with Noah
and all creatures. The modern Cartesian disjunction between cosmos
(or nature) and the self is an aberration, not at all what the New
Testament envisions.

Cosmos and self, nature and history, belong together. Human beings,
we said above, can be understood only in global terms. The clincher for
this statement is located in the New Testament conviction that when
God addressed us through his Word, the Christ, what was revealed was
the very meaning of the whole cosmos, which had been "hidden since
all eternity" (Matt. 13:35). This is an interpretation that was given
new life by Scholastic theologians in what is known as the "twelfth-
century Renaissance" and further developed by Franciscan friars like
Bonaventure (1217–74) and Duns Scotus (1266?–1308). The meaning
of Christ, this tradition says, is not limited to being the remedy for sin.
That is only one dimension. From all eternity, it is said, God intended
the Incarnation of the Word — whether there had been a "fall" or not.

The claim is that from all eternity the fundamental aim of God in
creating is disclosed in Christ, that Christ embodies the secret heart
and purpose of all things, "the mystery hidden from the beginning"
(Eph. 1:9; Col. 1:26). The revelation of Christ thus pertains to the very
nature of the cosmos. Or as Bonaventure and Duns Scotus would put
it, what God intends in creating is manifest in Christ. Or as St. Paul has
it, "God was in Christ reconciling the world to himself" (2 Cor. 5:19).
The deepest potential of the universe, we could say — the meaning of
15 billion years of evolution — is that all of nature is somehow to be
united to God. Nothing is to be left out.

It's certainly possible to discover this big surprise, as did Moses or
Jesus or John Muir, out in the wilderness. In fact, ever since Puri-
tan theologian Jonathan Edwards's conversion experience there's been
something very American about discovering God in nature. "God's
excellency, his wisdom, his purity and love seemed to appear in everything," said Edwards (1703–58) after encountering God's presence in
the fields and woods of his father's New England farm, "in the sun,
moon, and stars; in the clouds and blue sky; in the grass, flowers, trees;
in the water, and all nature." Just as often, however, the breakthrough

occurs, as in the story of the Jesus' disconsolate disciples on the way to Emmaus, after the bottom has dropped out of one's world, through that "stranger" encountered on the road, the fellow traveler who makes the heart glow, as if on fire (Luke 24:13–32). It's discovered at a common table, in the "breaking of the bread" with someone whose love for you is unquestionable. From such everyday experience, one moves back to the idea that creation is "very good," that the universe is for us, that indeed we and the earth are loved with an eternal love. This doesn't guarantee a happy ending; this isn't optimism.

Eucharist: Oneness with Earth

In contrast to a Manichaean or gnostic spirituality that would have us despise the earth and escape our prison-bodies, Jesus identifies with the earth. And consecrates the earth to new purposes. Of bread and wine, he says, "This is my body, take and eat.... This is my blood, take and drink."

There are no theatrics here, no magic, simply the highly charged action of a man who knows he will die on the morrow and must make every word and gesture count. Two great movements converge in what Jesus shows us here: the everlasting desire of cosmic dust to mean something great, and God's promise that it shall be done. There is first a centripetal movement. We the followers and disciples center in on Jesus, identify, become one with him. Then there is the centrifugal, decentralizing movement. Jesus, both conduit of Spirit-Energy and cosmic dust himself, freely identifies himself with us and with the fruits of earth — the ash of a dying star present in bread and wine — and converts these gifts of earth, the work of human hands, into another story than the nightmarish one we have been telling with them. The point to highlight is that Jesus doesn't simply identify himself with his disciples around the table: he identifies himself with all the creatures of earth. It's as if he stepped out of the Hindu Upanishads, declaring "I am that" (*tat tvam asi*). Northrop Frye reminds us that the vision behind the eucharistic rite is apocalyptic, of the end-time when God will be "all in all" (1 Cor. 15:28). That is, it heralds "the way reality looks after the ego has disappeared."

> The apocalyptic vision, in which the body of Christ is the metaphor holding together all categories of being in their identity, presents us with a world in which there is only one knower, for whom there is nothing outside of or objective to that knower, hence nothing dead or insensible. This knower is also the real

consciousness in each of us. In the center of the table is the identification of the body and blood of the animal world, and the bread and wine that are the human forms of the vegetable kingdom, with the body of Christ.[9]

Jesus takes bread and wine, forms of matter-energy, and like any good poet, he metamorphoses them, transmutes them, breathes new meaning into them. In an allusion to the second chapter of the Book of Genesis, we are taken back to the original act of creation wherein "Yahweh God fashioned man of dust from the soil," and then "breathed into his nostrils a breath of life." Likewise, at the Last Supper Jesus breathes into inanimate earth-stuff (bread and wine) and converts them into signs of the eschatological "heavenly feast": a common table, a celebration of unconditioned love and forgiveness, communion among friends — a sign of plentiful, tangible grace. There is no longer any hierarchy here, no above and below. "You are my friends," John's Gospel has Jesus saying. "I call you servants no longer; a servant does not know what his master is about. I have called you friends, because I have disclosed to you everything that I heard from my Father" (John 15:14–15).

A solemn event? I suppose so, but a roiled, disputatious one by other accounts. Right in the middle of things, according to Luke's Gospel, "a jealous dispute broke out; who among them should rank the highest?" The disciples are rebuked: "The highest among you must bear himself like the youngest, the chief of you like a servant.... I am among you like a servant" (Luke 22:24, 26–27). John's Gospel actually echoes this scene; he has Jesus gird himself with a towel and, one by one, wash his disciples' feet (John 13:4–17) — as if, without saying so, John too is familiar with the story of the disciples wrangling over who was to be top dog.

When Jesus says, "This is my body ... This is my blood," and "Take and eat ... Take and drink," we have the centrifugal movement — outward from him to us. He is bidding us to take in, to discover in our own soul-space the same Spirit that works in and through him. "So should the just soul be equal to God and close beside God," says Meister Eckhart (1260–1329), "not beneath or above." "The Father," he goes on, "gives birth to the Son in eternity, equal to himself. 'The Word was

---

9. Northrop Frye, *The Great Code: The Bible and Literature* (New York: Harcourt Brace Jovanovich, 1981), 166, 165. For a similar experience of nonduality and communion, see Victor Turner's accounts of pilgrimages in *The Ritual Process: Structure and Anti-Structure* (Ithaca, N.Y.: Cornell University Press, 1977), 94–165; and *Dramas, Fields, and Metaphors: Symbolic Action in Human Society* (Ithaca, N.Y.: Cornell University Press, 1974), 231–99.

with God, and God was the Word' (John 1:1); it was the same in the same nature."

> Yet I say more: He has given birth to him in my soul. Not only is the soul with him, and he equal with it, but he is in it, and the Father gives his Son birth in the soul in the same way as he gives him birth in eternity, and not otherwise. He must do it whether he likes it or not. The Father gives birth to his Son without ceasing; and I say more: He gives me birth, his Son and the same Son. I say more: He gives birth not only to me, his Son, but he gives birth to me as himself and himself as me and to me as his being and nature. In the innermost source, there I spring out in the Holy Spirit, where there is one life and one being and one work.[10]

"Do this in memory of me," he commands. Equivalently, that is an invitation to remember ourselves, who we are and what we are here for. Serve one another (wash each other's feet). Be humble; that is, re-member you are born of the earth (*adama*). In effect Jesus is saying that the great work of transfiguring earth stuff in accord with the Cre-ator's dream is not his solitary work but fundamentally the work of "the Father in heaven." "May they all be one," John's Gospel has Jesus praying at the end. "Father, may they be one in us, as you are in me and I am in you" (John 17:21). The Father/Creator gives himself away in Jesus, as He would give himself away in all of us.

Swallow this, Jesus effectively declares: I am God's promise for the elements, the exemplary inside of nature, its secret wish fulfilled. As-sume my role. Swallow my words, let them resonate in the marrow of your bones, and you will tap into the same current of Spirit that moves me. Swallow me and you will have taken in what God imagines for matter: that it be spirited, that justice be done to all, according to the great vision of the rainbow covenant. We shall then be one body, matter and spirit reconciled. Come, he says, here is everlasting life — and the way, through the all-encompassing charity of God, to do jus-tice to the earth. No, there is no magic blueprint for what such justice would mean. It's this: the community is gathered — and the commu-nity includes all the earth, the ecosystem — and the question is put. It is up to us, trusting in the Spirit's guidance, to figure out how we must proceed. Don't just stare into heaven; use your wits!

The eucharistic moment, of course, is part of the Passover rite, the recollection of the ancient exodus event from Egypt, which created a

---

10. Meister Eckhart, *The Essential Sermons, Commentaries, Treatises, and Defense*, trans. and introduction Edmund Colledge, O.S.A., and Bernard McGinn (New York: Paulist Press, 1981), 187.

new people. The rite therefore models a new polity — which the Book of Revelation, chapters 21 and 22, imagines as a wild New Jerusalem, a radiant Ancient of Days at center, inner city, emanating the river of life down Main Street. Certainly this is a big part of what is going on: not simply a consolation farewell dinner for those left behind, but a commissioning, a renewal of the covenant. The community, which will be church, is charged to make over the earth into a symbol of what the Creator, from the beginning, imagined for star carbon to become: a truly human city, a place of justice and love that hums with Spirit-Energy. What we have here is a great eschatological vision. Come Holy Spirit, renew the face of the earth!

It is against this background that the Easter liturgy's Exsultet proclaims, "Exult, all creation, in shining splendor.... Christ has conquered [the forces of death]." For in him the 15-billion-year-long odyssey wherein great nature struggles to find its own voice and meaning as the Creator intended is anticipated and prefigured. Christ is that voice; star carbon and earth stuff that in him finds its purpose, its point — and, in the resurrection, its glory.

Why should we value the material world? All living things? Not because the universe is divine but because it holds a great promise. Because the universe is unfinished, imperfect, a mere installment on an extravagant future. To trash the earth or the creatures of earth is to trash their promise and our own future as well. The things of earth are ultimately not destined to pass away, to vanish without a trace. Christ is Alpha and Omega, the key to the beginning and the end of all creation. If he be raised up, it means all things are raised up. Hence death does not have the last word; it is vanquished. We see but through a glass darkly, we do not apprehend how, but all of creation is somehow taken up in Christ and the promise of the resurrection of the body. This is the vision, however mediated, without which the universe is doomed to futility.

Converting Matter-Energy into Sacrament

What is our function, our great work, in this vast cosmos? What are we here for? "Do this in memory of me," the man said. We have work to do — good work. We return here to that second sense of sacrament or stewardship we mentioned in chapter 2.

Let me backtrack a bit and pull a few things together. When ancient eighth-century Celts rose in the morning to pray, they prayed with a deep sense of connection to the material world: "I arise today through the strength of heaven: light of sun, radiance of moon, splendor of fire, speed of lightning, swiftness of wind, depth of sea, stability of earth, firmness of rock."[11] A post-Einsteinian cosmos reconnects us with these natural wonders. In contrast to the iron cage of classical physics, we can now understand ourselves as no longer alien intruders in the cosmos, but belonging. The universe's history, its groaning to give birth to something glorious, comes together in us, becomes conscious in us. The great outdoors is inside us, and we are its interiority, its cave of winds. Our adversary relationship to nature, then, is the hangover of the pernicious half-truths of a mechanistic era; it is no longer justified. We, too, like Francis of Assisi, are joined to nature at the hip. Indeed, our connection and belonging lie so deep that we cannot even define our identities without including — or should I say, paying grateful homage to — the whole great sweep of cosmic evolution. "I am that," we can now say with the Hindu Upanishads: stardust, earth stuff, a being literally conceived in far-off parts of the universe and seeded here on this planet to make a difference to the cosmos, to strike a chord, play a variation on the great themes of its music that has never been heard before. This truth and its challenge defined us before we ever babbled a word or took a step on our own.

It's as if all the stardust in our DNA, the microbes that swim in our cells, the humble algae that gave us a breathable atmosphere — yes, all of nature — were expectant, waiting on us to finish the cosmic symphony well (certainly with the injection of more than a little blues and jazz). "It was not for any fault on the part of creation," says St. Paul, "that it was unable to attain its purpose, it was made so by God; but creation still retains the hope of being freed, like us, from its slavery to decadence [entropy], to enjoy the same freedom and glory as the children of God. From the beginning till now the entire creation, as we know, has been groaning in one great act of giving birth" (Rom. 8:20–23).

We can now read this text, penetrate it, in light of complexity/chaos theory and the strong anthropic principle, and reread that principle itself not in a narrowly anthropocentric sense but as an intimation of the great design of which we are a part. We are members of the orchestra, the choir, in a great project, a "mystery hidden from the foundation of the world" (Matt. 13:35; Ps. 78:2; Col. 1:26; Eph. 1:9).

But what is that mysterious design, that great project?

Try this children's story about a great experiment: The dizzy subatomic particle-waves spinning wildly out of the big bang didn't know

---

11. From "The Deer Cry, " attributed to St. Patrick, cited in Thomas Cahill, *How the Irish Saved Civilization* (New York: Doubleday, 1995), 116–19.

what to make of themselves at first (no fault of theirs, God made them so), but the initial conditions were such that as they joined forces, split and joined again and again and again, corralling energy to form atoms, galactic clusters, molecules, chains of inorganic and organic compounds, simple life-forms — and on and on to *Homo sapiens* — they were implicitly carving out an inside, an interior to ferry and hold the energy of their Initial Conditioner, the message of the Aboriginal Dispatcher who set them loose in the first place and never ceases to sustain the diversifying process forward. From the very beginning, the trouble was that quarks, atomic nuclei, molecules, plants, and bacteria, as finely woven as they are, could contain only so much of the divine energy field. It came across like static; no clear message. They weren't up to it, didn't have sufficiently complex circuitry, to hear what this whole buzzing and proliferating confusion was about — the God-Sound in their midst. Animals were an enormous improvement, of course, but whatever they knew they couldn't say. Only with the emergence of the species *Homo sapiens* did you have the complex hard wiring — nervous system and brain — that could possibly tune in to Cosmic Mind and thus become mindful of the meaning of things. In short, it took the atoms awake, mindful, and free in us to begin to decipher the "mystery hidden from the foundation of the world."

Offspring of stars, children of earth, we cannot be here simply to express our small personalities. Before the earth belonged to us, we belonged to the earth. We are here to take on duties to our fellow citizens of the earth, among which we must include plants, animals, and the soil. The cosmos may have been designed, from the very beginning, for carbon-based life and consciousness. The probabilities may have been stacked in our favor. Why? So that we might at last gather together all flux and chance variation that have preceded us and tell their story, tell the story of quarks and stars, of cells and mitochondria, of photosynthesizing algae and invertebrates, of lizards and leopards.

We are great mothering nature's soul-space, her heart and vocal chords — and her willingness, if we consent to it, to be spirited, to be the vessel of the Holy One whose concern reaches out to embrace all that is created. When we fail in this soul-work, fail in extending our own reach of concern, nature fails/falls with us. But when it happens, when we say yes to the Spirit who hovers over our inner chaos, the mountains clap their hands, the hills leap like gazelles. They and the quarks have a big stake in us.

Remember, though, to be patient: In the condensed astronomical time of a cosmic year, our species has been around only for a minute

or two, and for much of that time we've been sleep-walking. Our cosmological task takes some waking up to, and getting used to. We have
manifold associations with the earth, and hence belong to multiple
biological and ecological communities, each of which we must become
familiar with, as with the human communities of which we are a part.
One step at a time.

Nonetheless, within the great span of evolution, we represent a turning point for nature, and a turning point for the Great Dispatcher as
well. Two significant events happen simultaneously, or converge, once
humans emerge from the prebiotic soup. First, as the team of Plato,
Aristotle, Augustine, and Aquinas would say, consciousness or mindedness — of whatever fleeting sort — would not be there except for
participation in the mindfulness of the Poet-Maker of all things. Darwinian evolution only explains our hard wiring, not how it is that
we are aware or minded. Secondly, as I have said, consciousness is
also nothing else than great nature more or less awake and reflec-
tive. That's a beginning; the spiritual task is to deepen our inwardness
and at the same time intensify our outer associations, and therewith,
stretch our imaginations and understandings to include as much of
this world as we can tend and care for. We are nature's black box, her
vessel of soul-space — and hence her last chance to become spirited,
to be the vessel of God, the carrier of the message that all creation
is not only "very good," but to be glorified. That's the script, the big
theo-logical drama.

We are the voice of nature, "the voice of the hurricane, this thermal
howl." And like the rest of nature, we are here to give a sign, if you
will, a high sign. This entails more than expressing our little, private
personality. It is a collective thing, a matter of public policy, carried
out through those institutional combinations we call government, legal
system, school, corporation, and church. The signs we give through
these vehicles of expression constitute public policy for the earth. The
earth, or what we as a species make out of earth, is our sign. We are
here in a shared project to move mountains, to make a metaphor of
earth. It is poet's work, the poet-maker and builder in each one of
us. This the great work of which Thomas Berry speaks, the task of
moving the human project from its devastating exploitation of nature
to a posture of benign presence to nature. As he says, it is a task given
to us, a project we did not first choose but for which we were chosen
"by some power beyond ourselves."

With this theme, we return to the issue of Steven Weinberg's pointless cosmos. Inevitably, we leave our graffiti scrawl, our stamp, our

mark, upon the planet during our brief passage here. How does our collective signature read? What sign have we chosen to give? Is it promise or curse? With these questions, we reach behind our factories and cities, behind our technology, to the vision — or lack of it — at their base.

Human history: what is it except the story of what we have made of matter/energy? Matter, Aristotle and Aquinas and Hegel and Marx thought, is sheer potency and means anything or nothing in particular until it has been filtered through the human imagination. We know today that this is not quite true; the vast galaxies, the subatomic underworld, the rain forests, and the bacteria swimming in our intestines give their own signals, carry their own sets of internal instructions, have their own organizational agendas, and do magnificent work. But it remains true that at least on this spiral arm of the Milky Way galaxy, it is we — the last in the great chain, the final transformers and interpreters — who voice nature's story, who are given the chance to make comedy or tragedy of it all, to make sense or make a mess of it by how we live, by what we do with our science and technology and culture.

Is the vast universe in which we dwell pointless? Or is it, as Jacques Monod put it, deaf to our music, indifferent to our hopes, our sufferings, even our crimes? Does nightmare history, the cries out of Auschwitz and Hiroshima, not count, not set the stars to weeping? Now I think the answer you give to such questions will depend on whether you are in touch with your own soul, that cavern in you where all the currents of the cosmos intersect and meet. Sunk in your body-temple, operating through your sympathetic nervous system, your soul is the basic depth-probe or antenna — better than any electron microscope or nuclear accelerator — through which you listen to the thermal howl, the microbes that swim in your cells, the humble blue-green algae, ancient forests now buried under the earth, the wildlife with whom you are kin. Do you not hear the entire creation groaning, aspirating in one great act of giving birth? And do you not hear the appeal, the request, that earth makes of us? Can you not read earth's sign language?

"Why, if this interval of being can be spent serenely / in the form of a laurel," asks Rilke in *The Ninth Duino Elegy*, "why then / have to be human — and escaping from fate, keep longing for fate?"[12] It is not, he says, because happiness exists, or out of curiosity, much less to improve ourselves.

---

12. I am using Stephen Mitchell's translation of this poem, from *The Enlightened Heart: Anthology of Sacred Poetry* (New York: Harper & Row, 1989), 140–43.

But because *truly* being here is so much; because everything here
apparently needs us, this fleeting world, which in some
   strange way
keeps calling to us. Us the most fleeting of all.
Once for each thing. Just once; no more. And we too,
just once. And never again. But to have been
this once, completely, even if only once:
to have been one with the earth, seems beyond undoing.

We are up to our neck in debt. Where would we be without star factories? Without blue-green algae? Without rain forests? Without the
mitochondria in our cells? Do you not hear the stars, the algae, the
forests and mitochondria calling out to you — to name them properly,
to understand them, to give them voice, to give them meaning by what
we make of this earth? "To say them," as Rilke puts it,

> oh to say them *more* intensely than the Things themselves
> ever dreamt of existing. Isn't the secret intent
> of this taciturn Earth, when it forces two lovers together,
> that inside their boundless emotion all things may
>   shudder with joy?

Isn't that what we're here for: the secret mission of the scientist's inquiries, the homemaker's labor, the builder's dream? To pour soul into
the soulless, into the chaos of nature, and make all creation "shudder
with joy," as the Creator-Poet did on the first day?

   What is the import of the new physics and cosmology — except to
bring forth questions like these? We are placed in a radically unfinished
universe, where it is our task to bring things to completion. Inanimate
nature has been about this transforming work since the beginning, and
now it is our turn, our chance at the job of making something either
absurd or beautiful for God. This is, after all, a possibly absurd planet
in a rhymeless universe. What have we made of our piece of the action?
What will we make of it in the time to come? We owe this diligent, unfinished world deliverance from absurdity, from pointlessness. And we
do that by freely letting it enter our hearts, by freely claiming it as our
body and blood. Shall the earth become a holy place, be transfigured?
To a great extent, that depends on us.

   Again, it seems that Rilke had it mostly right: To deliver the earth
from absurdity involves making a good story of our passage here,
telling "the unsayable one" (or at least an impressionable angel) of
"things." It might amount to a psalm.

Praise this world to an angel, not the unsayable one,
you can't impress *him* with glorious emotion....
So show him
something simple, which, formed over generations,
lives as our own, near at hand and within our gaze.
Tell him of Things. He will be astonished....
And these Things,
which live by perishing, know you are praising them;
    transient,
they look to us for deliverance: us, the most transient
    of all.
They want us to change them, utterly, in our invisible heart,
within — oh endlessly — within us! Whoever we may be at last.
Earth, isn't this what you want: to arise within us,
invisible? Isn't that your dream...?

T W E L V E

Citizens of Earth

Growth for the sake of growth is the ideology of the cancer cell.
— EDWARD ABBEY, *Desert Solitaire*

As a species, we seem to have an infinite capacity to postpone difficult decisions. But since these decisions are inevitable, we are simply leaving the next generation with far more difficult ones than any we now face. Decisions are being postponed in societies at all levels of industrial development and of every political persuasion.... In effect, we are behaving as though we have no children, as though there will not be a next generation.
— LESTER R. BROWN, *State of the World 1998*

From now on we are steering things that, in the past, we didn't steer. In dominating the planet, we become accountable for it. In manipulating death, life, reproduction, the normal and the pathological, we become responsible for them. We are going to have to decide about every thing, and even about Everything — about the physical and thermodynamic future, about Darwinian evolution, about life, about the earth and about time, about the filtering of possibilities — candidates to be evaluated for becoming realities — a process Leibniz described as characterizing the work of God the creator, in the secret of his infinite understanding.
— MICHEL SERRES, *Conversations on Science, Culture, and Time*

Throughout these pages, I have introduced each chapter with epigraphs, several of them selections taken from some of our best nature writers: John Muir, Aldo Leopold, Wendell Berry, Annie Dillard, Bill McKibben, and Thomas Berry. They are writers, as I described them in chapter 5, who belong to the arcadian tradition of Gilbert White. We could as easily identify them as belonging to the pastoral tradition of the Bible. In any case, the choice has been deliberate, an indication that the ecological crisis requires more than the quick fixes of science

220

and technology. Our ecological problems, I have said from the start, are essentially cultural — matters of how we think of ourselves in relation to nature. Solving these problems demands a new shape to that relationship. It will require a spirited response from and to the earth, from both scientists and men and women of faith.

I call upon the writers of the arcadian tradition because they do not ignore, much less denigrate, the scientific approach to nature; rather, like White himself, they presuppose and include a scientific understanding of the natural world. Instead of seeing a scientific approach to nature as hostile to an aesthetic or religious approach, a knowledge of physics, molecular and organic chemistry, geology, botany, or zoology is considered an asset, something that can only enhance and deepen our understanding and appreciation of the environment. Science in this view can only add to an aesthetic and spiritual valuation of the natural world. At the same time, however, these writers implicitly assume that there is something partial and incomplete — nay, very abstract — about a strictly scientific approach to physical reality. They perceive nature, I want to say, more concretely and fully than the scientific method allows. The scientific method goes out of its way to prescind from or ignore, as if it were not there, all nature's beauty, as well as its capacity to elicit a sense of the mystical. The nature writer is a humanist; he or she takes in that beauty, and as well the element of the sublime, the wonder-ful and the mysterious, the stupendous and the unutterably other. And let us say it: the holy.

We owe the rivers, fields, forests, and hills of our homeland our deepest love and affection. And our protection. Think of how the Hebrew psalmists felt about the hills and fields of Judea, Thoreau at Walden Pond or in the Maine woods, Willa Cather's love of the Nebraska prairie, John Muir's ecstasies in the high Sierras, the fondness of Annie Dillard for Tinker Creek, or Czeslaw Milosz's love of the Lithuanian countryside in the novel *The Issa Valley*. These powerful sentiments of place and homeland, usually established in childhood or early adolescence, form the basis and motivation for our obligations to nature, and thus constitute the foundation for any ecological ethic. The theological perspective I developed in the last chapter simply intensifies this foundation, gives it greater depth and scope.

The sciences need the humanities, claims Michel Serres, because the humanities remember the origins, the genesis of science, in the problem of evil. The humanities are the guardians of human pain, those who keep vigil over the cultures of woe and mourning, and they do not forget that "the problem of evil underlies the power we derive from our various means of addressing it."[1] The genesis story of science begins here, claims Serres, with the problem of evil: as an effort to overcome it. Science, therefore, cannot afford to forget its progenitors — the prophet Jeremiah's lament over the ruins of Jerusalem, Job howling from his dung heap, the horrors of the Trojan war, Ulysses in his wanderings, the Greek tragedians, the passion of Jesus Christ, the Black Plague of the fourteenth century, the history of European anti-Semitism, the tribulations of Native American tribes, the horrors of the slave trade, Auschwitz, Pol Pot's "killing fields" in Cambodia, Bosnian ethnic cleansing, and the Rwandan Holocaust — the great nightmare of history. Knowledge and misfortune cannot be separated. For it is out of the oceanic clamor of suffering that all our knowledge and practical activity springs. Human suffering, says Serres, "produces the background noise from which all our knowledge and the conditions of our practical activities spring. This is the origin of knowledge and our expertise." He goes on:

> No, we did not set out long ago to understand things and act upon their future because we felt and observed through the five senses, the way philosophy once amused itself by saying we did, or for other reasons just as cold. No — we did it because we suffered from our misery or our crimes, and because we were moved by the intuition of our untimely death. Knowledge is based on this mourning.
>
> Our capacities come from our weaknesses and our effectiveness from our fragilities. Our science has no other foundation than this permanent collapse, this lack, this endless slippage into the abyss of pain.[2]

At a foundational level, then, Copernicus and Darwin and Pasteur emerge from the same human agony and anguish as do the prophet Jeremiah, Sophocles and Aeschylus, Shakespeare and Balzac and Solzhenitsyn!

If scientific educators do not want to turn out monsters of inhumanity, they must remember the lessons of tragedy, the wisdom of the humanities. "Deprived of the terrible lessons emanating from this source," says Serres,

> the sciences would train our eminent experts to become brutes and savages, infinitely more dangerous (as our century has abundantly

---

1. Michel Serres with Bruno Latour, *Conversations on Science, Culture, and Time*, trans. Roxanne Lapidus (Ann Arbor: University of Michigan Press, 1995), 182.
2. Ibid. 181–82.

shown) than during the days when necessity dominated our paltry and ineffectual technologies. The future will force experts to come quickly to the humanities and to humanity, there to seek a science that is humane — since in our language the word signifying our genus also signifies compassion.[3]

Love of the Wild

In commenting about the Book of Job in my first chapter, I pointed to the religious significance of wilderness in the experience of the Jews. Let me offer but a single example of its continuing importance, even for the contemporary secular spirit: the late Edward Abbey in his book *Desert Solitaire* of 1968, a now classic account of the three seasons Abbey spent as a park ranger in the Arches National Monument near the little town of Moab in southeast Utah. In the very first chapter, Abbey explains why he has left the city for the wilderness, and what he is seeking there. Without quite acknowledging it, for he calls himself a nonbeliever, he comes to the high desert of Utah like some third-century desert hermit-monk, seeking something like the vision of Moses on Sinai. He disdains his own habit of describing the fabulous rock formations in human terms, as looking like heads from Easter Island, "a stone god or a petrified ogre."

> The personification of the natural is exactly the tendency I wish to suppress in myself, to eliminate for good. I am here not only to evade for a while the clamor and filth and confusion of the cultural apparatus but also to confront, immediately and directly if it's possible, the bare bones of existence, the elemental and fundamental, the bedrock which sustains us. I want to be able to look at and into a juniper tree, a piece of quartz, a vulture, a spider, and see it as it is in itself, devoid of all humanly ascribed qualities, anti-Kantian, even the categories of scientific description. To meet God or Medusa face to face, even if it means risking everything human in myself. I dream of a hard and brutal mysticism in which the naked self merges with a non-human world and yet somehow survives still intact, individual, separate. Paradox and bedrock.[4]

Still, Abbey the hard-headed realist and agnostic can hardly help himself. When confronted by the works of nature in the concrete, the response is awe and wonder, even a sense that he is in the presence of

---

3. Ibid., 179–89.
4. Edward Abbey, *Desert Solitaire: A Season in the Wilderness* (New York: Touchstone Simon and Schuster, 1968), 6.

the holy. Here is Abbey standing before a monumental, eroded piece of sandstone, the so-called Delicate Arch, which looks like a "giant engagement ring cemented in rock, a bow-legged pair of petrified cowboy chaps, a triumphal arch for a procession of angels, an illogical geological freak." One may see in it, he concedes, a symbol, a sign, a fact, a "thing without meaning or a meaning which includes all things." Much the same could be said, he insists, "of the tamarisk down in the canyon, of the blue-black raven croaking on the cliff, of your own body."

> If the Delicate Arch has any significance it lies, I will venture, in the power of the odd and unexpected to startle the senses and surprise the mind out of their ruts of habit, to compel us into a reawakened awareness of the wonderful... that which is full of wonder.
>
> A weird, lovely, fantastic object out of nature like Delicate Arch has the curious ability to remind us — like rock and sunlight and wind and wilderness — that out there is a different world, older and greater and deeper by far than ours, a world which surrounds and sustains the little world of men as sea and sky surround and sustain a ship. The shock of the real. For a little while we are again able to see, as the child sees, a world of marvels. For a few moments we discover that nothing can be taken for granted, for if this ring of stone is marvelous then all which shaped it is marvelous, and our journey here on earth, able to see and touch and hear in the midst of tangible and mysterious things-in-themselves, is the most strange and daring of all adventures.[5]

This is ancient wisdom. The connection to nature is tied up with wonder, as something "older and deeper by far" than our world of artifact, a "world of marvels" that surrounds and sustains our little world. Such wonder, such "shock of the real," as Aristotle maintained, is the beginning of science and wisdom.

Abbey is something of a scold. He excoriates what he calls "Industrial Tourism," which means the Park Service for which he works, the motel and restaurant owners, the gasoline retailers, the oil corporations, the road-building contractors, the heavy equipment manufacturers, the state and federal agencies and the "sovereign, all-powerful automotive industry" that serves the mechanized tourists — "the Wheelchair Explorers who are at once the consumers, the raw material and the victims of Industrial Tourism." No more roads or cars, he argues, should be allowed in national parks. "We have agreed not

---

5. Ibid., 36–37.

to drive our automobiles into cathedrals, concert halls, art museums, legislative assemblies, private bedrooms and the other sanctums of our culture; we should treat our national parks with the same deference, for they, too, are holy places." "Holier than our churches," this atheist claims.

Nature, he argues, cannot be reduced to the managed resources of utilitarian reason. Wilderness is not disposable or dispensable. It is vital to the human spirit. Not by bread alone do we live.

> Wilderness is not a luxury but a necessity of the human spirit, and as vital to our lives as water and good bread. A civilization which destroys what little remains of the wild, the spare, the original, is cutting itself off from its origins and betraying the principle of civilization itself.

> If industrial man continues to multiply his numbers and expand his operations he will succeed in his apparent intention to seal himself off from the natural and isolate himself within a synthetic prison of his own making. He will make himself an exile from the earth and then will know at last, if he is still capable of feeling anything, the pain and agony of final loss. He will understand what the captive Zia Indians meant when they made a song out of their sickness for home:

> > My home is over there,
> > Now I remember it;
> > And when I see that mountain far away,
> > Why then I weep,
> > Why then I weep,
> > Remembering my home.[6]

What is the fascination in wilderness? What does it mean, and why is it so important? "The word," says Abbey, "suggests the past and the unknown, the womb of earth from which we have emerged," which for Abbey means the only "paradise" he ever wants. But Abbey does not romanticize this paradise. It includes "apple trees and golden women but also scorpions and tarantulas and flies, rattlesnakes and Gila monsters, sandstorms, volcanos and earthquakes, bacteria and bear, cactus, yucca, bladderweed, ocotillo and mesquite, flash floods and quicksand, and yes — disease and death and the rotting of the flesh." His paradise of wild nature is not a garden of bliss and changeless perfection where toothless lions lie down with lambs.

---

6. Ibid., 169.

It means something lost and something still present, something remote and at the same time intimate, something buried in our blood and nerves, something beyond us and without limit. Romance — but not to be dismissed on that account. The romantic view, while not the whole truth, is a necessary part of the whole truth.

But the love of wilderness is more than a hunger for what is always beyond reach; it is also an expression of loyalty to the earth, the earth which bore us and sustains us, the only home we shall ever know, the only paradise we ever need — if only we had the eyes to see. Original sin, the true original sin, is the blind destruction for the sake of greed of this natural paradise which lies all around us — if only we are worthy of it.[7]

Loyalty to the earth: that's the mantra we have been seeking. Without love of and loyalty to the earth, there can be no justice to the earth, no ecological ethic for our time. What we require is a new and enlarged social contract — a contract with the earth.

Extending the Social Contract to Earth

In a landmark essay published in 1949 and titled "The Land Ethic," the wildlife ecologist Aldo Leopold spoke of the need to extend the reach of ethics beyond relations to other individuals and society to our natural environment.[8] From my opening chapter, this has been one of the central issues: the idea of expanding our moral concern beyond the human circle to include the larger biological and ecological communities to which we belong.[9] As the Bible's Yahwist scribe insisted, we are creatures of the soil. To Leopold, "land" meant more than soil; it is a "fountain of energy flowing through a circuit of soils, plants, and animals."

Food chains are the living channels which conduct energy upward; death and decay return it to the soil. The circuit is not closed; some energy is dissipated in decay, some added by absorption from the air, some is stored in soils, peats, and long-lived forests; but it is a sustained circuit, like a slowly augmented revolving fund of life.[10]

7. Ibid., 166–67.

8. Aldo Leopold, *A Sand County Almanac and Sketches Here and There* (New York: Oxford University Press, [1949] 1989), 201–26.

9. See also Michel Serres, *The Natural Contract*, trans. Elizabeth MacArthur and William Paulson (Ann Arbor: University of Michigan Press, 1995).

10. Leopold, *A Sand County Almanac*, 216.

We have obligations to this whole complex circuit, this extraordinary "fountain of energy."

For Leopold, Darwinian competition was not the last word. Nor were economic considerations. The land demanded a moral response. For him, ethics meant social as opposed to anti-social behavior. Growing out of the "tendency of interdependent individuals or groups to evolve modes of co-operation," ethics places a "limitation on freedom of action in the struggle for existence." Over time, Leopold pointed out, we have evolved an ethics to deal with the relation between individuals — for example, the Mosaic Decalogue — and we have modified that code to deal with the relation between the individual and society, as in the Golden Rule and the institutions of a democratic polity. And yes, we have the rich legacy of social contract theory. But as yet, Leopold wrote, there is "no ethic dealing with man's relation to land and to the animals and plants which grow upon it." Land, he said, is like Odysseus's slave girls (whom he slaughtered with impunity on his return home), still property; and our relation to it remains entirely economic, "entailing privileges but not obligations."

What Leopold was after — and what this book has been about — is an extension of our ethical boundaries to the larger communities of which we are a part. Charles Darwin had a similar idea. In *The Descent of Man* (1871), he had argued that moral "sympathies" evolved — from the rudimentary "social qualities" and "mutual aid" within all animal species, which had direct survival value, to the ethics of human beings, who gradually broadened their concern to include "small tribes," then "larger communities," and eventually "nations" and "races." Against any dualism between human and other animal species, Darwin and his popularizers argued for the unity and continuity of all life, a universal kinship. It would be an idea championed in our time not just by Aldo Leopold, but by theologian-physician Albert Schweitzer (1875–1965), the bacteriologist René Dubos (1901–82), literary critic Joseph Wood Krutch (1893–1970), oceanographer Rachel Carson (1907–64), entomologist Edward O. Wilson, and philosopher Michel Serres.

In the 1980s, Edward O. Wilson wrote about a "deep conservation ethic" based on "biophilia," a deep-seated tendency of the human mind to affiliate with life-forms and the life process itself. Wilson maintained that this sense of kinship had been bred into our bone by the process of having co-evolved over millions of years with myriad other forms of life. And hence, he claimed, we still need them, even if subconsciously, for the continued survival of "the human spirit." I hope he is right.

As I noted above, especially in chapter 4, the notion that these life-forms — or Leopold's fulsome sense of "the land" — could have moral claims to make violates the fundamental rule of conventional social contract theory, which restricts duties and rights to other human agents. Once we have clarified our duties in justice to other members of the human race, say the social contract theorists, we have done the main work, covered the major issues, the big numbers. What is left out, we are led to believe, amounts to a small minority, which doesn't amount to a hill of beans — nothing to worry much about. But this is not the case.

Philosopher Mary Midgley has performed the useful service of making a list of some of the items that ought to involve us in noncontractual duties.[11] The scope of this list, as you will see, is considerable, in fact daunting. It turns out that social contract theory omits a great deal.

1. The dead
2. Posterity
3. Children
4. The senile
5. The temporarily insane
6. The permanently insane
7. Defectives, ranging down to "human vegetables"
8. Embryos
9. Sentient animals
10. Non-sentient animals
11. Plants of all kinds
12. Artifacts, including works of art
13. Inanimate but structured objects — crystals, rivers, rocks, etc.
14. Unchosen groups of all kinds, including families and species
15. Ecosystems, landscapes, villages, warrens, cities, etc.
16. Countries
17. The biosphere
18. Oneself
19. God

---

11. Mary Midgley, "Duties Concerning Islands," in *Environmental Ethics,* ed. Robert Elliot (New York: Oxford University Press, 1995), 89–103, esp. 97.

"As far as numbers go," says Midgley, "this is no minority of the beings with whom we have to deal. We are a small minority of them." Social contract theory is narrowly anthropocentric and omits the overwhelming majority of beings. And hence it is deficient as ethical theory, for it leaves out the greater part of our obligations.

Certainly, so far as importance is concerned, some of these listed beings demand more attention than others. The various kinds of claims are not all equal. We need a rating system, a set of priorities. My duties to bacteria are arguably not on the same level as my duties to cetaceans or young children. But what is clear, argues Midgley, is that we are involved in a whole range of different kinds of duties — to animals, to plants, and to the biosphere — and the different claims have to be understood and compared in detail, not written off in advance. It should also be clear that "duties of justice become more pressing, not less so, when dealing with the weak and inarticulate, who cannot argue back." Nor will the sharp antithesis that Kant drew between persons and things serve to map the huge continuum that ought to concern us.

> Duties need not be quasi-contractual relations between symmetrical pairs of rational human agents. There are all kinds of other obligations holding between asymmetrical pairs....To speak of duties to things in the inanimate and comprehensive sectors of my list is not necessarily to personify them superstitiously, or to indulge in chatter about the "secret life of plants." It expresses merely that there are suitable and unsuitable ways of behaving in given situations. People have duties as farmers, parents, consumers, tourists, potential ancestors, and actual descendants, etc. As such, it is the business of each not to forget his transitory and dependent position, the rich gifts which he has received, and the tiny part he plays in a vast, irreplaceable and fragile whole.[12]

Midgley here reminds us that to a great extent our obligations are determined by our multiple memberships in a whole series of communities, both human and nonhuman, and our complex relationships thereto. At an earlier period of history, say in the Middle Ages, it was a matter of course that responsibilities were gauged in terms of membership in family, group, tribe, guild, feudal hierarchy. The distinctive challenge of our time is to consider duties that arise out of our membership in complex biological and ecological communities that are to a great extent invisible to us. Consider, for instance, our relationship on the food chain to soil bacteria, fungi, algae, and protozoa. Without

---

12. Ibid., 101.

the crucial functions that these microorganisms perform (decomposing waste, transferring nutrients, etc.) for the plants we eat, we could not long survive on the planet. Yet for all practical purposes these microorganisms are out of sight and, unfortunately, out of mind. Midgley's list serves the useful purpose of enumerating a whole set of wholes of which we are a dependent part, and to which we owe our lives. We are literally parented by these ecosystems.

Leopold's land ethic is another way of making the same point. His description of it runs directly against the "imperial ecology" of Francis Bacon and remains worth repeating at some length:

> All ethics so far evolved rest upon a single premise: that the individual is a member of a community of interdependent parts. His instincts prompt him to compete for his place in that community, but his ethics prompt him also to co-operate (perhaps in order that there may be a place to compete for).
>
> The land ethic simply enlarges the boundaries of the community to include soils, waters, plants, and animals, or collectively: the land.
>
> This sounds simple: do we not already sing our love for and obligation to the land of the free and the home of the brave? Yes, but just what and whom do we love? Certainly not the soil, which we are sending helter-skelter downriver. Certainly not the waters, which we assume have no further function except to turn turbines, float barges, and carry off sewage. Certainly not plants, of which we exterminate whole communities without batting an eye. Certainly not the animals, of which we have already extirpated many of the largest and most beautiful species. A land ethic of course cannot prevent the alteration, management, and use of these "resources," but it does affirm their right to continued existence, and, at least in spots, their continued existence in a natural state.
>
> In short, a land ethic changes the role of *Homo sapiens* from conqueror of the land-community to plain member and citizen of it. It implies respect for his fellow-members, and also respect for the community as such.[13]

Human history has instructed us, Leopold continued, that the conqueror role is self-defeating. Why? "Because it is implicit in such a role that the conqueror knows, *ex cathedra,* just what makes the community clock tick, and just what and who is valuable, and what and who is worthless, in community life. It always turns out that he knows

---

13. Leopold, *A Sand County Almanac*, 204.

neither, and this is why his conquests eventually defeat themselves." An ethic of the land will be aware of all the scientific uncertainty; it requires the Yahwist's humility.

What a Sustainable Society Would Look Like

Has the environmental movement succeeded in converting Americans to a "land ethic"? The answer is probably no. Yet there has been headway made. As I have noted earlier on, there is survey evidence that in the realm of cultural ideas the old industrial social paradigm, with its low regard for nature and its no-limits-to-growth economics, is breaking down. It no longer dominates the popular American ethos. In its place has arisen a new ecological paradigm, which involves at least the following elements:

- the importance of maintaining the balance of nature;

- the reality of limits to growth;

- the need for noncoercive population control;

- the seriousness of anthropogenic environmental damage;

- the desirability of controlling industrial growth and developing clean technology.

Surprisingly, researchers are finding that ecological beliefs and values of this sort are widely held in the United States, and may even be displacing the older industrial paradigm.[14] All this is good news, and promising for the future.

What would a sustainable society look like? The news is that in general terms — and even allowing for scientific uncertainties — we know the answer. It would meet the needs of the present without compromising the ability of future generations to meet their own needs. It would be a system that respects the limits, the carrying capacity, of natural systems. It would be powered by renewable energy sources and, so far as possible, would emulate nature, where one organism's waste is another's sustenance. And it would be a reuse/recycle economy. As hard as it might be to pull off politically, a sustainable society would:

- Generate and nurture a culture of beliefs, values, and social paradigms that define and legitimize the following natural, economic, and social structures. Natural environments would be cognized

---

14. See M. E. Olsen, D. G. Lodewick, and R. E. Dunlap, *Viewing the World Ecologically* (Boulder, Colo.: Westview Press, 1992).

as ecological systems to be preserved and maintained. Virtues of material frugality and material sufficiency would replace a culture of consumerism. There would be stress on quality of life, richer human relationships, communities, outlets for artistic and cultural expression; individualism would be tempered by communitarianism.

- Reduce population growth and stabilize its size, primarily by improving women's economic and educational status, and health care.

- Conserve and restore fertile soil, grasslands, fisheries, forests, fresh water, and water tables. Preserve significant wild ecosystems and redesign agriculture to mimic nature in its diversity and natural organic recycling rather than degrading agrosystems with monocultures and industrial chemicals.

- Minimize or phase out the use of fossil fuels. Depend on a variety of renewable energy sources: hydrogen fuels, solar, wind, geothermal, biomass, and hydroelectric.

- Invest in energy efficiency with regard to transportation, machinery, offices, appliances, maximizing the recycling of material and wastes so that the economy functions more like an ecosystem (cyclically). Converting the existing throwaway economy to a reuse/recycle economy will be crucial, for it would reduce the environmentally disruptive flow of raw materials from mines and forests to smelters and mills, as well as the huge one-way flow of discarded solid waste to landfills. With a reuse/recycle structure, mature industrial economies with stable populations can operate for the most part on the existing stock of steel, aluminum, glass, paper, and other materials already in circulation. In order for these changes to happen, the tax system will have to be restructured, decreasing corporate and personal income taxes while increasing taxes on environmentally destructive activities.

- Develop social forms compatible with these natural, technical, and economic characteristics — a mix of coordinated, decentralized small-scale networks and flexible centralization. High density settlement encouraged; urban sprawl discouraged.

- Cooperate internationally with other societies to maintain environmental commons, with appropriate regimes, treaties, regulatory agencies, multinational governmental and nongovernmental organizations. This will involve reinventing institutions like the

World Bank and the International Monetary Fund so that they are more effective in providing debt relief and aiding poor countries, and reengineering the rules of the World Trade Organization so that fair labor practices and safety and environmental concerns are no longer mere side agreements but central to the rules governing international trade.[15]

We have seen, in Part IV, that there are major shifts occurring in the area of our cultural beliefs. It is taking a long time to sink in, but thanks to the new vision of the hard sciences themselves (the new cosmology), our relation to nature has changed radically over the last fifty years. There are also promising signs, as well, that industry is changing its ways. It is simply untrue that hard economic considerations and cost-benefit analysis will always come down against environmental aims. It is also not true that "realism" forces us to choose between trees and jobs.

In the United States, the transition to a reuse/recycle economy is well under way, and it has meant jobs. For instance, in the steel industry, electric-arc furnaces now feed on scrap metal. In 1996, 55 percent of the steel output came from scrap. Abandoned cars are melted down to produce soup cans, and when the cans are discarded they can be melted down to produce refrigerators, and when they wear out they can be reused to produce cars. And so on. A steel industry that feeds on scrap minimizes the disruption associated with mining and transporting virgin ore and reduces energy use by some 60 percent. Energy efficiency means reduced costs and jobs. The U.S. steel industry used to be concentrated in western Pennsylvania, close to iron ore and coal fields. Modern electric-arc mini-mills that feed on locally available scrap metal are now scattered all across the country.

What is true of steel is also true of paper. Instead of felling forests, paper companies are increasingly negotiating long-term contracts with local communities for scrap paper. The result is that recently few paper mills have been built in the heavily forested northwest or in Maine. Instead, mills are appearing near heavily populated areas where waste paper is abundant. In densely populated New Jersey, for instance, where there is little forested area and no iron mines, there are now thirteen paper mills that use wastepaper and eight steel mills relying

---

15. See Charles L. Harper, *Environment and Society* (Upper Saddle River, N.J.: Prentice Hall, 1996), 269–72. Also Lester R. Brown et al., *State of the World 1998: A Worldwatch Institute Report on Progress toward a Sustainable Society* (New York: W. W. Norton, 1998), esp. 168–87. See also Al Gore's proposals for a "strategic environmental initiative" in *Earth in the Balance: Ecology and the Human Spirit* (New York: Houghton Mifflin, 1992), 319–60.

on scrap iron, which collectively produce $1 billion worth of products, providing both local jobs and substantial tax revenues.

But the news is not all positive, as we have seen in Part III. Nor will scientific hubris and good intentions make up for the destruction wreaked by the failure to acknowledge our ongoing ignorance. The penalties of ignorance are severe. We need all the scientific understanding we can get, yes; but there will never be enough. One example: Some decades ago regional authorities in the vicinity of Lake Victoria in Africa decided they would like to improve the living conditions of those living around the lake. A noble intention. What better, they thought, than to import the Nile perch. Well, the Nile perch proved to be a very predatory fish that promptly consumed the native fish, its own food supply. As things turned out, the perch destroyed the local fisheries and drove the surrounding population to fell the shoreline forests in order to smoke the oily and distasteful perch, which otherwise they would not eat. The whole experiment, undertaken without regard to the subtle relationships among the local biological community, was an unmitigated economic and ecological disaster.[16] Rule of thumb: We usually think we know more than we do.

We continue, meanwhile, to put unparalleled pressure on the planet's resources. We are nearing the end of a half-century of unprecedented economic growth. Between 1950 and 1997, the global output of goods and services expanded sixfold, from just under $5 trillion annually to more than $29 trillion. During that same period, diets generally improved and life expectancy shot up from forty-seven years to sixty-five years. The trouble is, as the world economy grew, so did the stress on the earth's ecosystems. Between 1950 and 1997, the use of lumber tripled, paper consumption increased sixfold, the fish catch rose fivefold, grain consumption tripled, the burning of fossil fuel quadrupled, and air and water pollution multiplied several times. The fact is inescapable: As the world economy continues to grow at an exponential rate, the natural systems upon which it relies do not keep up. If the world economy continues to expand, it will eventually destroy the natural support systems — the Great Economy — upon which we depend.

Consider the case of China, with a fifth of the globe's population. Will China, the world's fastest growing economy during the 1990s, reach parity with U.S. consumption levels? And will the planet be able to stand it? If China continues to double its gross national product every eight years, as it has since 1980, it will overtake U.S. output by the

---

16. See Robert E. Ricklefs, *Ecology,* 3d ed. (New York: W. H. Freeman, 1990), 3.

year 2010. From 1992 to 1995, China registered double-digit economic growth rates each year — 12 percent, 14 percent, 11 percent, and 10 percent. In the consumption of such basic items as grain, red meat, fertilizer, steel, and coal, China already outstrips the United States, which with only 5 percent of the world's population now consumes 40 percent or more of the planet's resources. Five years ago, Beijing's Ministry of Heavy Industry decided to make the auto industry one of the five "pillar" industries that would spur economic development in the next few decades. If China continues along this automobile-centered path, modeled after the industrial West and Japan, and if car ownership and oil use reach U.S. levels, the country would require 80 million barrels of oil per day. In 1996 the world produced only 64 million barrels a day.

If we had a care for the next generation of animals and plant-life on this planet, we would take a warning from the collapse of natural systems that is already occurring, for example, the serious aquifer depletion in the Punjab, India's breadbasket, or the collapse of Canada's cod fishery off Newfoundland. In other words, governments would calculate as best they can (undeterred by uncertainties) the approximate sustainable yield of aquifers, fisheries, forests, and rangelands, and out of a commitment to future generations would see to it that these yield levels are not exceeded. As Lester R. Brown puts it in *State of the World 1998*:

> The ecological principles of sustainability are well established, based on solid science. Just as an aircraft must satisfy the principles of aerodynamics if it is to fly, so must an economy satisfy the principles of ecology if it is to endure. The ecological conditions that need to be satisfied are rather straightforward. Over the long term, carbon emissions cannot exceed carbon dioxide (CO_2) fixation; soil erosion cannot exceed new soil formed through natural processes; the harvest of forest products cannot exceed the sustainable yield of forests; the number of plant and animal species lost cannot exceed the new species formed through evolution; water pumping cannot exceed the sustainable yield of aquifers; the fish catch cannot exceed the sustainable yield of fisheries.[17]

The "cannot" translates into "must not" — for to continue to over-harvest the natural world is to do violence to the earth. It is to sin against creation.

---

17. Lester R. Brown, *State of the World 1998*, 170.

We have the technologies needed to make a sustainable society happen. The question is whether we have the political will. Do we care enough about the next generation to take the necessary steps? Do we care enough about our grandchildren to make some hard choices now?

The Great Work

To correct a short-sighted, egoistic anthropocentrism, as I said above, we need to expand our moral concern to include plants and animals, air and water and soils. If this be biocentrism or ecocentrism, I am all for it. What we are after is a new social contract with earth — which does not entail downplaying the human species or exaggerating the intrinsic wisdom of nature left to itself. The dichotomy some environmentalists want to draw, however, between the natural (wild and good) and the artificial (domesticated and generally bad) simply won't work. We are either part of nature, one species among others, or we are not. If we are, and all that I have been driving at in these chapters supports this, then everything we do is part of nature, and is natural in that primary sense. Whether what we do is prudent, sensible, or moral is another question. But given the demographic trends and the rise of megacities like Mexico City, Lagos, and Manila, leaving nature alone is simply not a viable option.

The ecocrisis of our time will not be remedied by either leaving things to nature (whatever that would mean), or by underestimating the central role we humans have to play, especially now, at this juncture in history. Ironically, in these last few pages, we return to the issue of human dominion over the earth. If the term "dominion" makes you flinch, use the word "responsibility" or "service" instead — either one is closer to what I have in mind. The fact is that we cannot undo the rate of technological advance. And this means that more and more the future of the planet depends upon us. Are we ready to accept the responsibility? Are we smart enough, wise enough for what Thomas Berry speaks of as the Great Work of our time?

Since the beginning of human history we have regulated our actions on the basis of distinguishing between the relatively few matters that depended on us and the huge array of matters that in no way depended on us. For most of recorded history — and this is clearly depicted in the Bible — the world eluded our control; it was an unforgiving place to which we had to submit. A few things in our vicinity (the neighborhood, the near and adjoining) we could influence; but those global things that philosophers like to speculate about (the spatially distant, the far-off future, the earth, the universe, matter, life, humanity as a whole) were produced by a necessity quite independent of us. Then the seventeenth-century scientific revolution occurred, and the industrial revolution in its several phases. Now, thanks to Bill Gates and his friends, the information revolution is underway. And we are no longer subject to the same comprehensive, external necessity. With every passing day, our decisions carry more weight, have more social and environmental impact, determine more and more of the world around us.

In the last half century, since the end of World War II, physics, biology, medicine and pharmacology, and the technologies they give rise to have brought about a stunning sea-change in the human situation. Increasingly the affluent West and Japan have been living like the immortals on Mount Olympus. The G-7 nations have been holding a great feast for themselves. In biblical terms it's the parable of Dives (the rich man) and Lazarus (the poor man) from the Gospel of Luke (16:19–31). Anesthetized by our good fortune, intoxicated by consumerism, we live like veritable gods, confident that nearly everything that matters (to us) lies within the reach of our knowledge and under our technical control. At least in the short term, everything does depend on us. We have eliminated much that was once beyond our powers. The force of gravity, distance, our planet's position in the solar system, hereditary diseases, and procreation were once considered natural things, unalterable by human intervention; they are no longer so. Pushing back the limits, we have succeeded in controlling our sexuality, prolonging life, eliminating diseases, relieving pain, reducing stress, abolishing neediness (for some). We are capable of feeding, caring for, and healing 6 billion human beings on this planet (not that we do so). We are now growing organs for transplants. At the same time we are capable of blowing everything up; we can disturb the climate, punch holes in the ozone layer, choose to give birth only to baby boys or only baby girls, genetically engineer our food supplies and create laboratories to produce deadly biological viruses that will spread with the wind.

The old necessities no longer rule. Like it or not (and most environmentalists will not), we are the masters of earth. Through rockets, satellites, television, fax machines, and the Internet, we dominate space. Tomorrow we will be able to choose the sex of our children and clone ourselves. In brief, we are now in charge of many of the aspects of our former dependence: earth, life, matter, time and history, good and evil, life and death. And it's all a bit scary, and an invitation to arrogance. The rate of technological innovation accelerates, and we move rapidly, often unthinkingly, from what is possible and can be done to the more dubious proposition that it is desirable and will be done. Projects can backfire, even with ample good intentions. Or, as with genetically engineered agricultural products, there can be unforeseen consequences. Technology outstrips us, and there's a sense we've all become sorcerer's apprentices. Science invents possibilities that immediately become actualities (or new market-driven necessities), and we find ourselves blindly swept away and along by the fate of the hard sciences. Increasingly, we find, we are in the hands of "the experts." Will they be fully human, humane experts? Or Frankensteins and Strangeloves?

The new adage: Everything depends on us. It is virtually impossible not to decide everything, if only by act of omission. Impossible not to determine the objective facts of our children's and grandchildren's future. Like it or not, planet earth is largely under our management. We cannot pretend it is not. Are we managing well or ill? (Part III of this book suggested that we are poor managers.) But inevitably it is we (and that, for the most part and sadly, means "we" in the affluent world) who will decide what the climate will be in the next century, whether there will be any wilderness left in the new millennium, what the "balance of nature" (if any) will be like, what the state of the soil, the air, the water will be, the health and variety of wildlife, yes, the very conditions of life and survival on the planet. The lives of our descendants will be conditioned by an earth we have programmed, decided, produced, modeled on our computer simulations. The Roman emperor did not carry the burden of the earth on his shoulders. We do. As Michel Serres states our situation,

> From now on we are steering things that, in the past, we didn't steer. In dominating the planet, we become accountable for it. In manipulating death, life, reproduction, the normal and the pathological, we become responsible for them. We are going to have to decide about every thing, and even about Everything — about the physical and thermodynamic future, about Darwinian evolution, about life, about the Earth and about time, about the filtering of possibilities — candidates to be evaluated for becoming realities — a process Leibniz described as characterizing the work of God the creator, in the secret of his infinite understanding.[18]

I suppose the obvious question is: What kind of gods will we choose to be? Will we be like the Olympian deities, feasting on Parnassus but coldly indifferent to human misery and suffering below? Or will we be like the God of Moses, who hears the cry of the poor? Or the God of

---

18. Serres with Latour, *Conversations on Science, Culture, and Time,* 173.

Isaiah and Hosea, who demands justice for the grieving earth and the people of the earth?

For if we are the new masters of earth, we also have to accept the fact that it is we who are now constructing an unforgiving world with a few winners and a great mass of losers. Just because it lies within our knowledge and power to make it otherwise, the massive misery of our world is our doing — something we at least connive in, passively accept, refuse to think much about, or actively oppose. One-fifth of the world's population is what the World Bank calls "absolutely poor," meaning totally destitute and famished; and at least another two-fifths is barely subsisting. And these have-nots are precisely the people who suffer most from environmental degradation and destruction. Sitting at our great feast on Parnassus, stuffed and drugged with the good food and wine of this world, has the first world and its expertise become inhumane, hardened and deaf to the lamentations of the land and the cry of the poor of the land?

Every generation not only defines itself, but chooses its Other, and in our time, it is clearly the weak, the indigent, the defenseless, the starving, those without reserves or shelter. These "others" are precisely those who are most afflicted by environmental devastation. These "others" constitute the majority of the human race; they define who and what humanity is today. Does our new global economy include them, take account of them? Or shut them out? Can we do no better? Do we manage the world only for the prosperous? And shall the world once again be unforgiving, but this time around not because of nature but because of our hard hearts?

What knowledge and wisdom will we bring to the task, the duty, the responsibility, of constructing the future? For insiders and outsiders? On behalf of the entire planet? For with this new mastery goes an equal, virtually crushing level of moral responsibility for the objective conditions of the earth. It will require every bit of scientific knowledge we can muster and every bit of humane wisdom. For under these new circumstances morality can no longer be conceived as a subjective matter. Our responsibility to direct ourselves, to shape our own character, turns out to form but a small part of our obligation. Morality must now mean accepting responsibility for constructing the basic givens — the objective facts — of life, things like the weather, the state of ocean fisheries, and a breathable atmosphere. Morality, says Michel Serres, is passing from the subject to the object, from the relatively minor task of governing our private lives to the public project of maintaining the life and health of the planet. The foundation of morality, he says, is now located in the realm of physics! Will we choose to

honor the laws of physics or not? That's the moral question of the
twenty-first century.

Why behave this way rather than that? The astonishing answer: So
that the earth can continue, so the air will remain breathable, so the
seas will abound in fish and the rainforests flourish with millions of
species as yet unnamed, so that the land will continue to be fertile, so
time will continue to flow and life will keep on propagating. So the
causes of things will continue to give rise to their results. These things
are now our tasks, our moral duties. We can no longer pretend that
we do not know why or how all these wonders happen, or why they
cease to happen. The difference we can make in the creative, generative
process — or the cessation of the process — is crucial. From now on,
the categorical imperative will reside in objective scientific laws, which
it will be our duty to honor, promote, and keep. This is the new social
contract with the natural world, which will continue to thrive only
with our active cooperation and support. As Serres puts it, "We have
become the authors of ongoing creation."

The question is: how to master our new mastery. Too much is happening, it seems, that escapes our powers, that is simply driven by
a science that has become indifferent as to whether it creates or de-
stroys. We require the light of science, surely, but also the light from
ancient humanistic texts. Do our scientific experts represent the theory
of a sanitized world, a world without evil? An elite that keeps itself
insulated from the suffering of the masses? Have our experts become
chilled, dehumanized, brutalized, effectively cut off from the anxiety
and anguish that gave rise to the whole enterprise of understanding to
begin with? Have they forgotten the lessons of the humanities? "Our
capacities," argues Serres, "come from our weaknesses, and our effectiveness from our fragilities. Our science has no other foundation than
this permanent collapse, this lack, this endless slippage into the abyss
of pain."

How will it all turn out? What will happen? Will it be nightmare
or curse? Will spacetime mean something beautiful? Be a passage to
life? The earth awaits the decisions of *Homo sapiens,* our science, our
wisdom. I dare say even God may await our decisions, not knowing
what we will do — and hoping that this time creation will work.

The Relationship between Science and Religion

The conciliatory language of "Preserving and Cherishing the Earth: An Appeal for Joint Commitment in Science and Religion" suggests that the conflict between science and religion — always much exaggerated in the Anglo-American world — is over. But is this true? What is the relationship between science and religion today? Actually, it comes in at least three different varieties: that of conflict, independence (or contrast), and interaction.

First, *conflict:* there are still those, biblical literalists on one side and scientific materialists on the other, who see science and religion as unalterably opposed to each other. In this view, science and religion are thought to be squabbling over the same turf, each making rival and monopolistic claims on it. When scientists talk about that turf, they call it "nature." When biblical believers talk about it, they call it "creation" and mean the handiwork of God. As fundamentalists would have it, the "creation science" derived from the opening chapters of the Book of Genesis and Darwinian evolution by natural selection cannot both be true; it's a question of either/or. Science and religion are thus seen as being at absolute loggerheads. But the scientific materialist typically agrees.

The biblicist assumes that Scripture contains the infallible truth about how the earth and human beings came to be; and the scientific materialist presumes that only the scientific method, as followed by Darwin and the "new synthesis," can deliver the truth of how we evolved. As the philosopher of science Ian G. Barbour expressed it in his 1989 Gifford Lectures: "In a fight between a boa constrictor and a wart-hog, the victor, whichever it is, swallows the vanquished. In scientific materialism, science swallows religion. In biblical literalism, religion swallows science."[1]

---

1. See Barbour, *Religion in an Age of Science: The Gifford Lectures 1989–90* (San Francisco: HarperSanFrancisco, 1990), 1:4, 3–92. For a slightly different but complemen-

Independence or Contrast: Conflict can be avoided, however, if science and religion occupy different territories. This is the second position, that of mutual independence or contrast. In this view science and religion each possess their own legitimate but contrasting approach to reality. They do not, as the biblical literalist assumes, make rival claims about the same field. They ask different kinds of questions, use different methods of inquiry, involve different "language games" and attitudes of mind, and refer to different kinds of experience. The Book of Genesis is not a tract on astronomy. Religion is concerned with questions of meaning and purpose, ultimate origin and destiny, and recommends a way of life and a set of moral principles — things that science, concerned with issues of prediction and control, is ill-equipped to provide. Accenting the contrast between these disciplines, the message of this position is that science and religion should keep off each other's turf.

There is much to be said in favor of stressing the differences of science and religion. The domains and methods of the two are undeniably distinct, and direct conflict can thus be avoided. But if science and religion are conceived as totally separate and compartmentalized, then one avoids conflict at too steep a price. Constructive dialogue and mutual enrichment become impossible. Can the scientific part of our lives be so neatly divided from the religious part — without damaging both? I think not. And for this reason we have to discriminate a third way of relating science and religion, namely, that of interaction.

Interaction: Proponents of this position, of which I am one, generally believe that faith and reason are basically congruent with each other, or that science and religion are fundamentally complementary.

Advocates of the interactionist position will also underscore the similarities between the methods of science and religion, stressing, for instance, that faith has a cognitive element and need not entail wild leaps into the irrational. Conversely, science, like religion, is theory-laden in its inquiries, and is dependent upon prevailing theoretical paradigms that control what counts as evidence and good theory. Moreover, as Michael Polanyi has shown, scientific method involves many of the features once thought confined to religious thinking, namely, personal participation in a community of inquiry, learning by example and practice, commitment to communal standards, and so forth.[2] Conversely, even though religious beliefs are not amenable to empirical testing, they can be approached with some of the same spirit of inquiry found in science. The scientific criteria of coherence,

---

tary breakdown, see John F. Haught, *Science and Religion: From Conflict to Conversation* (Mahwah, N.J.: Paulist Press, 1995), 9–46.

2. See Michael Polanyi, *Personal Knowledge* (Chicago: University of Chicago Press, 1958).

comprehensiveness, and fruitfulness have their parallels in religious thought.

In practice, we find influence moving both ways, from religion to science and from science to religion. Perhaps Albert Einstein put the interactionist position best:

> Now, even though the realms of religion and science in themselves are clearly marked off from each other, nevertheless there exist between the two strong reciprocal relationships and dependencies. Though religion may be that which determines the goal, it has, nevertheless, learned from science, in the broadest sense, what means will contribute to the attainment of the goals it has set up. But science can only be created by those who are thoroughly imbued with the aspiration towards truth and understanding. This source of feeling, however, springs from the sphere of religion. To this there also belongs the faith in the possibility that the regulations valid for the world of existence are rational, that is, comprehensible to reason. I cannot conceive of a genuine scientist without that profound faith. The situation may be expressed by an image: Science without religion is lame, religion without science is blind.[3]

---

3. Albert Einstein, "Science and Religion," an address at a Conference on Science, Philosophy, and Religion, New York, 1940; reprinted in *Ideas and Opinions* (New York: Crown, [1954] 1982), 44–49.

The Churches in the Environmental Movement

Environmentalists have begun to notice that church and synagogue have been working at developing an environmental ethic and have become politically active in defending environmental public policy. A few examples: Protestant theologians have been actively developing a theology of stewardship for over fifty years, ever since forester and hydrologist Walter C. Lowdermilk (1888–1974), speaking in Jerusalem in June 1939, announced an "eleventh commandment." Lowdermilk's formulation still merits attention. His new commandment read:

> Thou shalt inherit the holy earth as a faithful steward, conserving its resources and productivity from generation to generation. Thou shalt safeguard thy fields from soil erosion, thy living waters from drying up, thy forests from desolation, and protect the hills from overgrazing by thy herds, that thy descendants may have abundance forever. If any shall fail in this stewardship of the land, thy fruitful fields shall become sterile stony ground and wasting gullies, and thy descendants shall decrease and live in poverty or perish from off the face of the earth.[1]

In the 1950s, Joseph Sittler, a systematic theologian at Chicago's Lutheran Theological Seminary, wrote a series of groundbreaking articles exploring our relationship to nature, contending that God's purpose in redemption extended beyond human souls to "all things" and urging Christians to "take joy in the things themselves," caring for the earth as a religious imperative. Sittler's pioneering work was followed up in the 1960s by Richard A. Baer Jr., who stressed that the world belongs to God, that God likes what he has created, and that to destroy the relational "web of life" is to sin against the very structure of the world

---

1. Cited in Roderick Frazier Nash, *The Rights of Nature: A History of Environmental Ethics* (Madison: University of Wisconsin Press, 1989), 97–98.

that God has created. For some years Baer was a leader of the Faith-Man-Nature Group sponsored by the National Council of Churches, which not only nurtured the ecotheology of theologians like H. Paul Santmire, Philip Joranson, and John B. Cobb Jr., but also influenced the direction of the World Council of Churches throughout the 1970s and '80s.

The World Council of Churches has been at the forefront of organized Christian action and reflection on environmental issues since the 1970s when the council's Church and Society division put out the document on "Just, Participatory and Sustainable Society." Throughout the 1980s and 1990s the council has regularly created programs to promote "Justice, Peace, and the Integrity of Creation," and the theme of the 1991 General Assembly in Camberra, Australia, was "Come, Holy Spirit, Renew the Whole Creation."

On the local front, the National Council of Churches has recently taken a stand on global warming, declaring that the Kyoto Protocol of 1997 is "an important move toward protecting God's children and God's creation" and promising to lobby hard for its ratification by the Senate. The Central Conference of American Rabbis has said that preventing desecration of the Headwaters Forest in northern California is "part of the covenant with the Creator" and has called on Congress to reaffirm the Endangered Species Act. A coalition of evangelical Christians was instrumental in halting Congress's attempt to throttle that Act in 1996.

In his New Year's message of 1990 — in fact, just before the Sagan "Joint Appeal" was issued — Pope John Paul II addressed the ecological situation for the first time in his pontificate. "In our day," wrote the pope,

> there is a growing awareness that world peace is threatened not only by the arms race, regional conflicts and continued injustices among peoples and nations, but also by a lack of due respect for nature, by the plundering of natural resources and by a progressive decline in the quality of life.... Faced with the widespread destruction of the environment, people everywhere are coming to understand that we cannot continue to use the goods of the earth as we have in the past.[2]

The text addressed specific problems: the "greenhouse effect," acid rain, soil erosion, destruction of marine life, tropical deforestation, and

---

2. See "The Ecological Crisis: A Common Responsibility," reprinted in *"And God Saw That It Was Good": Catholic Theology and the Environment,* ed. Drew Christiansen and Walter Grazer (Washington, D.C.: United States Catholic Conference, 1996), 215; cf. 215–22.

the waste of resources consumed by arms spending. But for the first time, official Catholic teaching moved to analyze the root causes of the ecological crisis; the pope offered a critique of technology and warned that consumerism and a philosophy of instant self-gratification lie at the heart of the environmental predicament.

> Modern society will find no solution to the ecological problem unless it takes a serious look at its life-style. In many parts of the world, society is given to instant gratification and consumerism while remaining indifferent to the damage which they cause.... Simplicity, moderation, and discipline, as well as a spirit of sacrifice, must become part of everyday life, lest all suffer the negative consequences of the careless habits of the few. (par. 1)

The pope's 1990 statement represented a big shift for the Catholic communion. When Pope John XXIII convened the Second Vatican Council in the fall of 1962 — just months after Rachel Carson's epoch-making book *Silent Spring* was published — the environment did not rate mention on the agenda. When it came to the accomplishments of modern science and technology, the tone of the Vatican II documents was unequivocally celebratory. "Through his labors and his native endowments," said *Gaudium et Spes* (Constitution on the Church in the Modern World), "man has ceaselessly striven to better his life. Today, however, especially with the help of science and technology, he has extended his mastery over nearly the whole of nature and continues to do it" (par. 33). In the years following the council, Pope Paul VI generally treated the environment with benign neglect. No critical questions were raised about human "mastery" or about the harmful effects of modern science, technology, and industrialization, until well after the first Earth Day in 1970. (E. F. Schumacher's popular critique of technology, *Small Is Beautiful,* remember, did not appear until 1973.) It was not until 1979, in his encyclical *Redemptor Hominis,* that a new pontiff, Pope John Paul II, expressed a fear that the dominant economic order was "depleting the earth's resources of raw materials and energy at an ever-increasing rate and putting intolerable pressures on the geophysical environment" (par. 5–16).

Since 1980, Catholic bishops' conferences around the world have rallied behind the international environmental movement. In the late 1980s and early 1990s, the bishops of the Dominican Republic, Guatemala, the Philippines, Northern Italy, Australia, and the United States have all issued strong statements alerting their communities to the moral dimension of ecological problems. "Eco-justice" has permanently and officially joined the traditional list of Catholic social concerns.[3]

At a symposium on religion and science held in Santa Barbara in 1997, Bartholomew I, patriarch of the 250-million-member Eastern Orthodox (Christian) Church, declared: "To commit a crime against the natural world is a sin." It was at this same conference that Carl Pope, the executive director of the Sierra Club, issued an apology: "The environmental movement for the past quarter of a century has made no more profound error than to misunderstand the mission of religion and the churches in preserving the Creation."[4]

---

3. See Marvin L. Hrier Mich, *Catholic Social Teaching and Movements* (Mystic, Conn.: Twenty-Third Publications, 1998), 385–413.

4. Cited in Trebble Johnson, "The Second Creation Story," *Sierra: The Magazine of the Sierra Club* (November/December 1998): 52. For a general account of how the churches have become involved in the environmental movement, see "The Greening of Religion," a chapter in Nash, *The Rights of Nature,* 87–120.

Index

Abbey, Edward, 67, 223–26
Abraham, 29–30
acid rain, 81, 97
Ackerman, Diane, 41, 67
action. *See* preventive action
Adidas (shoes), 118
Aeschylus, 222
Agenda for Development (UN), 119
agriculture
  Hebrew Bible on, 19
  increased production by, 113–14
  industrial, 85–86
air quality, 81
Alt, Albrecht, 17
animals, 19, 65–66
anthropic principle, 173–77
anthropocentrism, 33, 110
anti-Semitism, 207, 222
apocalyptic thought, 14
aquifers, 235
Aquinas, 148
  on the atemporality of God, 134
  on creatures' existence in relation to God, 76
  on matter, 217
  on mindedness, 216
  on nature, 34
  on negative knowledge of God, 197
  a spirituality of ascent and, 25
arcadian tradition, the
  members of, 41
  overview of, 64–67
  science and, 221
  task of writers of, 220–21
Aristotle
  on the beginning of science and wisdom, 224
  as interested in the things of earth, 26
  on the male principle, 148
  on matter, 217
  on mindedness, 216
  on the Poet-Maker, 33
  on the Unmoved Mover, 24, 147
ascent, a spirituality of, 199–202
asceticism, 23
Asian financial crisis, 124
Augustine, St., 25, 33, 133–34, 216

Bacon, Francis, 3, 48–49, 59, 64, 230
Baer, Richard A., Jr., 244–45
Balzac, Honoré de, 222

Barbour, Ian G., 32, 130, 241
Barfield, Owen, 143–44
Barrow, John, 176
Barshevsky, Charlene, 124
Bartholomew I, 247
Benedictine tradition, the, 75
Benedict of Nursia, 75
Berry, Thomas
  the arcadian tradition and, 220
  on earth as the primary mode of divine presence, 37–38
  Easterbrook's critique of, 80
  on the eschaton and the obsession with progress, 150n.22
  on the Great Work, 1–2, 236
  on humans' new power to change the universe, 74, 216
  on the point of the universe, 177
Berry, Wendell, 55, 67, 107, 220
Bethe, Hans, 9
Bible, the
  comparison of Yahwist and Priestly accounts of nature in, 17–21
  environmental movement's critical assessment of, 10–15
  fundamentalists on, 241
  the future and, 153–54
  God's relation to earth according to, 196–98
  on human agency vis-à-vis nature, 39–40
  images of God in, 199–202
  the prophets' view of the universe in, 135–37
  recent reassessment of nature and, 15–17
  science's causality and the vision of the, 151–55
  See also Hebrew Bible, the
big bang, the
  the anthropic principle and, 173–77
  background of the theory, 138–39
  cosmic pessimism and, 162
  relation to the rest of the history of the universe, 141–42
biocentrism, 37, 68, 88
biodiversity, 88–91
biophilia, 88
biotechnology, 113
black holes, 162
Blake, William, 67
Bonaventure, St., 25, 35, 134, 202, 209
Botkin, Daniel, 106

Boutros Boutros-Ghali, 119
Bowler, Peter J., 73
Brief History of Time (Hawking), 144
Brown, Lester R., 235
Brueggemann, Walter, 29
Brundtland Commission, 93, 107, 119
Buddhism, 110, 204
Buenos Aires conference, 102
butterfly effect, 168, 185

Campbell, Joseph, 128
cancer, 97
capitalism
    classical physics and, 55–57
    dominant social paradigm of, 62–64
    Marx on, 112–13
    nature's degradation and, 56–57
    the new colonialism and, 116–18
    quantification of success of, 59–60
    See also corporations; economics; markets
carbon dioxide, 99–100, 101, 102
carrying capacity
    affluent countries' expropriation of poorer
        countries', 116–18
    current scientific uncertainty regarding, 73,
        106
    defined, 56, 104
    effects of exceeding, 104–5
    Malthusians on, 115
    necessity for gauging, 109
    Summers on, 56
Carson, Rachel, 64, 67, 71, 227, 246
Carter, Brandon, 174–75
Cather, Willa, 221
Catholic Church, 114, 245–47. *See also*
    churches; John Paul II; Vatican II
causality, 150–55
Central Conference of American Rabbis, 245
chain of being, the, 35, 76
chance, 168–70, 180–81
chaos theory, 170–71, 185–86
chemistry, 165
Chenu, M. D., 23
China, 234–35
Christianity
    ambivalence toward creation, 22–26
    cosmic time and, 143–44
    the environmental movement and, 10–15,
        244–47
    an evolving universe and, 146–50
    theocentrism of, 26–27
    two traditions of God in, 195–98
    See also Bible, the; religion; theology
christology, 205
churches, 244–47. *See also* religion
City of God (Augustine), 134
Clausius, Rudolph, 134, 161
Clements, Frederick, 72
Clinton administration, 102
Clough, Shepherd, 59–60

Club of Rome, 113
coal, 96
Cobb, John B., Jr., 93, 245
colonialism, 116–18
Commoner, Barry, 114
The Communist Manifesto, 62
complexity theory. *See* chaos theory
Condorcet, Marquis de, 111, 112, 115
Confucianism, 1
consciousness
    the beginning of the cosmos and, 215
    the big bang and, 174
    literacy and Western, 46–48
    nature and, 216
consumerism
    idolatry of, 237
    John Paul II on, 246
    as a source of environmental degradation,
        110
    a sustainable society and, 232
"Continuing the Conversation" (L. White),
        15–16
covenant, 27–29
Copernicus, 222
corporations
    attacks on environmental movement by,
        76–77
    deforestation and, 87
    expropriating third world nations' carrying
        capacity, 118
    globalization and, 123–24
    voluntary emissions reductions by, 102–3
cosmology
    different types of, 128
    medieval sacramental, 32–36
    overview of the new, 127–31
    process, 148–49
Council on Foreign Relations, 124
creation
    the Bible's different views of, 10–15
    ex nihilo, 26, 145
    Paul on, 214
    religious understanding of, 144–45
creation science, 241

D'Allonnes, Olivier Revault, 29–30
Daly, Herman, 80, 93, 94, 109
Dante, 25
Darwin, Charles, 138
    agony as the basis of the work of, 222
    ecology and, 67–70, 71
    on moral sympathy for nonhuman
        life-forms, 227
    and notions of God, 146, 147
    time in the outlook of, 54
    on the violent side of nature, 66
Darwinism, 161, 164–66. *See also* Darwin,
    Charles
Davies, Paul, 163
Dawkins, Richard, 2, 160, 162–64, 170

DDT, 71
deforestation, 114. *See also* forests; rain
 forests
deism, 57–58
Descartes, René, 48, 49–50, 163
descent, a spirituality of, 202–5
The Descent of Man (Darwin), 227
Desert Solitaire (Abbey), 223
determinism, 171
de Vaux, Roland, 17
developing world. *See* third world, the
development, 119–21. *See also* growth
Dickinson, Emily, 200
Dillard, Annie, 41, 67, 172–73, 220, 221
Discordant Harmonies (Botkin), 106
Discourse on Method (Descartes), 50
DNA, 169, 183, 188
Donne, John, 47–48
Dostoyevsky, Fyodor, 207
Drucker, Peter, 56
dualism
 of environmentalists, 83
 history of Christian, 12
 Newton on the mind/body, 43
 science's findings as eliciting, 157
 of scientific knowledge and everyday life,
  158
Dubos, René, 75, 227
Duns Scotus, 34, 209
dynamic ecology, 72
Dyson, Freeman J., 9, 176–77

Earth First! 39, 80
Earth Summit on Environment and
 Development (Rio de Janeiro), 93
Easterbrook, Gregg, 3, 80–84, 103
Eastern Orthodox Church, 247
Eckhart, Meister, 211–12
"The Ecological Crisis: A Common
 Responsibility" (John Paul II), 114–15
ecology
 arcadian, 64–67
 assessment of the effectiveness of, 71–74
 Darwin and, 67–70
 defined, 70–71
 environmentalism distinguished from, 71
 four factors contributing to the
  predicament of, 4–5
 sustainable communities and, 120–21
 a sustainable society and, 231–36
 uncertainty of current goals of, 105–7
The Ecology of Eden (Eisenberg), 16–17
economic materialism, 55–57. *See also*
 materialism
economics
 civilizing global, 121–25
 classical physics and, 55–57
 as ignoring nature's Great Economy, 107–9
 Marx on, 112–13
 the new colonialism and, 116–18

optimists' view of, 111–12
 population control and, 113–16
 recent rate of growth and, 234
 and resistance to limiting growth, 92–94
 See also growth
ecorealism, 81
ecosystems, 65–66, 72
Edwards, Jonathan, 36–37, 209
Ehrlich, Anne, 189
Ehrlich, Paul, 80, 113, 114, 189
Einstein, Albert, 54, 135, 138, 243
Eiseley, Loren, 48
Eisenberg, Evan, 16–17
Eliot, T. S., 154
Endangered Species Act, 245
energy
 consumption of, 94–97
 entropy and, 161
 history and, 217
 randomness and, 180–81
 unpredictability of, 180
energy efficiency, 232
Enlightenment, the, 2
entropy, 161, 165–66, 171–73
environmental crisis, the
 assessment of the scope of, 84–91
 driving forces behind, 109–11
 economic growth and, 119–21
 the end of nature and, 79–80
 four factors contributing to, 4–5
 as hype, 80–84
 new colonialism and, 116–18
 the poor and, 239
environmental movement, the
 on Christianity as a problem, 10–15
 the churches and, 244–47
 false choice presented by, 2
 original vision of, 105
equilibrium, 166–67
eschatology
 as the center of Christian faith, 150
 defined, 24n.6
 escapist, 24
 Western ideas of progress and, 150n.22
Essay on Population (Malthus), 112
ethics, 226–31
Eucharist, the, 210–13
evangelical Christians, 245
Everett, Hugh, 174
evolution
 Christian spirituality and, 146–50
 God and, 149–50
 history of, 141–43
 limitation of theory of, 216
 novelty and, 153
 pointlessness of, 160–61
 process cosmology on, 148
 randomness and, 168–70
 sources of Darwin's theory of, 69
 time and, 165–66

extinction. *See* species extinction
Exxon Valdez, 97

Faith-Man-Nature Group, 245
famines, 113–14, 114n.10
Ferris, Timothy, 128–29n.1, 174
fertilizer, 86
Finnegans Wake (Joyce), 188
first world, the
  environmental responsibility and, 239
  growth of, sustained by externalizing costs
    to the third world, 118
  positive environmental trends in, 81, 85
  third world pollution and, 102, 114
fish, 86
food production, 85–86. *See also* agriculture
Foreman, David, 80
forests
  current state of, 87–88
  importance of, 89–90
  paper mills and, 233
  See also deforestation; rain forests
fossil fuels, 96, 99. *See also* petroleum
Francis of Assisi
  as a biocentrist, 37
  challenge to the anthropic principle, 16
  comparison of his universe with ours, 199
  on divine immanence, 23
  the ecological tradition and, 25
  sacramentality of nature and, 35–36
freedom, 29–30
Freud, Sigmund, 203
Freudian psychoanalysis, 184
Friedman, Thomas L., 122
frontier paradigm, 109, 118
Frye, Northrop, 140, 151–52, 154, 210–11
fundamentalism, 241
The Fundamentals of Ecology (Odum), 72
future, the, 151, 153–54, 173

Gaia hypothesis, 73
Galapagos Islands, 67–70
Galileo, 71
garbage, 97–98
Gates, Bill, 237
Gaudium et Spes, 246
Gell-Mann, Murray, 188
General Agreement on Tariffs and Trade
    (GATT), 93, 123
genetic engineering, 237–38
globalization, 121–25
global warming, 79–80, 84, 98–101, 245
gnosticism, 22
God
  Christianity's ambivalence toward the
    relation of the cosmos and, 23–26
  Christianity's two traditions on, 195–98
  deism on, 57–58
  evolutionary theory and, 146–47, 149–50,
    160–61

images of, 199–202, 199n.5
  medieval concepts of the atemporality of,
    134
  medieval sacramental theology on, 32–36
  process thought on, 148–49
  science and, 174
  scientists' and atheists' misunderstanding
    of, 144–46
  a spirituality of descent and, 202–5
  Yahwist view of nature and, 20–21
Gödel, Kurt, 128n.1
Gore, Al, 77, 80
Gothic architecture, 15
Gould, Stephen Jay, 9
Gramm, Phil, 122
grand unified theories, 128
gravity, 175
The Great Chain of Being (Lovejoy), 23–24
Great Economy, the, 55, 107–9
Greek thought, 195–96, 197
greenhouse effect, 99
green taxes, 116
Greider, William, 123
Gross National Product, 93–94, 116
growth
  China's, 234–35
  current blindness to effects of, 92–94
  a new ecological paradigm on, 231
  recent rate of economic, 234
  as source of environmental degradation,
    110
  See also development
Gutenberg, Johannes, 46

Haeckel, Ernst, 70
Hartshorne, Charles, 148
Haught, John, 149, 152–53, 155
Hawking, Stephen
  on the anthropic principle, 176
  on the constants at the earliest seconds of
    the universe, 175
  on Hubble, 138
  misunderstanding of creation, 144, 145
  on randomness and science, 180
  on space-time as boundaryless, 174
  on the unification of physics, 128–29n.1
Hebrew Bible, the
  environmental movement's critique of,
    10–15
  on the land, 27–29
  the prophets' view of the universe in,
    135–37
  recent reassessment of its position toward
    nature, 15–17
  science's causality and the vision of the,
    151–55
Hegel, G. W. F., 14, 50, 199, 217
Heisenberg, Werner, 180
herbicides, 86
Heschel, Abraham, 136–37

Hiebert, Theodore, 12, 18, 20
Hill, Carla, 124
Hinduism, 110
"The Historical Roots of the Ecological
　Crisis" (L. White), 10–15
historicity, 165
Holy Spirit, the, 15–16, 203
Hopkins, Gerard Manley, 34, 198, 203
Hoyle, Fred, 138, 139
Hubble, Edwin, 138
humanities, the, 221–23
Hume, David, 61

Ignatius of Antioch, 205
imperial ecology, 48–50, 230
Incarnation, the, 198, 209
Index of Sustainable Economic Welfare,
　93–94
Indians. *See* indigenous peoples
indigenous peoples
　deforestation and, 114
　environmental myths and, 15
　on sustainable growth, 120–21
industrialism
　how it works, 62–64
　as ignoring the Great Economy of nature,
　　108–9
　nature's degradation and, 56–57
　quantification of success of, 59–60
information physics, 182–83
information revolution, the, 237
information theory, 167
institutional arrangements, 110
Intergovernmental Panel on Climate Change,
　99–100
International Monetary Fund, 121–25, 233
Internet, the, 237
invertebrates, 88–89
Irenaeus, 25
Islam, 110

Jantsch, Erich, 179
Jesus Christ
　Christianity's view of the divine-cosmos
　　relation and, 23
　the cosmic clock and, 144
　eucharist, the earth, and, 210–13
　meaning in the universe and, 205–10
　the Old Testament and, 151
Joachim of Floris, 49
John Paul II, 113, 114–15, 132–33, 245–46
Johnson, Elizabeth A., 13
John XXIII, Pope, 246
Joranson, Philip, 245
Joyce, James, 188
Judaism
　negation as a principle of freedom in,
　　29–30
　source of critical relation to social
　　paradigms, 30–32

theocentrism of, 26
　on time, 135–37
　See also Hebrew Bible

Kant, Immanuel, 48, 158, 229
Kepler, Johannes, 51
Koyré, Alexandre, 53
Krutch, Joseph Wood, 227
Kyoto treaty, 102, 245

land, 27–29, 226–31
"The Land Ethic" (Leopold), 226
landfills, 98
Landscape and Memory (Schama), 15
Laplace, Pierre Simon de, 53, 181
Lasch, Nicholas, 145
Leibniz, G. W., 53
Lemaître, Abbé Georges, 139
Leopold, Aldo, 67, 71, 220, 226–27, 230–31
Linde, Andrei, 145, 174
Linnaeus, 69
literacy, 46–48
Locke, John, 61
Lopez, Barry, 41, 67
Lovejoy, Arthur, 23–24
Lovelock, James, 73, 158
Lowdermilk, Walter C., 244
Lyell, Charles, 68

Maitland, Sara, 177
Malthus, Thomas, 65, 111, 112
Malthusians, 113–14
Marcuse, Herbert, 31
Margulis, Lynn, 73
markets, 115–16, 123–25. *See also*
　economics
Marx, Karl, 31, 50, 56, 62, 111, 112, 116,
　217
materialism
　biblicists on, 241
　cosmic pessimism and, 160–61
　physics and economic, 55–57
　as a source of environmental degradation,
　　110
　suppression of novelty by scientific, 153
　Whitehead on, 53–54
　See also scientific materialism
McFague, Sallie, 34–35
McKibben, Bill, 79–80, 83, 220
McNamara, Robert S., 122
Melville, Herman, 69, 70
Merchant, Carolyn, 80
Metaphysics (Aristotle), 24
Middle Ages, the, 32–36
Midgley, Mary, 61, 228–30
Mills, C. Wright, 30
Milosz, Czeslaw, 221
mind
　the anthropic principle and, 176–77
　the big bang and, 174

misanthropy, 83–84
Mitchell, George, 77
Moltmann, Jürgen, 149–50
A Moment on Earth (Easterbrook), 80–84
Monod, Jacques, 2, 159, 161, 162, 163, 164,
    168–69, 217
morality, 25–26
Muir, John, 41, 67, 209, 220, 221

National Council of Churches, 245
national parks, 15, 223–26
Native Americans, 222
natural gas, 95–96
natural history, 64–67
The Natural History of Selborne (G. White),
    64–65
natural philosophers, 65n.5
natural selection, 69, 73, 161, 169–70
nature
    anthropocentrism and, 110
    apocalyptic thought on, 14
    the arcadian and, 64–67, 221
    Bacon on, 48–49
    basic features of the new cosmology's
        understanding of, 130–31
    chaos theory and, 173
    the coming together of human culture and,
        183
    comparison of sacramental and
        materialistic view of, 41–42
    comparison of Yahwist and Priestly
        accounts of, 17–21
    criticism of Christianity's relation to,
        11–15
    Darwin on, 67–70
    Descartes on, 49–50
    ecorealism on, 81–82
    the end of, 79–80
    industrial capitalism's view of, 62–64
    John Paul II on, 245–46
    lack of respect for the Great Economy of,
        107–9
    literacy and detachment from, 46–48
    the new science on the dynamics of, 179
    Newton and, 50–54
    overview of mechanistic view of, 42–44
    recent reassessment of the Bible and, 15–17
    as sacrament, 32–40
    Sagan et al. on religion and, 9–10
    science's cosmic pessimism and, 161–63
    scientists' current view of, 2
    Smith (Adam) on, 111
    sustainable development and, 107, 231–32
    wilderness and, 223–26
negation, 29–30
Nelson, Gaylord, 77
neoclassical economists, 115
neo-Platonism, 22
net primary production, 95
new colonialism, 116–18

Newton, Isaac
    and the death of nature, 50–54
    on the dualism of mind and body, 43
    ecologists and, 71
    environmental problems and the ideas of,
        3
    as focused on integral systems, 184
    thermodynamics as negating the work of,
        165
    twenty-first-century science contrasted
        with that of, 130–31
Nicea, Council of, 197
Nietzsche, Friedrich, 61
Nike (shoes), 118
nonequilibrium thermodynamics, 166–67,
    170–71
North American Free Trade Agreement
    (NAFTA), 92–93, 120

oceans, 81
Odum, Eugene P., 72–73
oil companies, 102
Old Testament. *See* Hebrew Bible
optimists, 111–12
organisms, 171–72, 186–87
Origen, 25

Paley, William, 69
panentheism, 149
Pannenberg, Wolfhart, 150
pantheism, 32, 197, 198
paper companies, 233–34
parks. *See* national parks
Pasteur, Louis, 222
Paul, St., 24, 25, 33, 208, 209, 214
Paul VI, Pope, 246
Peacocke, Arthur R., 169, 172
perfection, 148, 195–96
pessimism, 2, 159–64
pesticides, 86
Peters, Ted, 150
Peterson, Pete, 124
petroleum, 95–96, 232
physics
    chance and quantum, 180–81
    chaos theory and order in the new, 184–86
    economic materialism and classical, 55–57
    Hellenic notions of God likened to
        classical, 196
    Judeo-Christian critique of classical, 135
    morality and, 239–40
    Newton and classical, 51–54
    pessimism of classical, 159
    thermodynamics and, 165
Planck, Max, 180
Plato, 23, 24, 152, 216
poetry, 189–90
Polanyi, Michael, 242
Polkinghorne, John, 139
Pollock, Jackson, 181

pollution, 97–98, 102, 114. *See also* environmental crisis
Pope, Carl, 247
population
  debates over growth of, 113–16
  ecorealism on, 82
  environmental damage and, 109–10
  famine and, 114n.10
  history of growth of world, 4–5
  a sustainable society and the growth of, 232
poverty, 113–15, 119. *See also* third world, the
preventive action, 101–3
Priestly account, 11, 17–21
Prigogine, Ilya, 170
Principia Mathematica (Newton), 52
printing press, the, 46
process cosmology, 148–49
process thought, 165
progress, 150n.22. *See also* growth
promise, 135–37
prophets, the
  post-Einsteinian physics and, 184, 186
  source of their critical relation to social paradigms, 30–31
  on time, 135–36
Protestantism, 114. *See also* Puritans
Puritans, 36–37

quantum mechanics, 129n.1, 180–81
quantum physics, 190

Rahner, Karl, 149
rain forests
  species extinction and, 89–90
  state of, 87–88
  urban dwellers' reliance on, 117
  See also deforestation
randomness, 168–70, 180–81
Rasmussen, Larry, 55–56, 108, 120
Rawls, John, 60
Reagan administration, 103
recycling, 81, 98, 231, 232, 233
Redemptor Hominis, 246
Rees, William E., 117
relativity, theory of, 138, 129n.1
religion
  cosmic time and, 143–44
  creation as understood by, 144–45
  the environmental movement and, 244–47
  evolution as undercutting, 160–61
  an evolving universe and, 146–50
  Sagan et al. on nature on, 9–10
  science on the pointlessness of, 159
  science's relation to, 241–43
  Whitehead on, 204
resources, 118, 234. *See also* carrying capacity
Ricardo, David, 112

Rifkin, Jeremy, 80, 107
Rilke, Rainer Maria, 189–90, 217–18, 219
Rolston, Holmes, III, 90–91
romanticism, 83
Romantic movement, 64–65
Ruether, Rosemary, 23

sacramentalism
  arcadian ecology and, 67
  human agency and, 38–39
  medieval theology on, 32–36
  problems with, 38
sacramental theology, 32–36
Sagan, Carl, 22, 26
  appeal to religious leaders from, 9–10
  cosmic clock of, 140–43
  on limitations of science, 45–46
  on science and religion, 10n.2
  on science as friend to nature, 5
Salinas de Gotari, President, 120
salvation, 14
Santer, Benjamin D., 100
Santmire, H. Paul, 24, 38, 245
Schama, Simon, 15
Schleiermacher, Friedrich, 145
Schumacher, E. F., 246
Schweitzer, Albert, 227
science
  the arcadian tradition and, 221
  the Bible's vision contrasted with the causality of, 151–55
  cosmic pessimism of some, 159–64
  on creation, 144–45
  ecological, 70–74, 105–7
  on evolution and God, 146–50
  God and, 174
  history of ecological destructiveness of, 45–46
  the humanities and, 221–23
  humans' dualistic means of dealing with the findings of, 157–58
  on nature, 2
  nature and seventeenth-century, 48–50
  the new cosmology and, 127–30
  Newtonian science contrasted with new, 130–31
  professionalization of, 65n.5
  religion's relation to, 241–43
  suffering as the basis of, 222–23
  theology and, 132–33
  uncontrolled nature of, 238
  on the universe as expanding, 137–39
  Vatican II on, 246
  White (L.) on, 13
scientific materialism, 42–44
scientific method, 242
scientism, 43
semiotics, 182–84
Sen, Amartya, 114n.10
sensitivity to initial conditions, 168, 171

Serres, Michel, 54, 171–72, 183, 186–87, 191, 221–23, 227, 238, 239, 240
Shakespeare, William, 222
Sierra Club, 247
signs, 32–38, 182–84
Silent Spring (Carson), 71, 246
Simon, Julian, 115
Sittler, Joseph, 244
Small Is Beautiful (Schumacher), 246
Smith, Adam, 3, 55, 56, 111–12, 115
smog, 81
Smolin, Lee, 180–81
Snyder, Gary, 41
social contract theory, 60–61, 226–31
soil, 81, 85
solar energy, 232
Solzhenitsyn, Aleksandr, 222
Sophocles, 222
soul, the, 24
space and time, 136–37
species extinction
  current rate of, 88–89
  ecorealism on, 82
  improvements in decreasing, 81
spirituality
  of ascent, 199–202
  of descent, 202–5
  in an evolving universe, 146–50
State of the World Report (Worldwatch Institute), 119
steel industry, 233–34
structuralism, 113, 114–15
Summers, Lawrence, 56
sustainability
  contrast of conventional and indigenous notions of, 119–21
  defined, 104
  economics and, 115–16
  See also sustainable development; sustainable society
sustainable development
  critique of ideology of, 120
  defined, 105
  ecologists' "new permissiveness" regarding, 105–7
  See also sustainability; sustainable society
sustainable society, 231–36. *See also* sustainability; sustainable development

technology
  John Paul II on, 246
  optimists' view of, 112
  as a source of environmental degradation, 110–11
  uncontrolled nature of, 237–38
  Vatican II on, 246
  White (L.) on, 13
Teilhard de Chardin, Pierre, 149

teleology, 176–77
theocentric utilitarianism, 38
theocentrism, 26–27, 38
theology
  evolution and, 146–50
  neglect of nature in twentieth-century, 13
  science and, 132–33
  in a static cosmos, 132–33
thermodynamics
  cosmic pessimism and, 161–62
  nonequilibrium, 166–67, 170–71
  poetry and, 190
  time as conceived by, 164–66
third world, the
  deforestation in, 87
  ecorealism on the environmental crisis in, 81
  energy consumption in, 96
  fighting for the right to pollute, 102
  the first world's expropriation of carrying capacity of, 116–18
  landfills in, 98
  population in, 113–15
Thomas, Lewis, 189
Thomas of Celano, 35
Thoreau, Henry David, 41, 67, 70, 221
Timaeus (Plato), 24
time
  classical physics on, 53–54
  Darwinian and thermodynamic conceptions of, 164–66
  the Hebrew Bible and science on, 151–52
  Heschel on, 136–37
  human beings' relation to universal, 139–44
  the prophets on, 135–36
Tipler, Frank, 176
tourism, 224
Toynbee, Arnold, 150n.22
trade, 116–18. *See also* economics; growth; markets
tragedy, 157, 222–23
transcendence, 24–25, 31–32
transubstantiation, 186
Trinity, the, 197–98
Turner, J. M. W., 181
Twain, Mark, 41

uncertainty principle, 180
United Nations, 119
universe, the
  Berry (T.) on the point of, 177
  Christian spirituality and the evolution of, 146–50
  as expanding, 137–39
  Heschel on, 136–37
  history of, 139–44
  the prophets on, 135–36
urban sprawl, 232
utilitarianism, 38

Vanhoozer, Kevin J., 196
Vatican II, 246
von Humboldt, Alexander, 17, 68, 73
von Rad, Gerhard, 17

Wackernagel, Mathis, 117
Ward, Keith, 162n.8
Washington consensus, 122
water, 86–87, 97
Watson, Robert, 102
The Wealth of Nations (Smith), 111
weather, 98–101. *See also* global warming
Weinberg, Steven, 168
    cosmic pessimism and, 2, 162, 164
    critique of the thinking of, 170
    Dyson and, 176
    on the pointlessness of the cosmos, 216
    on science and religion, 159–60
    on the universe as hostile, 161
Whewell, William, 65n.5
White, Gilbert, 64–67, 68, 70, 220
White, Lynn, Jr., 10–16, 42
Whitehead, Alfred North
    on the "century of genius," 3
    on the divine "lure," 38–39, 204
    on the fallacy of misplaced concreteness,
        129n.1
    on fourth-century theologians, 23
    on God under the aspect of power, 149, 202
    on mechanistic materialism, 53–54
    on the mentality of the modern age, 51
    on nature as meaningless, 58
    on principles and facts, 127
    on process cosmology, 148
    on scientific materialism, 42
    on tragedy and science, 157

wilderness, 223–26
Wilson, Edward O., 70–71, 88, 89, 227
wind energy, 232
Wittgenstein, Ludwig, 205
women
    Aristotle and Aquinas on, 148
    population control and, 114
    a spirituality of descent and, 203–4
    in traditional cultures, 121n.8
Wordsworth, William, 67
World Bank
    bashing of, 121n.18
    globalization and, 121–23
    misunderstanding economic growth, 120
    need to reinvent, 233
World Council of Churches, 109, 114, 120,
    245
World Trade Organization, 93, 122, 123,
    233
Worldwatch Institute, 119
Worster, Donald
    on the arcadian tradition, 64
    on Darwin, 68, 70
    on ecology's "new permissiveness," 106
    on imperial ecology, 48
    on industrial capitalism and the
        preservation of nature, 56–57
    on the root of the environmental crisis,
        111
    on sustainability, 106–7
    on White (G.), 66
Wright, G. Ernest, 17

Yahwistic thought, 11, 12, 13, 14, 17–21

Zapatista rebellion, the, 120